TEACHER'S EDITION

Progress™
English Language Arts

1

**For additional online resources, go to www.SadlierConnect.com
and enter the Teacher's Access Code:**

State	Access Code	State	Access Code
Alabama	SBPI01ALGD	Missouri	SBPI29MOBI
Arizona	SBPI04AZCB	New Jersey	SBPI34NJ9U
Arkansas	SBPI05AR3T	New York	SBPI36NYY6
California	SBPI06CA87	North Carolina	SBPI37NC4F
Colorado	SBPI08CO4O	Ohio	SBPI39OHGV
Connecticut	SBPI09CT2C	Oklahoma	SBPI40OKPR
Florida	SBPI12FLL9	Pennsylvania	SBPI42PA9K
Georgia	SBPI13GAN4	South Carolina	SBPI45SC2G
Illinois	SBPI17IL2W	Tennessee	SBPI47TN4W
Kentucky	SBPI21KY3C	Texas	SBPI48TX4M
Louisiana	SBPI22LAX8	Virginia	SBP51VISX2
Massachusetts	SBPI25MA1X	Wisconsin	SBPI55WI4P
Michigan	SBPI26MI9Y		
Mississippi	SBPI28MS2M	All Other States	SBPINA23BV

D1211623

S Sadlier School

TEACHER'S EDITION

Progress™
English Language Arts

Cover: *Series Design:* Studio Montage; *Title Design:* Quarasan, Inc. **Photo Credits:** Cover: age fotostock/Martin Ruegner: *right*. Getty Images/ Zhang Bo: *left*; James Brey: *center*. Used under license from Shutterstock.com/nikolarisim: *background*. Interior: Blend Images/Jose Luis Pelaez Inc: T3; Corbis/Ocean/2/Dave J. Anthony: T15; Ocean/2/Siede Preis: T15 *computer inset*. Dreamstime.com/Nyul: T17; Yobro10: T9. Masterfile (Royalty Free Division): T12; age fotostock/Aflo Foto Agency Royalty Free/Project with viguor/A: 246; ARCO/K Wothe: 58; Corbis: 40 *top*; Eastphoto: 163 *bottom right*; Jeff Greenberg: 67; hemis/LEMAIRE Stphane: 53, 55; Hunststock Inc.: 163 *bottom left*; ImageMore: 39, 41; Image Source: 10 *top*, 73 *bottom left*; Image Source/Justin L: 76; Joe Fox: 168 *bottom*; Dennis McDonald: 219; Michael L. Nolan: 74 *bottom right*; J Peltomaeki: 130; PhotosIndia.com: 45; Purestock: 42, 43; Martin Ruegner: 71 *bottom right*; Guy Russell: 166 *top left*; Konrad Wothe: 73 *top right*. Alamy/Blend Images/Collin Anderson: 164 *bottom left*; Les Breault: 148 *top*; Eddie Gerald: 149 *top*; Natural Visions/Heather Angel: 72 *top left*; Parrot Images: 59; PhotoAlto: 74 *bottom left*; Photoshot Holdings Ltd.: 87; Radius Images: 98 *top*; Michael Routh: 154, 171 *top left*; Andrew Shurtleff: 166 *bottom left*; M. Sobreira: 173. AP Images/Associated Press/The Telegraph/John Badman: 160, 171 *top right*. Corbis/Stefan Christmann: 72 *top right*; Golden Pixels LLC/Kai Chang: 156; JGI/Jamie Grill: 146 *top*; J. Nettis: 165 *top right*; Ocean: 176 *top*; Jose Luis Pelaez, Inc.: 145, 147; PhotoAlto/Michele Constantini: 190 *top*; Tomas Rodriguez: 232 *top*; Ariel Skelley: 84 *top*; Somos Images/Steve Hix: 252 *bottom*. Dreamstime.com/Cammeraydave: 250 *bottom right*; Djburrill: 249 *bottom right*, 250 *bottom left*; Tom Dowd: 149 *bottom*; Joseph73: 56 *bottom*; Mexrix: 89; Monkey Business Images: 251 *bottom*, 255 *bottom*; Jiri Vaclavek: 8 *top right*. ESO: 234, 255 *top left*. Fotolia.com/Alexandr79: 56 *top*; Mikael Damkler: 62 *bottom*; hurleysb: 77, 79 *bottom*; Michael Jung: 163 *top right*; pegbes: 81. Fotosearch: 218. Getty Images/Terry Alcorn: 166 *bottom left*; Steve Allen: 236; Asia Images: 216 *top*; Thomas Barwick: 175, 177; Dan Bigelow: 68; Blend Images - KidStock: 128 *top*; Zhang Bo: 8 *center*; Mark Bowler: 86; Tom Carter: 165 *bottom left*; Joseph T. Collins: 70; Sylvain Cordier: 71 *bottom left*; Driendl Group: 151; Andrew Furlong: 164 *bottom left*; Fuse: 166 *top right*; French School: 247 *bottom right*; Will Gray: 215, 217; hemis.fr/Sylvain Cordier: 171 *top left*; Nancy Honeycutt: 159; Jetta Productions: 167; Jupiterimages: 178; Thomas Kokta: 72 *bottom right*; John Lamb: 163 *top left*; Goldmund Lukic: 230 *top*; Luxx Images: 253; Ian McKinnell: 247 *top left*, 247 *bottom left*; Lawrence Migdale: 73 *top left*; Eri Morita: 252 *top*; Doug Perrine: 73 *bottom right*; Photo Researchers: 155; Les Piccolo: 127, 129; Rayes: 54 *top*; Francesco Reginato: 248 *bottom left*; Paul Simcock: 179; Ariel Skelley: 165 *top left*; VisitBritain/Martin Brent: 164 *top left*; Yin Wang: 229, 231. Glow Images/Aflo/Yukihiro Fukuda: 75; Juniors Bildarchiv: 74 *top right*. Masterfile/Robert Kapa: 233. NASA: 257; H. Richer (University of British Columbia): 247 *top right*. PhotoEdit, Inc./Tony Freeman: 248 *bottom right*. Punchstock/Photodisc: 8 *bottom left*. Science Source/J.-L. Klein & M.-L. Hubert: 72 *bottom left*; Photo Researchers, Inc./Aaron Haupt: 168 *top*, 171 *bottom*. Used under license from Shutterstock.com/Scisseti Alfio: 221; Tatiana Belova: 165 *bottom right*; Binkski: 249 *top left*; Blend Images: 97, 99; Anna Bogush: 61, 79 *top left*; Critterbiz: 106, 123 *top left*; cynoclub: 152; Ian Doktor: 250 *top left*; Flame of life: 241; Jana Guothova: 10 *bottom*, 40 *bottom*, 54 *bottom*, 84 *bottom*, 98 *bottom*, 128 *bottom*, 146 *bottom*, 176 *bottom*, 190 *bottom*, 216 *bottom*, 230 *bottom*; Grandpa: 65, 79 *top right*; Eric Isseleе: 220 *bottom left*; Anton Ivanov: 220 *top right*; Igor Kovalchuk: 267; Yuriy Kulik: 249 *top right*, 251 *top left*; Mike Liu: 238–239; Monkey Business Images: 162; Christopher Meder: 220 *top left*; Natursports: 249 *bottom left*; nikolarisim: 1, 8 *background*; Nixx Photography: 242; ollyy: 240; outdoorsman: 265; Micha Rosenwirth: 250 *top right*; Pal Teravagimov: 220 *bottom right*; Harald Høiland Tjøstheim: 169; Tsekhmister: 8 *bottom right*; Gert Very: 239 *top*; Valentyn Volkov: 62 *top*; Vaclav Volrab: 8 *top left*; Jeff Whyte: 150; Jan Martin Will: 71 *top right*; WilleeCole: 74 *top left*; YANGCHAO: 148 *bottom*. SuperStock/Biosphoto: 131; Angelo Cavalli: 251 *top right*; Cusp: 158; Exactostock: 164 *top right*; Marka: 248 *bottom right*; SuperStock: 83, 85. **Text Credit:** Common Core State Standards © Copyright 2010. National Governors Association Center for Best Practices and Council of Chief State School Officers. All rights reserved. **Illustration Credits:** Amy Adele: 37. Alistar: 244. Scott Angle: 22, 23, 24. Fian Arroyo: 27, 28. Ingvard Ashby: 192, 193. Bandelin-Dacey Studios: 60, 79. Constanza Basaluzzo: 50, 51, 194, 195, 196, 197, 211. Tim Beaumont: 207, 208, 209, 211. Anni Betts: 114. Tracy Bishop: 94, 95, 203, 204. Robin Boyer: 12, 13, 138, 139. Holli Conger: 26, 115, 116. Mike Dammer: 119, 120, 121, 123. Jane Dippold: 29, 30. Guy Francis: 189, 191, 202. Peter Francis: 110, 111, 112, 123. Wednesday Kirwan: 14, 15, 16, 35. Sophie Kittredge: 268. Aga Kowalska: 125. Karen Lee: 66, 117, 118, 188, 189. Joe LeMonnier: 232, 233, 235, 243, 248. David Leonard: 205, 206. Luciana Navarro Powell: 18, 19, 20, 35. John Nez: 9, 11, 102, 103, 104, 105. Merrill Rainey: 100, 101. Carol Schwartz: 76. Apryl Scott: 226, 227. Mary Sullivan: 213. Jomike Tejido: 107, 108, 123. Sue Todd: 198, 199, 200, 211. Sally Vitsky: 57. Julia Woolf: 63, 64. Kevin Zimmer: 31, 32, 33, 35. **Lexile Trademark and Copyright Statement:** LEXILE®, LEXILE® FRAMEWORK, LEXILE® ANALYZER and the LEXILE® logo are trademarks of MetaMetrics, Inc., and are registered in the United States and abroad. The trademarks and names of other companies and products mentioned herein are the property of their respective owners. Copyright © 2012 MetaMetrics, Inc. All rights reserved.

For additional online resources, go to sadlierconnect.com.

William H. Sadlier, Inc.
9 Pine Street
New York, NY 10005-4700

Printed in the United States of America.
ISBN: 978-1-4217-3061-5
1 2 3 4 5 6 7 8 9 WEBC 18 17 16 15 14

Contents

Access Your Digital Resources

Get Started

1. Go to www.SadlierConnect.com

2. Log in

Don't have a username and password? Teachers click "Get Started!" in the Teacher Registration section.

3. Select your program to begin accessing content.

With one username and password, you now have access to all your Sadlier Mathematics and English Language Arts content.

Contents

continued next page

Contents

Unit 4 | Text Types and Purposes:
Write Informative Texts

Unit 5 | Reading Literature:
Craft and Structure

continued next page

Contents

Unit 6 — Text Types and Purposes:
Write Fictional Narratives

Unit 7 — Reading Informational Text:
Craft and Structure

Contents

continued next page

Contents

Unit 11 | Reading Informational Text:
Integration of Knowledge and Ideas

Program Overview

Research indicates that high student performance results from alignment of curriculum, instruction, and assessment. *Progress English Language Arts* is a reading/language arts program that puts standards-based instruction into practice by aligning curriculum, instruction, and assessment in every unit, and at each grade level, K–8.

The foundation of *Progress English Language Arts* is the analysis and integration of state and national standards, curriculum guides and/or frameworks, current research on instruction and best classroom practices. Instruction in reading, writing, vocabulary, conventions of standard English, and speaking and listening is prioritized to create an instructional focus for each unit. Each element of the unit—including direct and guided instruction, and independent work—focuses on these critical skills, and provides students the range of encounters, varied practice opportunities, and levels of application necessary to gain the proficiencies required by the standards.

In *Progress English Language Arts*, children will:

- Engage in close reading of high-quality, challenging informational and literary texts through a gradual release of responsibility, leading to independent and proficient reading.
- Analyze grade-appropriate writing models and construct both informational and narrative essays with a focus on appropriate language usage.
- Cite evidence from complex texts to respond to text-dependent questions and support critical thinking.
- Develop strong foundational skills (phonological awareness, phonics, high-frequency words, and fluency) through Foundational Skills Read Togethers and Readers that transition them to read increasingly more rigorous texts.
- Acquire and use general academic vocabulary accurately.
- Practice analytical and writing skills with Performance Tasks that reflect the structure of standardized test tasks.

With the support of a comprehensive Teacher's Edition, teachers will be able to:

- Scaffold a child's learning with easy-to-use, comprehensive lesson plans.
- Use a child's assessment data, both observational and formal, to inform and redirect instruction.
- Understand the progression of English Language Arts requirements across grade levels and tailor instruction to grade-level standards.
- Support diverse learners, including English language learners, struggling learners, and those needing extended learning opportunities.
- Access online and professional development resources to enhance their instruction.

Founded on the Standards

Progress English Language Arts draws on a rich research base and aligns with the Standards for the English Language Arts jointly published by the National Council of Teachers of English (NCTE) and the International Reading Association (IRA) in 1996 and reaffirmed in 2012 by the NCTE Executive Committee, supports the Guiding Visions, and recognizes the central role of the learner in the standards and the four dimensions of language learning: **content, purpose, development,** and **context** that lead to the attainment of the standards. These dimensions are integrated throughout the program and are integral to *Progress English Language Arts* and the sound foundation it provides for student success.

NCTE and IRA Guidance and Standards-Focus		How Addressed in *Progress English Language Arts*
Content Addresses what students should know and be able to do in regards to English Language Arts	The development of literacy and the attainment of English Language Arts standards depend on experience with and systematic study of a wide array of texts.	*Progress* units expose students to a collection of rigorous texts, fifty percent of the texts are informational and fifty percent are literary and encompass a wide range of genres and topics. Through *Progress*, students learn a range of processes and strategies for comprehending and producing texts. Program instruction is centered on texts and skills rather than on related activities that draw attention from texts. Repeated readings and analysis of complex, content-area texts expose all students to new information and ideas. Writing instruction builds on student models and supports students in responding to an array of texts and becoming skilled with writing narrative, informational, and opinion essays, as well as research papers. In addition, *Progress* includes study of the systems and structures of language and of language conventions, including grammar, punctuation, and spelling. Students learn how to apply their knowledge of the systems and structures of language depending on the context.
Purpose Addresses why students use language	English Language Arts instruction should focus on four purposes of language use: for obtaining and communicating information, for literary response and expression, for learning and reflection, and for problem solving and application.	*Progress* integrates reading, writing, language and speaking and listening instruction with the goal of developing students who are independent learners, critical thinkers with deep knowledge, effective communicators, skilled problem solvers, and therefore, prepared for success in college and careers. With *Progress*, students' knowledge of history/social studies, science, and technical subjects and their academic and domain-specific vocabulary increase through reading rich, content-area texts.

NCTE and IRA Guidance and Standards-Focus		How Addressed in *Progress English Language Arts*
Purpose (continued)		Relevant and meaningful opportunities for speaking and listening engage students in developing lifelong oral communication skills. Writing units ensure students develop effective written communication skills for a broad range of purposes. Integrated language instruction develops students' knowledge and use of conventions of standard English. Through a variety of carefully planned tasks that increase in their cognitive demand, students apply and extend the acquired knowledge and skills.
Development Addresses how students develop competencies in English Language Arts	Students acquire knowledge and develop language competencies with practice over time. The quality of students' performance improves over time as students learn to use language clearly, strategically, critically, and creatively.	*Progress* is grounded in research-based learning progressions. Skill-based lessons reflect a gradual release of responsibility instructional model in which students assume increasing independence in reading and analyzing text, writing—including in response to text, developing and using vocabulary, employing the conventions of standard English, speaking, and listening. The program's scope and sequence balances instruction and practice so that students grow in their language competencies and effectively integrate all aspects of language development to learn, think and communicate effectively. For example, the readability of texts increases across units. Guided practice and independent practice are scaffolded and allow students to successfully engage with tasks that increase in cognitive demand.
Context Influences all areas of learning and encompasses the three preceding dimensions	Language is by definition social. Reading, writing, speaking, and listening take place in a context which influences the learning process and the resulting knowledge, skills, and communication. Students' interests and motivations are integral to English Language Arts instruction, practice, and application.	*Progress* is designed to engage and motivate the students who use the program. The magazine-like format was developed with today's learners in mind. The diversity of content, characters, and topics represented is inclusive and the selection was intentional. Each passage, each writing text, each speaking and listening activity was developed with the audience in mind and was purposefully selected with relevance to the participants in mind. Similarly, instruction was developed to guide students to think of the purpose and audience when communicating.

Flexible Program Use

Progress English Language Arts serves as a flexible resource for supporting schools in meeting English Language Arts standards. Reading selections incorporate a variety of genres and reflect English Language Arts expectations regarding text complexity. Writing units reflect English Language Arts text types and language expectations.

Progress English Language Arts can be used as:

- An alternative core English Language Arts program that provides the standards-based instruction, which can be supplemented with independent reading materials for additional practice.

- Supplemental lessons to fill curriculum gaps in a current core English Language Arts program.

- Targeted preparation materials for state-standardized assessments.

Linking Reading and Writing

Reading and writing units are linked by theme and, where appropriate, by reading genre/writing type. Children are first introduced to key concepts in reading selections based around a theme, usually a social studies or science topic based on grade-level standards. In the related writing unit, they encounter a Student Model, exemplifying excellent grade-level output in the same theme.

Writing types in *Progress English Language Arts* include:

- Nonfictional narrative text that reflects the theme of a related reading unit.

- Informative/explanatory text with the idea-detail structure of related reading selections.

- Fictional narrative text reflecting the sequential narrative structure of text within the related reading unit.

- Opinion piece modeled after a reading selection with a structure identifying an opinion and related supporting reasons.

- Research report whose research topic reflects the theme of the selections within the reading unit.

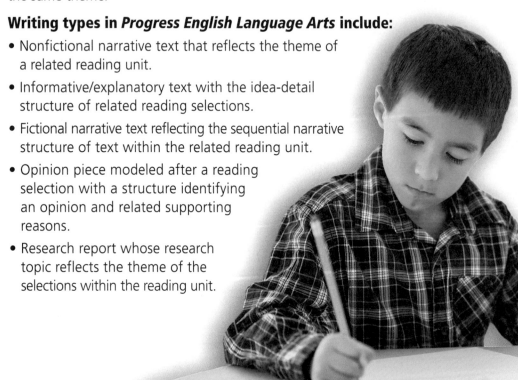

Diverse Grouping Models

The *Progress English Language Arts* program employs diverse grouping and instructional models to help teachers provide effective instruction in key English Language Arts skill/concepts.

Guided Instruction The program uses **whole-class** instruction to provide direct skill instruction and think-aloud modeling while children **read along** with the teacher. Discussion-based comprehension checks provide an opportunity for learners to ground skill instruction in collaborative academic discourse.

Guided Practice Lessons incorporate **partner reading in heterogeneous pairs** for scaffolded practice as the teacher circulates to provide targeted support as needed. Written comprehension checks offer multiple-choice and short-answer questions for pairs to work through together and then share their thinking with the class.

Independent Practice Lessons offer **independent reading application with callout support** as the teacher circulates to ensure that all readers are on task and effectively engaging with text. Written comprehension checks offer multiple-choice and short-answer questions as opportunities to demonstrate standard mastery.

➡ Alternative grouping models are suggested for struggling learners and English language learners, such as **heterogeneous pairing** with more proficient readers or **small group work with the teacher**.

Foundational Skills

Foundational skills on-level instruction is provided in the following ways in *Progress English Language Arts:*

- **Print concepts** are integrated into Foundational Skills Read Together and Language activities.

- **Phonological awareness** skills are reinforced through Foundational Skills Read Together and classroom activities.

- Explicit, targeted instruction in grade-level **phonics** and word analysis skills are taught through a Foundational Skills Read-Together.

- Foundational Skills Readers provide direct application of phonic skills and **high-frequency word** recognition.

- **Fluency** instruction and practice are integrated at point-of-use within reading selection instruction. In addition, the Foundational Skills Reader provides independent practice in developing fluency.

Student Worktext

(in print and eBook formats) Colorful, engaging standards-based instruction including complex, rigorous reading selections and structured writing models. ▶

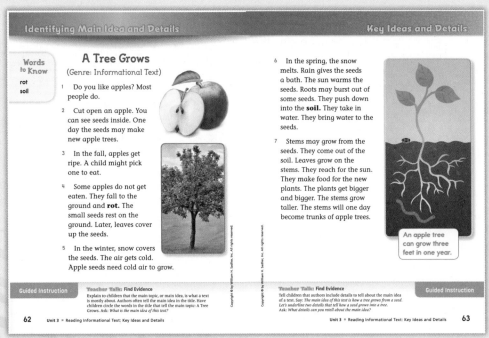

Grade 1 Pages 62–63

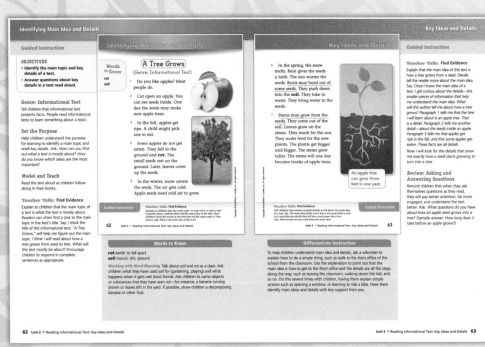

Grade 1 Teacher's Edition Pages 62–63

◀ Teacher's Edition

(in print and eBook formats) Teacher-friendly lesson plans with targeted standards instruction and supportive features suitable for both novice and experienced teachers.

Progress Monitor* (Optional Purchase)

Four benchmark assessments to identify instructional needs as benchmarked against grade-level English Language Arts skills and concepts.

*Items are mapped to CCSS.

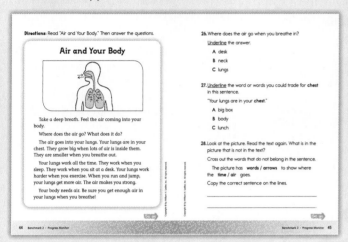

Grade 1 Progress Monitor Pages 44 and 45

Online Resources

A rich array of online resources at **www.SadlierConnect.com** supports program implementation and extends learning opportunities.

- **Home Connect Activities** support family member involvement.
- **Unit Performance Tasks** provide a wealth of practice opportunities for standardized Performance Tasks related to the content of each unit.
- **Performance Task 1 and 2** enable students to use downloadable unseen text with in-book Performance Tasks and provide teachers with robust evaluation support. These tasks can be used for mid-year and end-of-year assessment purposes.
- **Additional Practice** offers opportunities to augment program practice.
- **Full-Length Reading Selections** provide continuous text passages for fluency practice.

iProgress Monitor* (Optional Purchase)

This dynamic assessment component is available for enhancing grade-level English Language Arts skills and concepts. See page T17 for more information.

*Items are mapped to CCSS.

eBooks (Optional Purchase)

Student Worktext eBook The eBook provides the same quality content as the print Student Worktext. Delivered via Sadlier's one-stop platform at **www.SadlierConnect.com**, the eBook format also provides access to robust tools that allow students to:

- Read Text
- Make notes and highlight important information
- Search for key words
- Zoom in on specific content

Teacher's Edition eBook The eBook provides the same quality content as the print Teacher's Edition. Delivered via Sadlier's one-stop platform at **www.SadlierConnect.com**, in addition the eBook format also provides access to robust tools that allow teachers to:

- Toggle between the Student and Teacher's Edition
- Use Full-screen Mode to project the Student Edition onto a whiteboard to focus on instruction
- Assign lessons to an entire class or a specific group of students to take offline (in PDF format)
- View digital resources at point of use
- Make notes and highlight important information
- Search for key words
- Zoom in on specific content

Progress English Language Arts **Grade 1 eBook**

Progress English Language Arts contains many formative and summative assessment opportunities to help teachers gather evidence of students' progress toward mastering grade-level skills and concepts and prepare for the new state-standardized assessments.

Integrated, Ongoing Assessment Opportunities

Lesson Observational Diagnostics appear at point-of-use within lessons, reminding teachers to observe student response to instruction and offering a reteaching prescription. ▶

Assess and Respond

If students have difficulty answering the questions in the Comprehension Check . . .

Then have pairs of students review the story and create a list of the inferences they made as they read. Students should identify the clues they used to make their inferences.

Unit II Review

Read along with the following selection.

Kids in Space

1　Do you think a kid will be able to go into space someday? I do. Many people have traveled safely into space. Animals have traveled into space, too. Astronauts have even walked on the moon.

2　Scientists are planning how people can live in space. Astronauts are working, cooking, and playing in space. They have stayed at a space station for a few months. I think that someday a family may be able to live in space. That would be really cool for a kid!

Astronauts can do many things in space.

Fill in the circle of the correct answer choice for questions 1 and 2.

1. Which key idea of the text does the picture show?

○ Astronauts have walked on the moon.

○ Animals have traveled in space.

○ Astronauts have lived in space.

Unit 11 ▪ Reading Informational Text: Integration of

Grade 1 Page 257

◀ **Unit Reviews** are provided with each unit and offer an opportunity for children to encounter standardized test practice for the skills that have been taught within the unit.

Directions: Read "The Ants in Danger." Then answer the questions.

The Ants in Danger

I am busy. I work all day with other ants. We are a big ant family. When we leave our nest, I like to go first.

One day, I poked my head out of the nest. "Oh no!" I cried. "Danger!"

I saw a long nose. I saw two big claws and a furry body. It was an anteater, an animal that eats ants. It was looking for my family to eat. I was scared. Then I felt a tickle. I turned around.

"Oh no!" I cried. "Another anteater!" Now two of them wanted to eat my family.

I ran inside. The anteaters began to fight about who would eat my family. That gave us time to get away.

Go on▶

14　Benchmark 1 · Progress Monitor

Grade 1 Test 1 from Progress Monitor

◀ **Benchmark Assessments*** in Progress Monitor (an optional purchase) provide comprehensive assessments that can be administered periodically throughout the school year to evaluate children's knowledge and skill level relative to grade-level English Language Arts skills and concepts.

*Items are mapped to CCSS.

Unit Performance Tasks provide a wealth of practice opportunities to expose children to standardized Performance Tasks related to the program's instructional reading units.

Performance Tasks 1 and 2 ▶ provide tasks that introduce children to formats that they will later encounter on standardized assessments. The tasks incorporate both text items and an extended response question—which assesses children's ability to think critically about text as well as write to sources, using supporting evidence. Performance Tasks 1 and 2 are also available online at **www.SadlierConnect.com**. These Performance Tasks can be used for mid-year and end-of-year assessment purposes. They play a vital role helping you determine if children are able to integrate skills and concepts being taught and apply them.

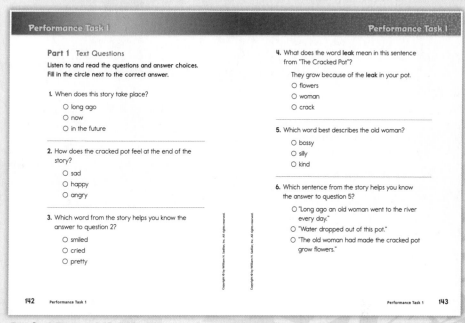

Grade 1 Pages 142–143

iProgress Monitor* (Optional Purchase)

Augment your assesment resources with customized assignments and test-building power!

With the **iProgress Monitor**, teachers can:

- Assign, evaluate, and monitor student progress with preformatted program assessments in an interactive format.
- Build custom assessments with a built-in test generator.
- Track students' progress and guide instruction with real-time data.

*Items are mapped to CCSS.

Student Worktext

With a full-color, magazine-like design, the engaging Student Worktext gives children opportunities to:

- Read both informational and literary texts
- Encounter increasingly rigorous and complex texts
- Answer text-based questions and engage in academic discussions about text
- Write in a clear and coherent manner using the conventions of standard English
- Build academic vocabulary

Organized by ELA standards, the reading and writing units are linked by theme and, where appropriate, genre. The reading units address a rich variety of genres while the writing units focus on the standards-supported writing types.

A Unit Introduction That Focuses on Standards

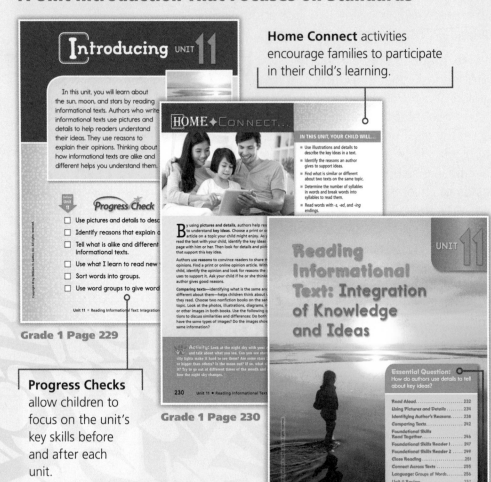

Home Connect activities encourage families to participate in their child's learning.

Grade 1 Page 229

Grade 1 Page 230

Grade 1 Page 231

Progress Checks allow children to focus on the unit's key skills before and after each unit.

A Read Aloud to Set the Stage for Standards

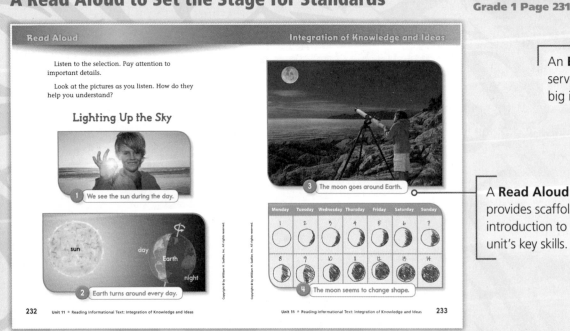

Grade 1 Pages 232–233

An **Essential Question** serves as a hook into the big idea of the unit.

A **Read Aloud** provides scaffolded introduction to the unit's key skills.

Encountering Complex Reading Text: Gradual Release of Responsibility

Each standard is taught using one continuous text following a gradual release of responsibility instructional model. By gradually decreasing the level of support within each text, children are prepared for independent encounters with complex text and can best master complex standards.

Guided Instruction: Direct standard instruction

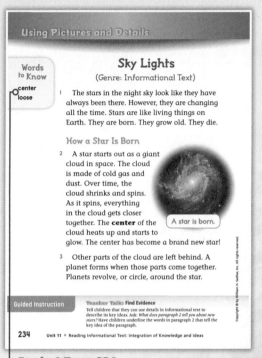

Guided Practice: Scaffolded standard practice in a partner-reading environment

Complex **informational texts** with a rich array of text features comprise half of each grade's reading selections.

Embedded questions support rigorous, standards-based **conversations about text** in the context of selections.

Grade 1 Page 234

Grade 1 Page 236

Academic vocabulary is introduced in a text-based context with the appropriate standards-based instruction.

Text-dependent questions require children to respond with evidence from the text to support their answers.

Each unit contains multiple opportunities to **write to text sources.**

Integration of Knowledge and Ideas

8 Sometimes the moon looks round and bright. It lights up the night sky. The stars light up the night sky, too. Together with the sun, they are our sky lights.

Comprehension Check 〔 MORE ONLINE 〕 sadlierconnect.com

1. Reread the "Hello, Neighbor!" section. Which detail does not belong in this part of the text?
   a. The moon is one of Earth's sky lights.
   b. Stars are born, grow old, and die.
   c. The moon is Earth's closest neighbor.

2. Look at the diagram on page 235. What planet is closest to the sun? How do you know?

_____

_____

_____

_____

Teacher Talk: Find Evidence
Have children circle the words *sky lights* in the last sentence. Ask them to underline the details in the last paragraph that name the sky lights.

Independent Practice

Unit 11 ▪ Reading Informational Text: Integration of Knowledge and Ideas   **237**

Grade 1 Page 237

Independent Practice: Extensive independent practice on standards enables children to build mastery.

Foundational Skills

These core skills focus on developing children's understanding of print concepts, phonological awareness, phonics, word recognition, and fluency. While children are developing these key foundational skills, they are also developing comprehension and vocabulary by listening to and reading various genres of texts.

Foundational Skills Reader 1

Grade 1 Pages 247–248

Children are provided a direct application of **phonics elements.**

Key **phonics elements** are presented in the context of literary and informational texts.

Foundational Skills Read Together

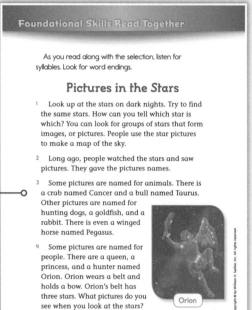

Foundational Skills Read Together

As you read along with the selection, listen for syllables. Look for word endings.

Pictures in the Stars

1   Look up at the stars on dark nights. Try to find the same stars. How can you tell which star is which? You can look for groups of stars that form images, or pictures. People use the star pictures to make a map of the sky.

2   Long ago, people watched the stars and saw pictures. They gave the pictures names.

3   Some pictures are named for animals. There is a crab named Cancer and a bull named Taurus. Other pictures are named for hunting dogs, a goldfish, and a rabbit. There is even a winged horse named Pegasus.

4   Some pictures are named for people. There are a queen, a princess, and a hunter named Orion. Orion wears a belt and holds a bow. Orion's belt has three stars. What pictures do you see when you look at the stars?

Orion

246   Unit 11 ■ Reading Informational Text: Integration of Knowledge and Ideas

Grade 1 Page 246

Foundational Skills Reader 2

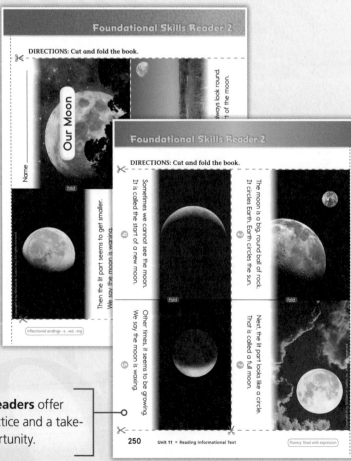

Grade 1 Pages 249–250

Foldable readers offer fluency practice and a take-home opportunity.

Close Reading for Critical Comprehension of Text

Close reading—careful, purposeful reading and rereading of text—requires children to integrate the unit's reading standards. In the Close Reading and the related Unit Review assessment, children analyze text, grow comfortable with increasing text complexity, and demonstrate an understanding of unit standards. A **language lesson** follows each Close Reading.

Close Reading

3. "Movements of the Sun, Earth, and Moon" explains that the moon mirrors back the sun's light. You also learned about moonlight in "Sunlight Is Better." Tell how the information is the same or different.

_____
_____
_____
_____
_____

4. What is the author's opinion about sunlight in "Sunlight Is Better"? What is a reason the author uses to support this opinion?

_____
_____
_____
_____
_____

254   Unit 11 ▪ Reading Informational Text: Integration of Knowledge and Ideas

Grade 1 Page 254

Text-dependent questions require application of the unit's standards and use of supporting evidence and link to a critical understanding of the text.

Connect Across Texts

Compare and Contrast Texts

Look at the pictures from the texts you have read. Be ready to talk about the pictures and the key ideas.

Sky Lights   Make a Model

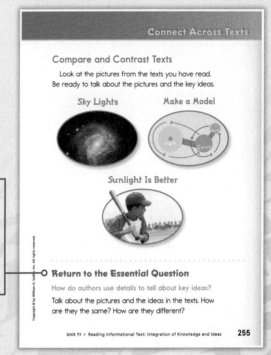

Sunlight Is Better

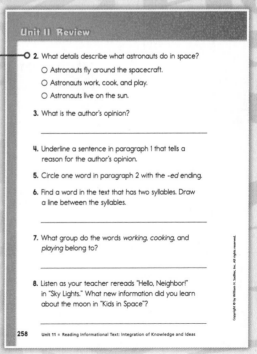

Return to the Essential Question

How do authors use details to tell about key ideas?

Talk about the pictures and the ideas in the texts. How are they the same? How are they different?

Unit 11 ▪ Reading Informational Text: Integration of Knowledge and Ideas   255

Grade 1 Page 255

Students engage in **rigorous academic discussion** as they talk about the unit's texts and Essential Question.

Language page develops **language skills** taught in the context of unit texts.

Language

Groups of Words

Guided Instruction Words that are the same in some way can be put into a group. Read this sentence from "Sunlight Is Better."

We eat plants like carrots and peas.

The group is **plants**. The plants in the group are *carrots* and *peas*. Each word in the group is different in some way. We can understand a word by saying what is different about it.

The words *dog* and *cat* belong to the group **pets**. A dog is a pet that barks. A cat is a pet that purrs.

Guided Practice Choose a word from the box to complete the sentence. Write the word on the line.

| animal | leaves | petals | wings |

1. A **tree** is a plant that has _____ .

Independent Practice Choose words from the box above to complete the sentence. Write the words on the lines.

2. A **fly** is a(n) _____ that has _____ .

256   Unit 11 ▪ Reading Informational Text: Integration of Knowledge and Ideas

Grade 1 Page 256

Multiple-choice questions, as well as other question formats, assess mastery of reading and language skills/concepts presented in the unit.

Unit 11 Review

2. What details describe what astronauts do in space?
   ○ Astronauts fly around the spacecraft.
   ○ Astronauts work, cook, and play.
   ○ Astronauts live on the sun.

3. What is the author's opinion?

   _____

4. Underline a sentence in paragraph 1 that tells a reason for the author's opinion.

5. Circle one word in paragraph 2 with the *-ed* ending.

6. Find a word in the text that has two syllables. Draw a line between the syllables.

   _____

7. What group do the words *working, cooking,* and *playing* belong to?

   _____

8. Listen as your teacher rereads "Hello, Neighbor!" in "Sky Lights." What new information did you learn about the moon in "Kids in Space"?

   _____

258   Unit 11 ▪ Reading Informational Text: Integration of Knowledge and Ideas

Grade 1 Page 258

Writing Units with a Standards Focus

Writing units, along with the Writing Handbook, reflect the key writing types in English Language Arts: opinion, informative/explanatory, narrative (both fictional and nonfictional), and research report. Language and Speaking and Listening pages are integrated to build children's accurate use of academic language in both written and spoken forms.

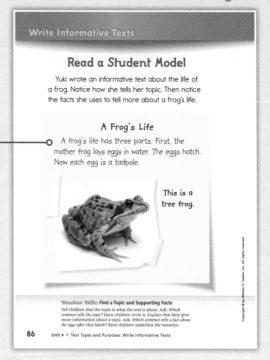

Student **writing model** provides a good example of the writing type while Teacher Talk supports children in understanding the elements of the type.

Integrated **Language** pages focus on conventions of English and knowledge of language through a gradual release model.

Speaking and Listening lessons support children as they use speaking and listening skills to present their writing and respond to classmates' writing.

Grade 1 Page 93

Grade 1 Pages 94–95

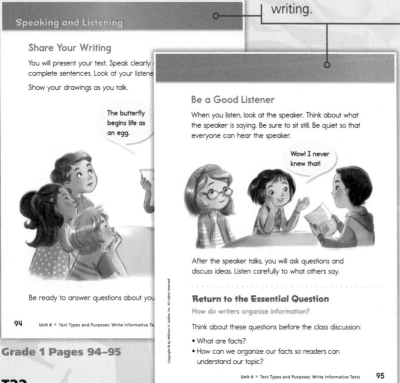

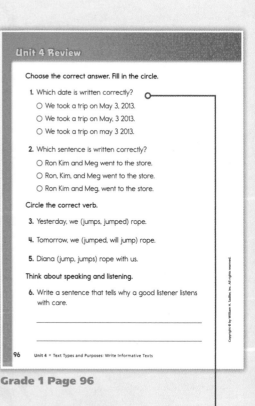

Grade 1 Page 96

Selected-response questions as well as other question formats assess mastery of language and speaking and listening skills/concepts presented in the unit.

Teacher's Edition

Teacher-friendly, easy-to-use lesson plans support teachers in providing systematic instruction, practice, and application of English Language Arts skills and concepts. The Teacher's Edition is also available in eBook format.

- Easy-to-use rubrics at point-of-use enable busy teachers to assess and modify instruction quickly.

At-a-Glance Unit Introduction Pages

Unit introduction pages, featuring student self-assessment, a home connection, a planner for understanding key concepts at a glance, and learning progressions for comprehension standards, provide a quick reference for busy educators!

Unit Planner

Grade 1 Teacher's Edition Page 229 and 230

The unit launches with support for a **child's self-assessment** and connects to home.

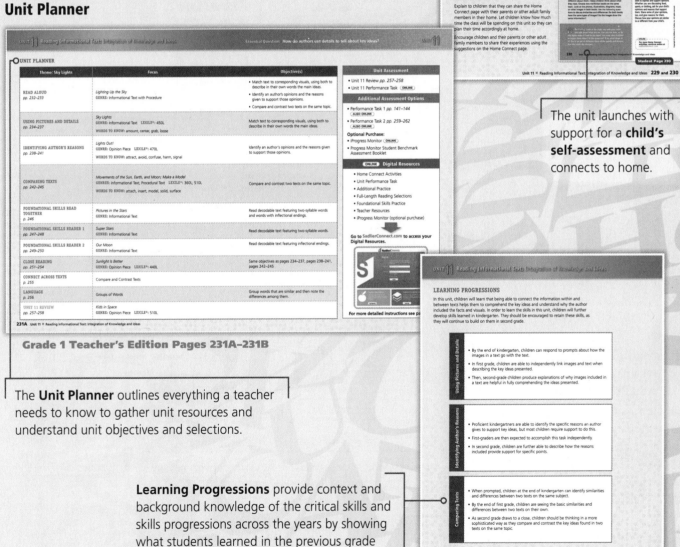

Grade 1 Teacher's Edition Pages 231A–231B

The **Unit Planner** outlines everything a teacher needs to know to gather unit resources and understand unit objectives and selections.

Learning Progressions provide context and background knowledge of the critical skills and skills progressions across the years by showing what students learned in the previous grade and connections to what they will learn in the next grade, building coherence within and across the grade levels.

Grade 1 Teacher's Edition Page 231C

On-the-Spot Lesson Support Makes Teachers English Language Arts Experts!

Teacher-friendly Lesson Plans provide targeted standards-based instruction and supportive features suitable for both novice and experienced teachers.

Think-alouds preview the unit's targeted reading skills.

Read Aloud

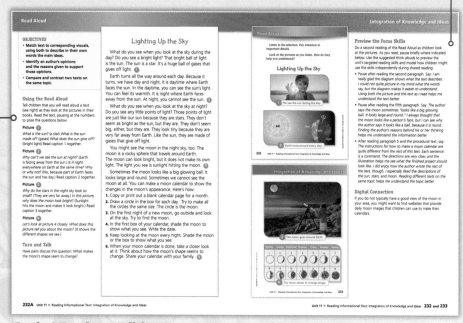

Scaffolded questioning aids in comprehension and strengthens the relationship between illustrations and texts.

Grade 1 Teacher's Edition Pages 232A–232 and 233

Think-alouds model a reader's approach, and an additional prompt **scaffolds skill application** for additional support.

Guided Instruction

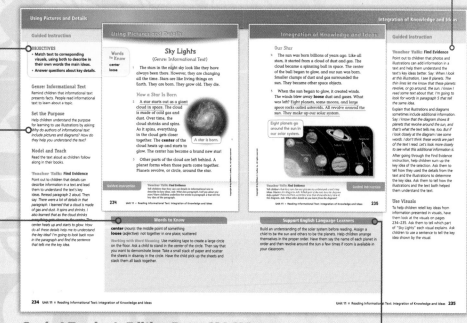

Each lesson segment has student **objectives** clearly noted.

Genre instruction supports close examination of the features of **text types**.

Academic vocabulary is defined, and vocabulary-building activities (e.g., Marzano's six vocabulary acquisition strategies) support acquisition.

Grade 1 Teacher's Edition Pages 234–235

Modifications for English language learners, struggling learners, and children who need challenges embrace all learners.

Successive Increase of Student Responsibility Leads to Success

Answer explanations support the teacher in helping children understand where they may still have gaps in applying the skill/concept effectively.

Guided and Independent Practice

Whole-class, partner, and individual instructional settings build scaffolding for all children to be successful with the skill/concept.

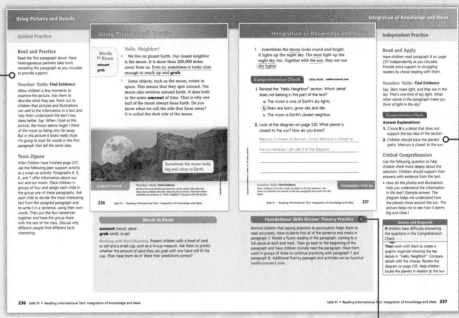

Grade 1 Teacher's Edition Pages 236–237

Foundational Skills practice is integrated at point-of-use in lessons.

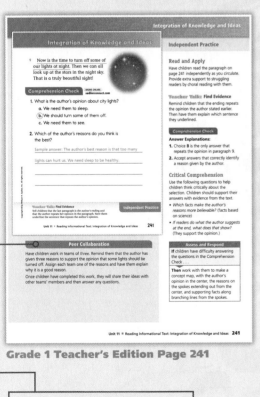

Grade 1 Teacher's Edition Page 241

Peer Collaboration provides opportunities for children to work together to share ideas.

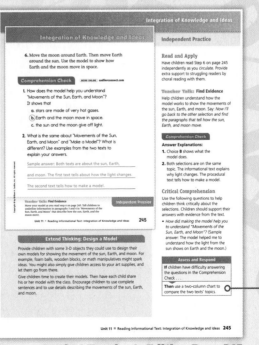

Grade 1 Teacher's Edition Page 245

If-Then diagnostics allow teachers to remediate immediately when children need additional support.

Explicit Instruction and Application Develops Foundational Skills

Foundational Skills Read Together

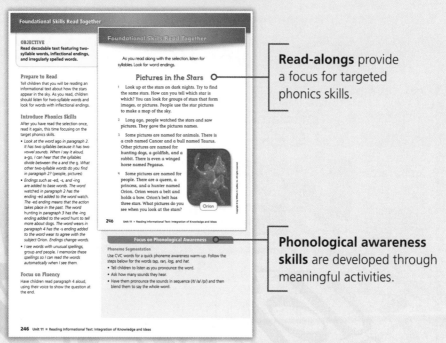

Grade 1 Teacher's Edition Page 246

Read-alongs provide a focus for targeted phonics skills.

Phonological awareness skills are developed through meaningful activities.

Foundational Skills Readers

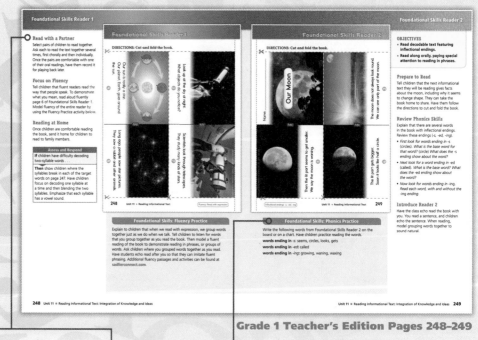

Grade 1 Teacher's Edition Pages 248–249

Partner reading allows children to practice for individual mastery of fluency skill.

Phonics practice with the readers reinforces the phonics skills.

Opportunities to Analyze Text to Determine Its Meaning

Strategy reminders assure children are monitoring their comprehension during and after reading.

Close Reading

Strategy check-ins support basic understanding of the selection.

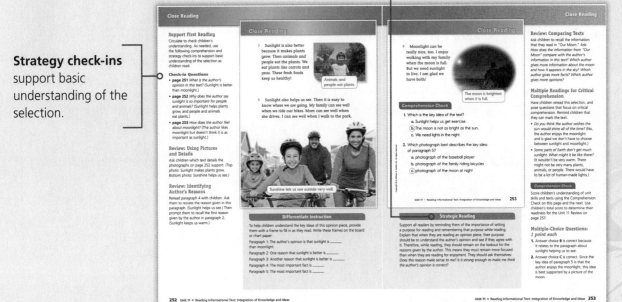

Grade 1 Teacher's Edition Pages 252–253

Assessment Tools Make Grading Simple

Progress English Language Arts supports busy teachers by offering easy-to-use rubrics for grading and charts that outline next steps after grading or assessing.

All assessment items are **aligned to an ELA standard** so that teachers can easily determine which standards are mastered.

Assessment rubrics for short-answer questions take the worry out of assigning grades to open-ended questions.

Analyze Scores charts detail next steps that teachers should take with children based on assessment results.

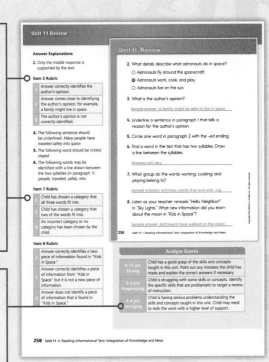

Grade 1 Teacher's Edition Page 258

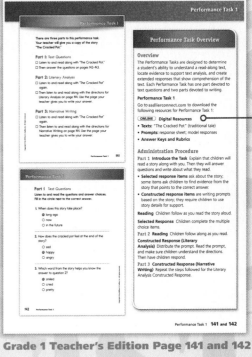

Grade 1 Teacher's Edition Page 141 and 142

Detailed **Performance Task rubrics** provide clear and thorough guidance on how to evaluate written performance tasks.

Weeks	Student Worktext	Online Resources to Enrich, Support, and Assess
1–3	Unit 1, pp. 9–38	Unit 1 Performance Task; Additional Practice; Full-Length Reading Selection; Foundational Skills Practice; Teacher Resources Optional purchase: iProgress Monitor
4–5	Unit 2, pp. 39–52	Additional Practice; Teacher Resources Optional purchase: iProgress Monitor
6–8	Unit 3, pp. 53–82	Unit 3 Performance Task; Additional Practice; Full-Length Reading Selection; Foundational Skills Practice; Teacher Resources Optional purchase: iProgress Monitor
9–10	Unit 4, pp. 83–96	Additional Practice; Teacher Resources Optional purchase: iProgress Monitor
11–13	Unit 5, pp. 97–126	Unit 5 Performance Task; Additional Practice; Full-Length Reading Selection; Foundational Skills Practice; Teacher Resources Optional purchase: iProgress Monitor
14–15	Unit 6, pp. 127–140	Additional Practice; Teacher Resources Optional purchase: iProgress Monitor
16	Performance Task 1	Performance Task 1 Selections, Rubrics, and Answer Key
17–19	Unit 7, pp. 145–174	Unit 7 Performance Task; Additional Practice; Full-Length Reading Selection; Foundational Skills Practice; Teacher Resources Optional purchase: iProgress Monitor
20–21	Unit 8, pp. 175–188	Additional Practice; Teacher Resources Optional purchase: iProgress Monitor
22–24	Unit 9, pp. 189–214	Unit 9 Performance Task; Additional Practice; Full-Length Reading Selection; Foundational Skills Practice; Teacher Resources Optional purchase: iProgress Monitor
25–26	Unit 10, pp. 215–228	Additional Practice; Teacher Resources Optional purchase: iProgress Monitor
27–29	Unit 11, pp. 229–258	Unit 11 Performance Task; Additional Practice; Full-Length Reading Selection; Foundational Skills Practice; Teacher Resources Optional purchase: iProgress Monitor
30	Performance Task 2	Performance Task 2 Selections, Rubrics, and Answer Key

Progress Monitor Student Assessments, an optional purchase, contains four comprehensive assessments that you may administer throughout the school year to assess children's mastery of grade-level skills/concepts.

Introducing UNIT **1**

In this unit, you will read stories about how characters learn that they are special. Authors include details in a story to make it more interesting. You can use those details to retell a story. When you retell a story, you tell about the characters, the setting, and story events. You tell the story your way!

Progress Check *Can I?*

Before Unit 1 / After Unit 1

- [ ] Ask and answer questions about story details. [ ]
- [ ] Retell a story. [ ]
- [ ] Describe characters, setting, and events. [ ]
- [ ] Use what I learn to read new words. [ ]
- [ ] Connect word meanings to real life. [ ]
- [ ] Use word clues in sentences to figure out new words. [ ]

Unit 1 ■ Reading Literature: Key Ideas and Details

Student Page 9

HOME ◆ CONNECT...

The Home Connect feature is a way to keep parents or other adult family members apprised of what their children are learning. The key learning objectives are listed, and some ideas for related activities and discussions are included.

Explain to children that they can share the Home Connect page with their parents or other adult family members in their home. Let children know how much time the class will be spending on this unit so they can plan their time accordingly at home.

Encourage children and their parents or other adult family members to share their experiences using the suggestions on the Home Connect page.

Progress Check

The Progress Check is a self-assessment feature that children can use to gauge their own progress. Research shows that when children take accountability for their own learning, their motivation increases.

Before children begin work on Unit 1, have them check the boxes next to any item that they feel they can do well. Explain that it is fine if they don't check any of the boxes. Tell them that they will have an opportunity to learn about and practice all of these items while studying the unit. Let them know that near the end of the unit they will have a chance to reconsider how well they can do each item on the list.

Before children begin their Unit 1 Review on page 37, have them revisit this page. You can use this information to work with children on any items they don't understand before they tackle the Review.

HOME ◆ CONNECT...

For young learners, **asking and answering questions** about a story helps them connect more closely with the story. As you read a story with your child, ask your child questions about important details in the text. Encourage your child to ask you questions about the story, too. These activities will help your child find, understand, and remember key details from a story.

Retelling a story helps children better understand and remember what they read. After your child has read a story, ask him or her to tell you what happened. Guide your child by discussing events that happen at the beginning, in the middle, and at the end.

Encourage your child to describe the **characters** and **setting** and to tell the **major events** in a story that he or she has read. After reading, ask your child to describe how a character acts and feels in a situation. Then ask your child to think about what he or she would do in that situation. Talk about the setting and ask your child to tell how this place is important to the story.

Conversation Starters: Ask your child to name his or her favorite cartoon or story character and tell what he or she likes best about that character. Then ask your child questions that will encourage him or her to describe what the character does and says. For example, ask your child, "What does the character do when trouble comes?" or "What does the character say at the end?"

IN THIS UNIT, YOUR CHILD WILL...

- Ask and answer questions to show understanding of key details in a text.
- Make text-to-text, text-to-self, and text-to-world connections.
- Retell stories.
- Describe characters, setting, and important events in a story.
- Read words with consonant blends, such as *stop* and *nest*.
- Read words with short vowels.
- Apply the meanings of words to real life.
- Use context clues to figure out a word's meaning.
- Compare and contrast three different stories on the same topic: an animal fantasy, a fable, and realistic fiction.

WAYS TO HELP YOUR CHILD

Talk to your child about stories that you read together. Ask: "What happens in the story?" "Who are the characters?" "Where does the story take place?" Then have your child retell the story and tell the central message. Model how to make connections by telling how you would act or feel if you were a character in the story. Encourage your child to make connections on his or her own.

ONLINE
For more Home Connect activities, continue online at sadlierconnect.com

10 Unit 1 ■ Reading Literature: Key Ideas and Details

Student Page 10

UNIT PLANNER

Theme: All About Me	Focus
READ ALOUD *pp. 12–13*	*I Want to Be* **GENRE:** Realistic Fiction
UNDERSTANDING KEY DETAILS *pp. 14–17*	*Bunny's Talent* **GENRE:** Animal Fantasy **LEXILE®:** 240L **WORDS TO KNOW:** fancy, talent, toward
RETELLING STORIES *pp. 18–21*	*The Elephant Dance* **GENRE:** Fable **LEXILE®:** 200L **WORDS TO KNOW:** prance, shower, spray, worry
DESCRIBING STORY ELEMENTS *pp. 22–25*	*Rocky's Boat Ride* **GENRE:** Adventure Story **LEXILE®:** 250L **WORDS TO KNOW:** caught, gather, heavy, rescue
FOUNDATIONAL SKILLS READ TOGETHER *p. 26*	*The Best in Me* **GENRE:** Narrative Poem
FOUNDATIONAL SKILLS READER 1 *pp. 27–28*	*At Bat!* **GENRE:** Realistic Fiction
FOUNDATIONAL SKILLS READER 2 *pp. 29–30*	*I Can!* **GENRE:** Realistic Fiction
CLOSE READING *pp. 31–34*	*Talk, Talk, Talk!* **GENRE:** Realistic Fiction **LEXILE®:** 180L
CONNECT ACROSS TEXTS *p. 35*	Compare and Contrast Texts
LANGUAGE *p. 36*	Word Meanings
UNIT 1 REVIEW *pp. 37–38*	*Frog's Wings* **GENRE:** Fantasy **LEXILE®:** 220L

Objective(s)

- Ask and answer questions about details in a story.
- Retell stories and identify their lessons.
- Describe the characters, settings, and main events in a story.

Ask and answer questions about details in a story.

Retell stories and identify their lesson.

Describe the characters, settings, and main events in a story.

Read decodable text featuring words with short vowels, *l* blends, *r* blends, *s* blends; and final blends.

Read decodable text featuring words with short vowels *a* and *i*, *l* blends, and *r* blends.

Read decodable text featuring words with short vowels *o, u,* and *e; s* blends; and final blends.

Same objectives as pages 14–17; pages 18–21; pages 22–25

- Use context to figure out word meanings.
- Connect word meanings to real life.

Unit Assessment

- Unit 1 Review *pp. 37–38*
- Unit 1 Performance Task (ONLINE)

Additional Assessment Options

- Performance Task 1 *pp. 141–144*
  (ALSO ONLINE)
- Performance Task 2 *pp. 259–262*
  (ALSO ONLINE)

Optional Purchase:

- iProgress Monitor (ONLINE)
- Progress Monitor Student Benchmark Assessment Booklet

(ONLINE) Digital Resources

- Home Connect Activities
- Unit Performance Task
- Additional Practice
- Full-Length Reading Selections
- Foundational Skills Practice
- Teacher Resources
- iProgress Monitor (optional purchase)

Go to SadlierConnect.com to access your Digital Resources.

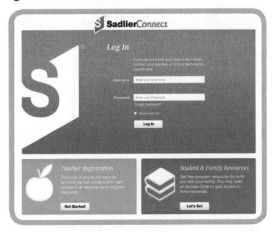

For more detailed instructions see page T3.

LEARNING PROGRESSIONS

In this unit, children will learn to use key details to describe characters, settings, and major events of a story. In order to learn the skills in this unit, children will further develop skills learned in kindergarten. They should be encouraged to retain these skills, as they will continue to build on them in second grade.

Understanding Key Details

- When prompted, children at the end of kindergarten can ask and answer questions about a text.

- By the end of first grade, children are able to ask and answer questions about key details in a text.

- In second grade, children will continue asking and answering questions such as *Who? What? Where? When? Why?* and *How?* to better understand key details in a text.

Retelling Stories

- Proficient kindergartners can retell stories with prompting and support.

- First-graders are able to retell stories and their key details and demonstrate understanding of a story's central message or lesson.

- In second grade, children can retell stories, including fables and folktales from diverse cultures, and determine central messages, lessons, or morals.

Describing Story Elements

- By the end of kindergarten, children can identify story characters, settings, and major events with prompting and support.

- In first grade, children are able to use key details to describe story characters, settings, and major events.

- Second-grade children can move beyond recall of key details to describe how characters in a story respond to major events and challenges.

Reading Literature: Key Ideas and Details

UNIT 1

Essential Question:
How do the details of a story work together?

Unit 1 ■ Reading Literature: Key Ideas and Details **11**

Essential Question:
How do the details of a story work together?

In this unit, children will learn how to identify and interpret key ideas and details when reading literature. Specifically, children will be able to identify details about characters, settings, and main events.

Theme: All About Me

Children will explore the unit theme, All About Me, through various genres of literature, including a fantasy story, a fable, and an adventure story. In each of the stories, children will learn how the characters come to appreciate their own uniqueness. Through analysis of the characters and story events, children will discover that every person has special gifts and talents.

Curriculum Connection: Social Studies

As children enjoy the selections in this unit, they will explore how each person is unique with his or her own abilities and skills.

Vocabulary Overview

caught 24, fancy 17, gather 22, heavy 23, prance 18, rescue 24, shower 20, spray 20, talent 14, toward 15, worry 19

OBJECTIVES
- **Ask and answer questions about details in a story.**
- **Retell stories and identify their lessons.**
- **Describe the characters, settings, and main events in a story.**

Using the Read Aloud

Tell children that you will read aloud a text (see right) as they look at the pictures in their books. Read the text, pausing at the numbers to pose the questions below.

Picture ①

What do you see in the picture? What does the picture and the poem tell you about Dorie? (Dorie likes to sing. You can see her smile and hear about her dream to be famous.)

Picture ②

What is Dorie doing in this picture? What details do you learn about Dorie and her mother? (Dorie is in a sailboat. You learn Dorie wants an adventure far away, but her mother wants her to stay close.)

Picture ③

What wish is shown in this picture? How did Dorie's mother respond to this wish? What does that tell you about her? (Dorie flying; she tells Dorie that she is afraid to fly, but she wants Dorie to be happy.)

Picture ④

How is what this picture shows different from the others? What does Dorie learn from her discussion with her mother? (This picture shows something Dorie is really doing; she learned to enjoy being a kid and being with her family and friends.)

Turn and Talk

Have pairs discuss this question: What are your dreams? What do you enjoy about being a kid?

I Want to Be

1 Mom, I want to be a singer,
You can see me on TV,
Perhaps I need some lessons,
Listen now, "Do-re-me!"

2 Dear Dorie, I'll teach you to sing,
I'll buy you a new TV,
But being a real singer,
Will take you away from me. ①

3 Okay, Mom, I'll be a sailor
And sail the sea so deep,
Wave to me from the shore,
I'll dream of you in sleep.

4 Daughter, how will I manage
When you sail so far away?
And don't forget this September,
You'll miss your first school day. ②

5 Okay, I can fly an airplane,
That would be really great,
Will you teach me to fly
And make the plane go straight?

6 Dorie, I am afraid of going up high,
I would have to stay down here.
But since I love you so much,
Go and fly away, my dear. ③

7 Oh, Mom, I've got years to decide
What to do and who to be,
For now, I'll stay with you,
And be a kid being me. ④

Listen to the poem. Pay attention to key details about the characters.

Which details tell what Dorie wants to do?
Which detail tells what she decides at the end?

I Want to Be

Key Ideas and Details

Preview the Focus Skills

Do a second reading of the Read Aloud as children look at the pictures. As you read, pause briefly where indicated below. Use the suggested think alouds to preview the unit's targeted reading skills and model how children might use the skills independently during shared reading.

- Pause after reading the second stanza. Say: *I look at the picture to see what Dorie is doing. She looks happy, which lets me know that she likes to sing. One thing I wonder when I look at this picture is who the boy taking a picture of Dorie is. At first I thought he might be her friend, but if she's imagining that she's famous, he might be a reporter or a fan. Thinking about the different parts of a story helps me understand the story and the characters.*

- Pause after reading the fourth stanza. Say: *I'm going to stop as I go through this poem to think about what has happened so far. I remember that Dorie has said that she wants to be a singer and a sailor; her mother says that both would take her too far away. Stopping to tell myself what has happened so far helps me remember and understand what I'm reading.*

- Pause after reading the sixth stanza. Say: *I also like to stop and think about the characters in the poem or story I'm reading. As I read, all the different things I learn about Dorie help me build up a picture of what she's like. I know from what I've read so far that she is adventurous and a dreamer.*

- Pause after reading the final stanza. Say: *After I finish a poem or story, I like to think about how it connects to me. I'm like Dorie because I've dreamed about what I want to be, even though I haven't dreamed about the exact same things. Thinking about the connections between you and a story makes the story more meaningful.*

Guided Instruction

OBJECTIVE
Ask and answer questions about details in a story.

Genre: Fantasy

Remind children that a fantasy story describes things that cannot happen in real life. In many fantasy stories, animals talk, think, and act like humans.

Set the Purpose

Help children understand the purpose for asking and answering questions by asking *How can asking questions help you understand a story? How does thinking about how the story connects to your life help you understand it better?*

Model and Teach

Read the text aloud as children follow along in their books.

Teacher Talk: Find Evidence

Explain to children that key details are the most important parts of a story. Say: *Key details tell who the main character is and what he or she does. I need to find the key details in a story. One way I do this is to ask myself questions and then answer them.*

First, I will ask myself "Who is this story about?" I will look for the names of the main character and his friends. I can also look at the picture to help me. What are the characters' names? (Bunny, Squirrel, Robin, Bear) Encourage children to respond in complete sentences, as appropriate.

Words to Know

talent
toward

Bunny's Talent
(Genre: Animal Fantasy)

1 Bunny likes his friends. Each friend has a **talent**. Each one can do something well. Squirrel can run up a tree. She jumps from branch to branch!

2 Robin can fly. He flaps his wings and takes off. He glides above the trees. He dives to the ground. Robin is good at flying.

3 Bear can catch fish. She puts her paw in the water. Then she grabs a fish. She eats it for dinner. Bear has a great skill.

4 Bunny cannot climb a tree. He cannot fly. He cannot catch a fish. He thinks and thinks. What talent does he have? What can he do well?

Guided Instruction

Teacher Talk: Find Evidence
Explain that key details are important pieces of information in a story. To find key details, readers can ask and answer questions. One kind of question asks *Who?* Ask: *Who is this story about?* Guide children to find and circle each animal's name in paragraphs 1–3.

14   Unit 1 ■ Reading Literature: Key Ideas and Details

Words to Know

talent (*noun*): something someone is good at doing
toward (*preposition*): in the direction of

Working with Word Meaning Ask children to stand in a circle. One child should say aloud one of his or her *talents*. Each child who shares that talent should take a step *toward* the speaker; those who do not should take a step away. Continue until each child has the chance to share a talent.

5   The friends are all thirsty. They go to the pond to drink. Suddenly, Bunny has a plan. He looks at the pond. Then he jumps into the water!

6   Bunny tries to swim. His feet go this way and that. He starts to sink to the bottom of the pond.

7   Bear swims out. Then she carries Bunny back to land. "Bunnies cannot swim," Bear says.

8   "I know that now," Bunny says.

9   Fox is thirsty, too. The friends see him across the pond. Fox sees them, too. He runs **toward** Bunny.

Teacher Talk: Find Evidence

Explain that readers can find key details to answer the questions *Where?* and *What?* Ask: *Where is Fox?* Have children put a box around the key detail that tells where Fox is. Then ask: *What does Fox do?* Guide children to underline the key detail that answers the question.

Guided Instruction

Unit 1 ■ Reading Literature: Key Ideas and Details   **15**

Support English Language Learners

Build an understanding of the word *talent*. Show pictures of famous athletes, writers, musicians, etc. Ask children to discuss: *What is this person's talent?* Have children work with a partner to discuss their own talents and how they use them.

Guided Instruction

Teacher Talk: Find Evidence

To support children in finding key details, say: *I am going to stop again and think about what I am reading to make sure I understand all the key details. I will ask myself "Where is Bunny?" and find a word that names a place.* (pond) *In paragraph 5, I see that the friends are at the pond. As I keep reading, a new character, Fox, appears. I ask myself "Where is Fox?" I will read on in paragraph 9 to find out.*

Explain that it's also important to ask about what happens in a story. Say: *I know that the events, or what happens in the story, are also important details. I can ask "What does Fox do?" to check my understanding of this detail. To answer the question, I will look for action words like* jumps, swims, carries, *and* runs. *Let's look in paragraph 9 to find out what Fox does.*

Finally, ask children to think about why Fox is running toward Bunny. Make sure that children realize that Fox intends to eat Bunny. Say: *Why is Fox running toward Bunny? Maybe he is Bunny's friend. But I also know that real foxes eat rabbits. Because he is running at Bunny, I think Fox might want to eat him. I will read on to find out if that's true. If Fox does want to eat Bunny, I wonder what Bunny will do. How can he escape Fox?*

Use Visuals

Use the visuals to help children make connections to what they read by asking them to explain what Bunny does in each picture. Say: *Good readers make connections between what the characters are feeling and the readers themselves. Have you ever tried new things like Bunny does? How did you feel when you tried something new?*

Guided Practice

Read and Practice

Remind children that they can ask and answer questions about the text to check their understanding. Have them study the picture and ask a question about what they think will happen. Then read the first sentence and discuss with children. Have heterogeneous partners take turns reading the rest of the text as you circulate to provide support. While they read the text, remind them to pay attention to key details that answer *who, what, where, when,* and *why.*

Teacher Talk: Find Evidence

Allow children time to read the page with their partners. Then go through the Find Evidence instruction. Point out that the question "What can Bunny do?" is asking for Bunny's talent. Remind children that asking and answering this question will help them understand the story. Say: *I know I am looking for a key detail. Bunny has been looking for his talent all along, so the question "What can Bunny do?" is asking about his talent. I will look in the text and in the picture to help me answer this question. The picture shows Bunny far ahead of Fox. It looks like he escaped! I'll read the text carefully to find out what Bunny did to get away.*

Team Jigsaw

Place children in groups of four, and assign each child in the group one character. Each child must decide the talent of that animal and describe it in a sentence, using his or her own words. Then, the four sentences are put together to be shared with the rest of the class. Discuss each animal's unique talent.

Understanding Key Details

Words to Know

fancy

10 (Bunny hops very fast.) Fox cannot run that fast. Fox stops. He shakes his head. Bunny gets away!

11 Bunny joins his friends again.

12 "Wow," Robin says. "You are fast."

13 Bear says, "You hop faster than anyone."

Guided Practice

Teacher Talk: Find Evidence
Review that readers can ask or answer a question to find a key detail. Have children find and circle the key detail that answers the question, "What can Bunny do?"

16   Unit 1 ■ Reading Literature: Key Ideas and Details

Words to Know

fancy (*adjective*): special

Working with Word Meaning Ask the children to tell something they can do that is fancy. Challenge children to dance regularly and dance fancy.

Key Ideas and Details

14   Squirrel says, "You did some **fancy** hopping just now!"

15   Bunny grins. "Thanks," he says. He is glad. He knows what he can do well.

Comprehension Check   (MORE ONLINE) sadlierconnect.com

1. Reread "Bunny's Talent." Which key detail in the story tells what Bunny tries to do?

   a. Bunny tries to fly.

   b. Bunny tries to catch fish.

   c. Bunny tries to swim.

2. Have you helped a friend know that he or she has a talent? Find key details in the story that tell how Bunny's friends help him. Then tell how you helped your friend.

   Sample answer: Bunny's friends tell him that he is a fast

   hopper. I told my friend that she is a good swimmer.

Teacher Talk: Find Evidence
Have children underline the key details that answer the question "Why does Bunny grin?"

Independent Practice

Unit 1 ■ Reading Literature: Key Ideas and Details   **17**

Foundational Skills Review: Fluency Practice

Tell children that part of reading is paying attention to punctuation marks because the marks can show where characters are talking and what characters are feeling and thinking. Direct children to paragraph 15. Point out the punctuation marks and ask children to listen for places where your voice shows excitement. Model reading the paragraph. Then have children chorally read the paragraph. Have them work in groups of three to continue practicing with another paragraph. Additional fluency passages and activities can be found at **sadlierconnect.com**.

Independent Practice

Read and Apply

Have children read paragraphs 14 and 15 independently as you circulate. After they have read the paragraphs, have pairs of children talk about the text.

Teacher Talk: Find Evidence

Say: *Think about reasons that someone might grin or smile—what would that person be feeling? What is Bunny feeling at the end of the story?* Use the directions in Teacher Talk so children can complete the activity.

Comprehension Check

Answer Explanations:

1. Choice **C** tells what Bunny tries to do.

2. Children should mention that Bunny's friends tell him that he is a fast hopper, and then relate a time they complimented a friend.

Critical Comprehension

Use the following question to help children think more deeply about the selection. Children should support their answers with evidence from the text.

- *What lesson can you learn from Bunny's experience?* (I can learn that everyone has unique talents. I should focus on what I can do best and not try to be like others.)

Assess and Respond
If children have difficulty answering the questions in the Comprehension Check . . .
Then work with them to create a 5W graphic organizer listing *who, what, where, when,* and *why.*

Unit 1 ■ Reading Literature: Key Ideas and Details   **17**

Guided Instruction

OBJECTIVES
- Retell stories and identify their lessons.
- Answer questions about key details in a text read aloud.

Genre: Fable

Tell children that fables are a kind of literature that often have animals as characters and end with a lesson or moral.

Set the Purpose

Help children understand the purpose for learning the reading skill by asking *Have you ever retold a story to a friend? How did you remember all the important parts?*

Model and Teach

Read the text aloud as children follow along in their books.

Teacher Talk: Find Evidence

Tell children that retelling a story helps us understand and remember it. To retell, we tell the most important events in our own words. So, we must understand the key details as we read. Say: *The first key detail is that this story is about a talent show. The next key details are what each animal does in the show. Lion is the first to show his talent. I will reread paragraph 4 to find out what trick he does and circle it.*

What do the other animals do? (Parrot tells jokes, and Monkey dances.) Encourage children to respond in complete sentences.

Retelling Stories

Words to Know

prance
worry

The Elephant Dance
(Genre: Fable)

1   It was a hot day in the forest. It was too hot to work.

2   "What can we do?" Lion asked.

3   "We can play. We can have a talent show," Monkey said.

4   Lion climbed a tree. He waved to his friends. Everyone clapped for Lion.

5   Parrot began to tell jokes. Her friends laughed at her jokes. She was very funny. Everyone clapped for Parrot.

6   Then Monkey started to **prance**. She waved her hands. Monkey could dance very well. Everyone clapped for Monkey.

Guided Instruction

Teacher Talk: Find Evidence

Tell children that when we retell a story, we tell it in our own words. We include important details. We tell the events in the order they happen. Ask: *What does Lion do?* Have children circle the words that tell what Lion does. Then discuss what the other animals do.

Words to Know

prance (*verb*): to dance and skip around
worry (*verb*): to feel upset about something or about what might happen

Working with Word Meaning Help children understand the words by acting them out. Ask children: Can you *prance* like a horse? Then, ask children to turn and talk to a partner and share something that may make them *worry*.

7   "Well done!" said Lion.

8   "You have talent," said Parrot.

9   "Thank you," Monkey said. "But now I am too hot!"

10   Elephant began to **worry**. What could she do? <u>She tried to climb a tree.</u> She slid right down. <u>She tried to tell a joke.</u> No one laughed. <u>Then she tried to dance a jig.</u>

11   Elephant's legs were heavy. She was not light on her feet. The ground shook. Elephant could not dance.

12   "You cannot dance!" Parrot yelled.

13   "You are not a monkey!" Lion roared. "Do something only an elephant can do."

Teacher Talk: Find Evidence

Explain that in a retelling, we include important details and the story's message. Ask: *What does Elephant try to do?* Have children underline the sentences in paragraph 10 that tell. Then explain that Elephant will be good at doing things only elephants can do.

Guided Instruction

Guided Instruction

Teacher Talk: Find Evidence

Explain that as we read and retell a story, we include important details and the story's most important message. Say: *The key details of a story can help me learn what the story's message is. I can think about how the main character feels, what he or she does, and what the character learns. Elephant is the main character in this story. To help myself understand her better, I'll look at her actions, or what she does in the story.*

In this part of the story, Elephant tries many things. I will reread this page to see what those are. Direct children to find and underline the sentences in paragraph 10 that explain the things that Elephant tries to do.

Review: Understanding Key Details

Remind children that it's important to look for the important details in a story as they read. They can find out these details by asking themselves questions that begin with *who, what, where, when,* or *why.*

Differentiate Instruction

For children who need more support retelling, provide sentence frames such as the following to guide their identification of key elements:

The animals _____.

Elephant felt _____.

Then she tried _____.

But she _____.

Guided Practice

Read and Practice

Have heterogeneous partners take turns reading page 20 as you circulate to provide support. Before children begin reading, remind them to pay attention to important events that happen at the end of the story that help Elephant realize her talent.

Teacher Talk: Find Evidence

Give children time to underline the key details about what Elephant can do. Remind them that they can look at the picture for a clue. Then say: *Now it is time to retell the story so far. When I start to retell a story, I think about the most important characters and events. I think about what the main character does and what he or she learns. I think about the message of the story. I can look back over the pages of the story to help me remember. I can even make my own notes or draw my own pictures to help myself retell the story.*

Then have children retell the key details and the central message of the story to a partner.

Retelling Stories

Words to Know
spray
shower

14 Elephant went to get water to drink. She got an idea. She drank more. Then she came back to her friends. She raised her trunk above them. She began to **spray** water on them. The water was like a **shower**.

15 Everyone clapped. "Thank you, Elephant!" Lion said.

16 "We were very hot," Monkey said. "Now we are not."

Guided Practice

Teacher Talk: Find Evidence
Elephant realizes that she can do something important. Have children underline the key details that tell what Elephant does when she realizes she can do something. Then have children retell the story, including its message, to a partner.

20 Unit 1 ■ Reading Literature: Key Ideas and Details

Words to Know

shower (*noun*): type of bath where water falls down from above
spray (*verb*): to squirt, like water from a hose

Working with Word Meaning Have children create illustrations for each word. Explain that they should draw a picture of a light rain shower and a picture of spray from a hose.

Key Ideas and Details

17 Parrot agreed. "That was a clever idea!"

18 Elephant laughed. ⭐"I just did what an elephant can do."

Comprehension Check

(MORE ONLINE) sadlierconnect.com

1. Which sentence tells a key detail that happens at the beginning of the story?

    a. Elephant tries to dance like Monkey.

    b. The animals clap for Monkey.

    c. Monkey dances for her friends.

2. What does Elephant learn in this story? Write three sentences that tell what she learns. Include key details from the story.

Sample answer: Elephant learns that everyone can

do something well. Some animals can climb, tell jokes,

or dance. Elephants can spray water.

Teacher Talk: Find Evidence
Have children draw a star next to Elephant's words that tell the central message of the story.

Independent Practice

Unit 1 ■ Reading Literature: Key Ideas and Details   **21**

Independent Practice

Read and Apply

Have children read the paragraphs on page 21 independently as you circulate. Provide extra support to struggling readers by choral reading with them.

Teacher Talk: Find Evidence

Explain that paying attention to key details can help readers figure out the lesson in a story. Say: *First, I'll think about key details that tell what Elephant does. Then I'll think about what she says.*

Comprehension Check

Answer Explanations:

1. Choice **C** tells the story detail that happens first.

2. Ask children what Elephant learns from each thing she tries.

Critical Comprehension

Use the following questions to help children think critically about the selection. Children should be prepared to support their answers with evidence from the text.

- *How did Elephant's friends help her learn the lesson?* (Her friends complimented her.)

- *What can you learn from the message?* (I can find my own talents.)

Assess and Respond

If children have difficulty answering the questions in the Comprehension Check . . .

Then have partners work together to mark each event. Have partners tell each other what Elephant tries, what happens, and what she learns from each thing she tries.

Peer Collaboration

Have children work in teams of three. Remind them that when retelling a story, they should include all the important events. Assign children in each group to focus on the events in the beginning, middle, and end. Each student writes a retelling of the events in his or her part of the story. Then, they share their writing. They make any changes and then combine them to create a team retelling that can be shared with the class.

Guided Instruction

OBJECTIVES
- Describe the characters, settings, and main events in a story.
- Answer questions about key details in a text read aloud.

Genre: Adventure Story

Explain that an adventure story tells about a character that solves an exciting problem through a series of events.

Set the Purpose

Help children understand the purpose for learning to describe characters, settings, and major events by asking: *What are the most important parts of a story? Can you imagine a story without a character or without a problem to solve?*

Model and Teach

Read the text aloud as children follow along in their books.

Teacher Talk: Find Evidence

Explain that the setting is where a story takes place. Say: *The first sentence tells me that the story takes place at a campground. To understand more about the setting, I look for details in the pictures and text. The picture shows woods in the background and a girl setting up a tent, a woman building a campfire, a man cooking, and a boy gathering wood.* Have children mark setting details in the text. Ask volunteers to tell what they know about the campground, encouraging them to respond in complete sentences.

Describing Story Elements

Words to Know

gather
heavy

Rocky's Boat Ride
(Genre: Adventure Story)

1   I was excited for our first day at the ★campground. Maria put up the tent. Mom built a campfire. Dad's job was to cook. I was everyone's helper.

2   "Milton, please **gather** some wood," Dad said.

3   I went to get some logs. Then I looked for Rocky, our dog. He had come along with me. But now I could not spot him.

4   I looked over at the river. I saw our red canoe. A big yellow ball of fur was inside the boat. It was Rocky!

5   "Rocky, come!" I yelled.

Guided Instruction

Teacher Talk: Find Evidence

Have children draw a star next to the word *campground*. Explain that this is the setting—where the story takes place. Key details tell about the setting. Ask: *What do you know about the campground?* Have children circle words and pictures that tell more about the setting.

Words to Know

gather (*verb*): to collect; pick up
heavy (*adjective*): hard to lift up

Working with Word Meaning   Ask children to tell about a time when they were asked to gather something. What did they gather? Was it heavy or light?

Guided Instruction

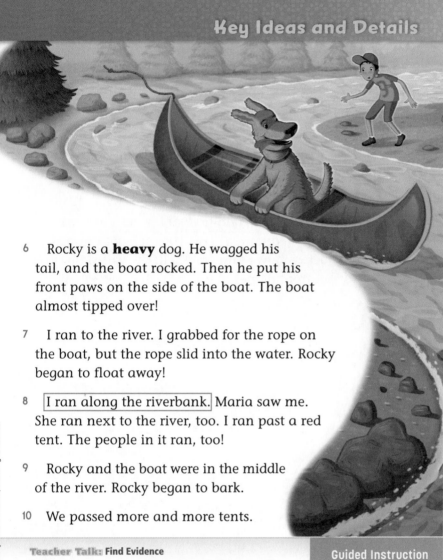

6   Rocky is a **heavy** dog. He wagged his tail, and the boat rocked. Then he put his front paws on the side of the boat. The boat almost tipped over!

7   I ran to the river. I grabbed for the rope on the boat, but the rope slid into the water. Rocky began to float away!

8   I ran along the riverbank. Maria saw me. She ran next to the river, too. I ran past a red tent. The people in it ran, too!

9   Rocky and the boat were in the middle of the river. Rocky began to bark.

10   We passed more and more tents.

Teacher Talk: Find Evidence

Explain that the characters are the people or animals in a story. The events are the things that the characters do. Have children put a box around the sentence that tells what Milton does when he sees Rocky float away. Ask: *What does this action tell us about Milton?*

Guided Instruction

Unit 1 ■ Reading Literature: Key Ideas and Details   **23**

Teacher Talk: Find Evidence

Tell children that characters are the people or animals that the story is about and that events are things that happen to the characters or that the characters do. Say: *As I read, I look for the names of people and animals that are doing things in the story. These are the characters. Usually a story focuses on one main character and the things he or she does. This story tells about the things Milton does and what happens to him. I've just read about an event that happens to Milton when his dog Rocky gets into a boat and starts to float away. I can look at how characters respond to an event to help me better understand a story.* Ask children to box the words that describe the action Milton takes when Rocky floats away. Say: *As I look at each event, I ask myself, "Why does the character do this?"*

In this paragraph, Milton chases after Rocky. What does this action say about Milton?

Review: Retelling Stories

Remind children that retelling stories helps us to check our understanding. A retelling does not include every detail. Instead it focuses on key events. Ask: *Why is it important to tell the events in the order they happen?* (The events build on one another. Telling the events out of order is confusing to the listener.)

Support English Language Learners

English language learners may benefit from using a graphic organizer such as a story map to identify the key elements. Model for children how to list the characters and do a close reading of the text and pictures to find words to describe the setting. Then, guide children in identifying the key events and placing them in order. After children understand the model, allow them to work with partners to complete a story map.

Guided Practice

Read and Practice

Have heterogeneous partners take turns reading page 24 as you circulate to provide support. Before children begin reading, read paragraphs 11 and 12 aloud and model identifying who these speakers are and what their words tell readers about the event.

Teacher Talk: Find Evidence

Remind children that key details in a story describe how events turn out and what happens in the end of the story. Then ask children to look for the events that show what happens to Rocky. Say: *Milton has a problem: he can't reach Rocky in the boat. The story tells me how the problem is solved. The problem and its solution are two key story details. I'm going to look for sentences that describe these important events.*

Team Jigsaw

Divide the class into groups of three. Assign each group member a drawing that shows characters, the setting, or the events. Then, the children should use the pictures to describe the story elements to the class.

Digital Connection

Allow children to use a word-processing program to create a newspaper article describing Rocky's rescue. Model how to create text boxes for images and text.

Describing Story Elements

Words to Know

caught
rescue

11 "Someone must **rescue** that dog!" a man yelled.

12 "The river is very deep," a woman said.

13 There was a large rock in the middle of the river. The boat hit the rock. Then it hit another. Rocky barked louder.

14 The boat began to float toward the bank. It moved slowly to us. The rope got **caught** between two large rocks. Rocky was right in front of me!

15 I waved my arms. I jumped up and down. Rocky saw me. He jumped out of the boat. Rocky was safe!

Guided Practice

Teacher Talk: Find Evidence

Point out that key details in the story explain what happens to the boat so that Rocky can get back on land. Have children underline the sentences that tell these details.

24   Unit 1 ■ Reading Literature: Key Ideas and Details

Words to Know

caught (*adjective*): stuck; trapped
rescue (*verb*): to save; help

Working with Word Meaning Ask the children to name ways that animals can get caught, such as in a net or in bushes. Then, have children explain how you can rescue the animals.

16   Maria pulled the boat to the bank. A woman helped her carry the boat back to our camp.

17   Mom and Dad ran to hug me and Maria. They patted Rocky.

18   "We are so thankful that you are safe," Dad said.

Comprehension Check

(MORE ONLINE) sadlierconnect.com

1. What is the best way to describe Milton in this story?

   a. He is worried about his dog.

   b. He is happy about camping.

   c. He is mad about the boat.

2. Retell the important events in this story. Include key details about the characters and the setting.

Sample answer: Milton's dog, Rocky, floated down the river

in a boat. Milton ran along the bank after him. The rope

on the boat got caught between two rocks. Then Rocky

jumped out on the shore.

Teacher Talk: Find Evidence
Have children put a box around the key details that tell what Mom and Dad do at the end of the story.

Independent Practice

Extend Thinking: Create an Award

Have children imagine that they are presenting Milton with an award for rescuing Rocky. Allow time for them to design an award, including an award name that reflects his actions. Then, allow them to share their awards with the class. They should note the specific events that led to Milton's receiving the award.

Independent Practice

Read and Apply

Have children read the three paragraphs on page 25 independently as you circulate. Provide extra support to struggling readers by choral reading the paragraphs with them.

Teacher Talk: Find Evidence

Have children find the names *Mom* and *Dad* in the story. Say: *Now that you've found the names of these two characters, reread the surrounding text to find out how they act when they see Milton and Rocky are back safe.*

Comprehension Check

Answer Explanations:

1. Choice **A** is correct. Milton is worried about his dog, Rocky.

2. Retellings should include the characters, setting, and key events, including the problem and how it is resolved.

Critical Comprehension

Use the following question to help children think critically about the selection. Children should support their answers with evidence from the text.

- *Is Milton a hero? Explain why or why not.* (Children should support their answers with an example from the text, such as the onlookers' cries for someone to help Rocky.)

Assess and Respond
If children have difficulty answering the questions in the Comprehension Check . . .
Then have them create an event ladder of the events. Ask them what each event tells them about Milton.

OBJECTIVE

Read decodable text featuring words with short vowels, *l* blends, *r* blends, *s* blends, and final blends.

Prepare to Read

Tell children that you will be reading a poem about some friends who have different interests but still enjoy spending time together. As you read, children should listen for short vowel sounds along with *r*, *l*, *s*, and final blends.

Introduce Phonics Skills

After you have read the selection once, read it again, this time focusing on the target phonics skills.

- *Look at the word* it. *The letter* i *stands for the /ĭ/ sound. Now look at* can. *The letter* a *stands for the /ă/ sound.* Present the short *o, u,* and e sounds with the words *not, bugs,* and *Jess.*

- *Look at the word* blocks. *It begins with the letters* b *and* l. *You blend the sounds of these two letters to make the /bl/ sound.*

- *Now look at the word* grace. *It begins with the letters* g *and* r *that stand for the /gr/ sound.* Present s blends and final blends with the words *skates* and *just.*

- Direct children to the second line in stanza 2 and explain that this line is a complete sentence—it begins with a capital letter and ends with a period or other end mark.

Focus on Fluency

Explain that reading correctly is important because it helps us and our listeners understand what we read. Read stanza 2 with no pauses and help children see that without a pause after *paint,* we may think that James is painting Jess. Prompt children to pay attention to punctuation as they read.

Foundational Skills Read Together

As you read along with the poem, listen for short vowel sounds and consonant blends.

The Best in Me

James can paint a picture just right.
Jess builds spaceships with blocks.
Dee skates on the ice with grace.
I collect snails, bugs, and rocks.

James shows us how to paint.
Jess shows us stars in the night.
Dee shows us how to skate.
I show them bugs that do not bite!

We do not do the same things,
But we have fun together.
We take turns doing what we like,
No matter what kind of weather!

It is fun to play with three friends
Who bring out the best in me.
I hope I do the same for them,
My buddies—James, Jess, and Dee.

Focus on Phonological Awareness

Distinguishing Long and Short Vowel Sounds

Read the list of single-syllable words below. Ask children to stretch their arms up tall if they hear the long vowel sound and to bend down low if they hear a short vowel sound.

dig (short)	cape (long)	team (long)	mask (short)	tug (short)
cone (long)	bed (short)	tube (long)	ripe (long)	top (short)

Foundational Skills Reader 1

DIRECTIONS: Cut and fold the book.

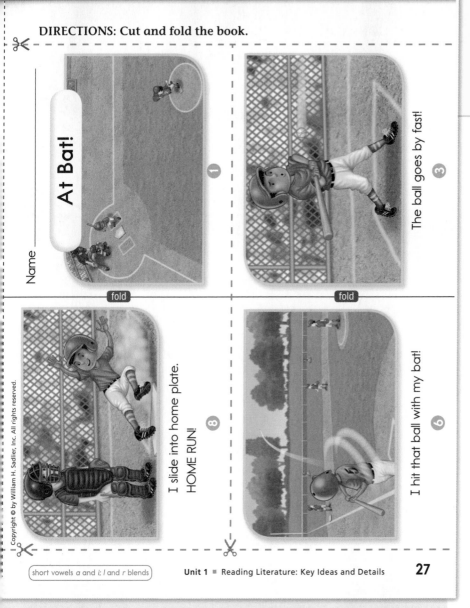

short vowels *a* and *i*; *l* and *r* blends   Unit 1 ■ Reading Literature: Key Ideas and Details   **27**

OBJECTIVES

- **Read decodable text featuring words with short vowels *a* and *i*, *l* blends, and *r* blends.**
- **Read along orally with accuracy and appropriate rate.**

Prepare to Read

Tell children that they will be reading a story about a child who is playing baseball. When they are finished reading, they can take the book home to share. Have them follow the directions to cut and fold the book.

Review Phonics Skills

Explain that this book features many words with the short and long vowel sounds and blends. Review the targeted phonics skills.

- *Remember that a and i can stand for a short vowel sound.*
- *Remember when you see l blends like* pl, sl, bl, fl, *and* gl, *you blend the sounds together. When you see r blends like* br, cr, dr, fr, gr, pr, *and* tr, *you blend the two sounds together, too.*
- Review the characteristics of sentences with children. Lead them in a shared writing activity to compose sentences with different end marks.

Introduce Reader 1

Divide the class into two groups. Assign each group to read even or odd pages. Have each group chorally read its corresponding page after you read each line aloud.

Foundational Skills: Phonics Practice

Write the following words from the Read Together and Foundational Skills Reader 1 on the board or on a chart. Have children practice reading the words.

Read Together **short vowels *a* and *i*:** can, ships; ***l* blends:** blocks, play; ***r* blends:** grace

Foundational Skills Reader 1 **short vowels *a* and *i*:** bat, fast, hit, with, ***l* blends:** play, flies; ***r* blends:** grab, strike, cries

Read with a Partner

Select pairs of children to read together. Allow each pair to read the text together several times: first chorally, and then individually. Once the pairs are comfortable with one of their oral readings, have them record it for playing back later.

Focus on Fluency

Remind children that fluent readers read correctly. These readers pay attention to punctuation to help them know when sentences end and begin. Model fluent reading by using the Fluency Practice activity below.

Reading at Home

Once children are comfortable reading the book, send it home for children to read to family members.

Assess and Respond
If children have difficulty reading words with blends . . .
Then write the words on index cards. Have the children cut the words into strips according to their sounds with the two letters of the blend on one chunk, e.g. gl/a/d. Then, read the words together.

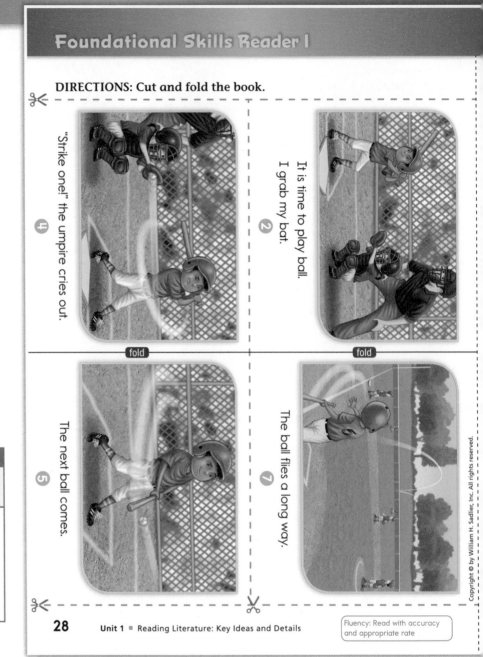

Foundational Skills Reader I

DIRECTIONS: Cut and fold the book.

"Strike one!" the umpire cries out.

④

It is time to play ball. I grab my bat.

②

The next ball comes.

⑤

The ball flies a long way.

⑦

28 Unit 1 ■ Reading Literature: Key Ideas and Details

Fluency: Read with accuracy and appropriate rate

Foundational Skills: Fluency Practice

Explain to children that reading accurately means not only getting the words right but also "showing" the punctuation marks with their voice. Discuss the common punctuation marks—comma, period, question mark, and exclamation mark. Work with children to identify the punctuation marks of "At Bat!" Model reading page 3, emphasizing reading with excitement to reflect an exclamation mark. Then chorally read the page. Follow this same procedure with another page. Additional fluency passages and activities can be found at **sadlierconnect.com**.

Foundational Skills Reader 2

DIRECTIONS: Cut and fold the book.

Name _____

I Can!

I can spell lots of words.

I will tell you this.
I can do anything!

I can hop like a bunny.

short vowels o, u, e; s blends; final blends

Unit 1 ■ Reading Literature: Key Ideas and Details **29**

OBJECTIVES
- **Read decodable text featuring words with short vowels o, u, and e; s blends; and final blends.**
- **Read along orally with accuracy and appropriate rate.**

Prepare to Read

Tell children that the next book they will be reading tells them about different things that some kids can do. Once they have read the story, they can take the book home to share. Have them follow the directions to cut and fold the book.

Review Phonics Skills

Remind children that you are focusing on short vowel sounds and words with blends.

- *The letters o, u, and e can stand for short vowel sounds. What are the short sounds of o, u, and e?*
- Write *sp* on the board. Say: *How would you read this blend? Circle the word on this page with this blend.* (spell)
- Write *ng* on the board. Say: *Pay attention to blends that come at the ends of words. How would you read this final blend? Circle the word on this page with this blend.* (anything)

Introduce Reader 2

Have the class echo read the book with you sentence by sentence. When reading, be sure to model how to observe punctuation. Consider holding up your hand in a stop motion to show a longer pause at a period. Children can hold up their hands as they echo read, too.

Foundational Skills: Phonics Practice

Write the following words from Foundational Skills Reader 2 on the board or on a chart. Have children practice reading the words.

Words with short o, u, or e: spell, lots, will, this, hop, bunny, swim, frog, run, just, funny

Words with s blends: swim, spell

Words with final blends: sing, just, anything

Read with a Partner

Form heterogeneous pairs of children so that stronger readers can help those who struggle. Have each pair read the text together several times. Once the pairs are comfortable with one of their oral readings, have them record it for playing back later.

Focus on Fluency

Remind children that fluent readers read with expression. Ask them to explain why this is important. (It makes the reading more enjoyable and helps them understand the text better.) Focus their attention on page 29. Ask them to follow along with their eyes as you read and raise their hands when they see a punctuation mark that shows excitement. Then chorally read the page with expression.

Reading at Home

Once children are comfortable reading the book, send it home for children to read to family members.

Assess and Respond
If children have difficulty decoding and pronouncing words with consonant blends . . .
Then allow them to pronounce the sounds separately when decoding the words, and then practice pronouncing the words with the consonant blends.

Foundational Skills Reader 2

DIRECTIONS: Cut and fold the book.

I can swim like a frog. ④

I can sing like a bird. ②

I can run, skip, or jump. ⑤

Or I can just be funny. ⑦

fold

fold

30   Unit 1 ■ Reading Literature: Key Ideas and Details

Fluency: Read with accuracy and appropriate rate

Foundational Skills: Fluency Practice

Review with children the punctuation marks used in the reader. Explain that a comma should be read with a short pause, and a sentence end mark should be read with a longer pause. Read one or two pages from the book in a dysfluent manner, omitting pauses for punctuation. Ask children to critique your reading, reinforcing that an accurate reading "shows" the punctuation marks in the text. Choral read the entire reader. Have children practice; then record them reading aloud. Additional fluency passages can be found at **sadlierconnect.com**.

Talk, Talk, Talk!

(Genre: Realistic Fiction)

1 I like to talk. I even talk when I watch TV.

2 "Silence, please!" my sister begs. "Please be quiet, Kento."

3 I talk at lunch.

4 "Stop talking!" my mother says. "You need to eat."

5 We go to a baseball game. I talk there, too. Music plays. The crowd cheers. I talk, but Dad cannot hear me.

6 I talk to my best friend, Sam. He likes to talk, too. We talk about trucks and dogs. We talk about planes and baseball.

Unit 1 ■ Reading Literature: Key Ideas and Details **31**

OBJECTIVES

- **Ask and answer questions about details in a story.**
- **Retell stories and identify their lessons.**
- **Describe the characters, settings, and main events in a story.**

Genre: Realistic Fiction

Remind children that realistic fiction tells a story with a setting and events that could happen in real life. Instruct children to identify the characters, setting, and events of the story as they read. While reading, they can ask and answer questions to check their understanding of the key details. Then, once they are finished, they can retell the story using the details they have learned.

Path Options

You may wish to have children read the text independently and apply the skills learned in this unit. Or you may wish to do a close reading with children; if so, use the supports provided on these pages. As a third option, set up a buddy system, with some heterogeneous and some homogenous pairs, to fit the needs of your class. Regardless, children should read the text more than once to facilitate understanding and to be able to answer the Comprehension Check questions correctly.

Support English Language Learners

If you decide to have children read the text on their own, be aware that English language learners may struggle to read it independently. You may wish to create a recording of this selection for children to listen to and follow along.

Support First Reading

Circulate to check children's understanding. As needed, use the following comprehension and strategy check-ins to support basic understanding of the selection as children read.

Check-in Questions

- **page 31** *How do you think Kento's family would describe him? Think about what his family members say.* (talkative) *Would your family describe you this way?*

- **pages 31–32** *Who does Kento like to talk to?* (his family, his friend Sam, his dog)

- **page 32** *What event is making Kento scared and shy?* (He is going to a new school, where no one will know him.)

Review: Understanding Key Details

Remind children that asking and answering questions helps them to better understand the key details of a story. Have them turn to talk with a partner to ask and answer a question that begins with *who.* Repeat with *where, what, when,* and *why.*

Review: Making Connections

Explain that good readers make connections to what they read. Ask children to reread paragraph 8. Ask: *How is Kento feeling?* (shy) *When is a time you have felt shy in a new place?*

Review: Retelling Stories

Remind children that when they retell a story, they should include the most important events in the order they happen. Pair children and allow them to practice retelling the story, using the pictures as support.

7   I talk to my dog. She listens. She wags her tail. She puts her paw on my lap. I talk some more.

8   Today, I am going to a new school. That is scary. I do not know anybody. No one knows me. For the first time, I do not talk. I feel shy.

9   We all sit in a circle. The teacher asks us what we did last summer. Everyone is quiet. Then I start talking. I talk about my dog. I talk about the baseball game and the home run I saw.

10   "Do you know what I liked best about summer?" I say. "The baseball game!"

11   "I like baseball," a girl says. "I also like to swim in the pool."

32   Unit 1 ■ Reading Literature: Key Ideas and Details

Differentiate Instruction

For children who struggle to retell a story, break the story into three parts: beginning, middle, and end. Have the children fold a piece of paper into three rectangles and draw a picture to represent the events in each part of the story. Then they may use the drawings to retell the story by describing the pictured events in the beginning, middle, and end.

12   Then everyone starts talking. Now I know something about all of my classmates.

13   My teacher speaks to me. She says, "Thank you for talking in our circle. You were a big help. Now everyone feels less shy."

14   "It is easy for me," I say. "I love to talk!"

Comprehension Check

1. Which detail from the story tells what Kento likes to do?
   a. He talks to everyone.
   b. He plays music.
   c. He swims in a pool.

2. What is the setting where most of this story takes place?
   a. at Kento's home
   b. in Kento's school
   c. at the ball park

Unit 1 ■ Reading Literature: Key Ideas and Details   **33**

Strategic Reading

Support all readers by reminding them of the importance of asking and answering questions as they read. Explain that if you ask questions you will be more actively engaged with the text. You will be looking for answers to your questions, which will help you understand and remember what you read. Help children create and complete a 5Ws/1H (Who, What, Where, When, Why, How) chart to help them ask and answer questions.

Review: Describing Story Elements

Use a story map to review the major story elements in "Talk, Talk, Talk!" Ask children: *Who is the story about? Where does the story take place? What are the major events? Do you think Kento learns a lesson in the story?*

Multiple Readings for Critical Comprehension

Have children reread this selection, and pose questions that focus on critical comprehension. Remind children that they can mark the text.

- *What is Kento's talent?* (talking) *How does Kento use his talent?* (He makes others feel comfortable talking in his new class.)
- *How does Kento's family respond to his talking? How do his classmates respond?* (Kento's family often asks him to be quiet, but his classmates like his talking and it encourages them to talk, too.)

Comprehension Check

Score children's understanding of unit skills and texts using the Comprehension Check on this page and the next. Use the children's total score to determine their readiness for the Unit 1 Review on page 37.

Multiple-Choice Questions: *1 point each*

1. Answer choice **A** is correct because the text tells about Kento talking to his friends, family, and dog.

2. Answer choice **B** is correct. This is where Kento's problem occurs and where he solves the problem.

Short-Answer Questions:
2 points each

Item 3 Rubric

2	Children list the key events in order, including the main character, his problem, and how he solves the problem.
1	Children retell some events from the story, but do not include all the key events, or tell them out of order.
0	Children cannot retell the key events from the story.

Item 4 Rubric

2	Children describe Kento and explain why he is like someone they know.
1	Children either describe Kento or a friend but not both.
0	Children are unable to describe Kento or make the connection to someone they know.

Theme Wrap-Up

Lead children in a discussion on what they have learned from the theme "All About Me." Ask them to share what they learned about people and their talents. Ask if this knowledge has affected how they think about others or about themselves.

Close Reading

3. Retell the key events that happen in this story.

Sample answer: Kento talks to everyone. Then he goes to a

new school. He sits in a circle with other kids. Everyone is

shy and quiet. Kento starts talking. Then everyone else

starts talking, too.

_____

_____

4. Who do you know that is like Kento? Use details from the text to tell what Kento is like. Then tell why you think the person is like Kento.

Sample answer: Kento is friendly. He likes to talk

to his family. He likes to talk to his friends. I am

like Kento. I like to talk to my family and friends.

_____

_____

_____

34   Unit 1 ▪ Reading Literature: Key Ideas and Details

Assess and Respond (pages 31–34)

If	Then
Children scored 0–2 points; they are **Developing** their understanding of unit skills …	Provide children with reading support and more intensive modeling of skills.
Children scored 3–4 points; they are **Improving** their understanding of unit skills …	Use children's scores to target areas that are weak and review those specific skills.
Children scored 5–6 points; they are **Proficient** in their understanding of unit skills …	Have these children move on. They are ready for the formal assessment.

Compare and Contrast Texts

Look at the pictures from three texts you have read. Think about the characters in each story. Be ready to tell how they are alike.

The Elephant Dance

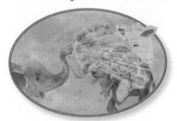

Bunny's Talent

Talk, Talk, Talk!

Return to the Essential Question

How do the details of a story work together?

How are the things the characters do and learn alike? Use details from each story in your answer.

Unit 1 ■ Reading Literature: Key Ideas and Details **35**

Compare and Contrast Texts

Read aloud the directions on page 35. Then provide some information about each of the featured texts, to help children as they recall the key details.

"The Elephant Dance" is the story about the animals having a talent show. Do you remember what Elephant did? (She sprayed water on everyone.)

The story "Bunny's Talent" is about Bunny, who was sad because he couldn't do things that other animals could do. What does Bunny do when he sees Fox? (He hops away.) *How does this make him feel better?* (He realizes he is a good hopper.)

The selection "Talk, Talk, Talk!" is the story about a boy who likes to talk. How does his love of talking help him? (He makes friends at his new school.)

Give children time to organize their thoughts about the texts. Have them ask questions about the texts before you begin to discuss them. Then lead the Essential Question discussion.

Support Essential Question Discussion

Read the Essential Question aloud. Then prompt children to share their ideas about their selections. Remind children to raise their hands and wait for you to call on them.

- *What problems do the characters in these stories have? How do they solve the problems?*

- *Which character reminds you of yourself or someone else you know?*

- *What lessons can people learn from these stories?*

Discussion Skills

As children read the texts, encourage them to make connections to themselves and other texts they have read. Review discussion skills with the children, reminding them that active participants listen to others' ideas, revoice them, and add their own reasoning. You can encourage these skills by asking questions such as the following:

Can you repeat what he or she just said in your own words?

Do you agree? Why?

Would you like to add another idea?

OBJECTIVES

- **Use context to figure out word meanings.**
- **Connect word meanings to real life.**

Guided Instruction

Read aloud the Guided Instruction section on page 36. Be sure children understand that they are defining the boldfaced word *silence.* Ask: *How does reading around the word help you understand its meaning?* (It helps me know that you need to be quiet so that there will be silence.)

Guided and Independent Practice

Explain that the children are to look for clues to the meaning of the boldfaced word.

If children struggle to find a clue to the meaning of the word *sprints,* ask: *What other action words do you see?*

Apply to Reading

Have children return to "The Elephant Dance." Point to the last word, *jig,* in paragraph 10. Ask children to read around the word to find the meaning. Then ask them to turn to a partner and discuss the clue that helped them find the meaning. Discuss with the class that the words before *jig* tell that it is a kind of dance. By rereading the sentence, they can understand what *jig* means.

Language

Word Meanings

Guided Instruction Sometimes you may not be sure of a word's meaning. You can look for a clue nearby. Then you can use the word when you write and speak. Read this sentence from "Talk, Talk, Talk!"

"**Silence**, please!" my sister begs. "Please be quiet, Kento."

The word *quiet* gives you a clue about the meaning of the word *silence.*

Guided and Independent Practice Underline the word or words that help you figure out the meaning of the word in **dark print**. Then write a sentence to answer the question.

1. A rabbit **sprints** across the yard. It runs too fast to catch.

   What is another animal that **sprints**?

   Sample answer: A horse sprints to win a race.

2. A fish **leaped** out of water. It jumped out to catch a bug.

   What can you **leap** across?

   Sample answer: I can leap across a sidewalk.

3. The **massive** elephant was as big as a school bus.

   Name something else that is **massive**.

   Sample answer: A whale is a massive animal.

Support English Language Learners

Guide children in visually exploring the connection between words and their use. For example, to gain a deeper understanding of the meaning of the word *fancy,* show pictures to the children of both plain and fancy clothing or jewelry. Verbally identify the fancy items with short phrases such as "fancy shoes" and "fancy necklace." Then, ask the children to name or draw pictures of things that are fancy. Have children model "plain hopping" and "fancy hopping."

Read along with the following story.

Frog's Wings

1   Frog and Bird are alike. They both eat bugs at the pond. But Bird can fly. Frog cannot.

2   One day, Frog tries to fly. He makes wings. He puts them on. He flaps and hops. One wing falls. Then Frog falls. He lands on the ground. "Help me!" Frog cries.

3   "Rest, my friend," Bird says. "You just cannot fly."

4   Now Frog will hop and snap up bugs.

Fill in the circle of the correct answer choice.

1. Which story word has the same vowel sound as the word *on*?

   ○ bugs

   ○ goes

   ● hop

Self-Assessment: Progress Check

Have children revisit the Progress Check on page 9 and respond to the questions again. Ask them to compare their Before and After responses.

Review children's responses to get an idea of their confidence with the unit skills. Based on these responses and on children's success with the Comprehension Check in Close Reading, you may want to conduct additional review and practice of one or more of the unit skills.

Unit Summary

Children have had instruction and practice in reading different types of literature, including fables and realistic fiction that have an "All About Me" theme. Children have learned that when reading, they can ask and answer questions about the text to improve their understanding. They can retell stories and describe the characters, settings, major events, and the central message, or lesson. Children have compared texts on the same topics. They have progressed toward completing an independent close reading of text, practiced applying concepts across texts, and explored the use of context clues.

They have read words with short *a, e, i, o,* and *u* vowel sounds, and practiced *l, r, s,* and final blends. They should be well prepared for the review section.

Introduce the Review

Explain to children that they will read a new story along with you that is related to the unit's theme and the selections they have already read. Then they will answer the questions on pages 37 and 38.

Answer Explanations

Scoring: Items 1, 2, and 6 on pages 37 and 38 are worth 1 point each. Explanations for the correct answers are given below and on the next page. Also see the rubrics on the next page for guidance in scoring the short-answer questions on page 38.

1. *On* has the short *o* vowel sound; *hop* also has the short *o* sound.

2. The second sentence states that the animals eat bugs at the pond.

Answer Explanations

Item 3 Rubric

2	Child underlines the context clue *both eat bugs* and names two animals that are alike.
1	Child either underlines the context clue or names animals that are alike but does not correctly answer both parts of the question.
0	Child does not underline the context clue and does not name animals that are alike

Item 4 Rubric

2	Retelling includes the characters, setting, and main events.
1	Retelling includes the characters, setting, or events, but not all elements.
0	Child is unable to retell the story.

Item 5 Rubric

2	Child notes that Frog learns he cannot fly.
1	Child notes that Frog hops or snaps up bugs.
0	Child is unable to answer.

6. *Just* and *rest* both end in the final blend *st*. *Rest* should be circled.

Item 7 Rubric

2	Child relates two or more character traits of Bird.
1	Child relates one character trait of Bird.
0	Child cannot relate any character traits.

Unit 1 Review

2. Where does this story take place?

○ at the park

◉ at the pond

○ at the zoo

3. Underline the words that help you find the meaning of the word *alike*. Name two animals that are alike.

Sample answer: Frog and Bird. They both eat bugs.

4. Retell the story by listing the important events.

Sample answer: Frog makes wings. He flaps the wings.

He tries to fly, but he cannot. So he does what frogs can do.

5. What lesson does Frog learn?

Frog learns that he cannot fly.

6. Circle the word in the story that has the same ending sounds as the word *just*.

7. Use details from the story to tell what Bird is like.

Sample answer: Bird is kind. He tells Frog to

rest. He helps him see what he can do.

Analyze Scores

9–11 pts Strong	Child has a good grasp of the skills and concepts taught in this unit. Point out any mistakes the child has made and explain the correct answers if necessary.
4–8 pts Progressing	Child is struggling with some skills or concepts. Identify the specific skills that are problematic to target a review of instruction.
0–3 pts Emerging	Child has difficulty understanding the skills and concepts taught in this unit. Child may need further instruction with a higher level of support and detailed explanation of the unit's skills and concepts.

Introducing UNIT **2**

In this unit, you will learn how to write a nonfictional narrative. A nonfictional narrative is a true story. You will write about something that has happened in your life.

A good nonfictional narrative is interesting to read. You share what you did, thought, and felt so readers can picture what happened.

 Progress Check *Can I?*

Before Unit 2 / After Unit 2

- [ ] Write events in the order they happened. [ ]
- [ ] Use time-order words to help readers follow events. [ ]
- [ ] Describe actions, thoughts, and feelings. [ ]
- [ ] Write a strong ending. [ ]
- [ ] Use common and proper nouns. [ ]
- [ ] Use possessive nouns. [ ]

Unit 2 ■ Text Types and Purposes: Write Nonfictional Narratives

Student Page 39

Progress Check

The Progress Check is a self-assessment feature that children can use to gauge their own progress. Research shows that when children take accountability for their own learning, their motivation increases.

Before children begin work on Unit 2, have them check the boxes next to any item that they feel they can do well. Explain that it is fine if they don't check any of the boxes. Tell them that they will have an opportunity to learn and practice all of these items while studying the unit. Let them know that near the end of the unit they will have a chance to reconsider how well they can do each item on the list.

Before children begin their Unit 2 Review on page 52, have them revisit this page. You can use this information to work with children on any items they don't understand before they tackle the Review.

HOME ◆ CONNECT...

The Home Connect feature is a way to keep parents or other adult family members apprised of what their children are learning. The key learning objectives are listed, and some ideas for related activities and discussions are included.

Explain to children that they can share the Home Connect page with their parents or other adult family members in their home.

Encourage children and their parents or other adult family members to share their experiences using the suggestions on the Home Connect page.

HOME ◆ CONNECT...

In this unit, children learn how to write a **nonfictional narrative** about an important experience they have had, such as a first sleepover or a summer vacation. Explain that people often enjoy retelling events that are important to them. Share with your child a memorable experience that you have had. Include your thoughts, actions, and feelings. You may also wish to read short nonfictional narratives or autobiographies with your child. Visit the library and help your child select an autobiography. As you read, decide with your child which experiences in the person's life are especially memorable.

When writing a nonfictional narrative, your child will be asked to tell events in the order in which they happened. As your child retells a special time, ask: *What happened first? What happened next? What happened last?* Help your child think of some details that describe his or her actions, thoughts, and feelings. Then encourage your child to end the retelling by explaining what made the time so special and how he or she felt when it was over.

Activity: Show your child examples of journals you may have kept or child-friendly blogs about experiences such as traveling or family games. Then buy your child an inexpensive notebook or help make one from notebook or blank paper. Encourage your child to use the notebook as a journal to keep track of events and/or thoughts and feelings he or she has each day. Entries can be as simple and fun as pictures of daily events or thoughts.

IN THIS UNIT, YOUR CHILD WILL...

- Write a nonfictional narrative that includes two or more events in the order they happened.
- Use time-order words, such as *next, then, last,* and *finally,* to show the order in which events happened.
- Include details that describe actions, thoughts, and feelings.
- Learn specific language skills and use them in writing a nonfictional narrative.
  - Use common, proper, and possessive nouns in his or her writing.
  - Capitalize proper nouns in his or her writing.

WAYS TO HELP YOUR CHILD

Help your child realize there are many events in life that he or she could use as a topic for writing a nonfictional narrative. Discuss special events your child has participated in. As you talk about them, help him or her explore what made them special. For example, instead of talking generally about a vacation, encourage your child to talk about his or her favorite part of the trip. Ask questions such as: *What did you see and hear? How did you feel?* The answers will help your child add details.

ONLINE
For more Home Connect activities, continue online at sadlierconnect.com

40 **Unit 2** ■ Text Types and Purposes: Write Nonfictional Narratives

Student Page 40

UNIT PLANNER

Theme: All About Me Curriculum Connection: Social Studies	Focus
WRITING MODEL *pp. 42–43*	*I Can Ride a Bike!*
WRITING ACTIVITY *pp. 44–47*	**ORGANIZATIONAL STRUCTURE:** Chart
LANGUAGE MINI LESSONS *pp. 48–49*	• Common and Proper Nouns • Possessive Nouns
SPEAKING AND LISTENING *pp. 50–51*	• Share Your Writing • Be a Good Listener • Return to the Essential Question
UNIT 2 REVIEW *p. 52*	Language Skills Summary

Objective(s)

Write a narrative about a true experience that will interest readers, stating the topic at the beginning, using time-order words and details to describe the experience, and including a strong ending.

- Plan a nonfictional narrative about a true experience, putting the events in time order and adding details that express feelings about the experience.

- Draw pictures, complete sentence starters, and compose text about a memorable experience.

- Correctly identify common and proper nouns.

- Correctly identify and write possessive nouns.

- Orally present a nonfictional narrative, speaking clearly and loudly and answering questions after the presentation.

- Participate respectfully in presentations as an active listener who waits his or her turn and asks questions and joins in the discussion.

Unit Assessment

- Unit 2 Review, *p. 52*

Additional Assessment Options

- Performance Task 1 *pp. 141–144*
  (ALSO ONLINE)

- Performance Task 2 *pp. 259–262*
  (ALSO ONLINE)

Optional Purchase:

- iProgress Monitor (ONLINE)

- Progress Monitor Student Benchmark Assessment Booklet

(ONLINE) Digital Resources

- Home Connect Activities
- Additional Practice
- Teacher Resources
- iProgress Monitor (separate purchase)

Go to SadlierConnect.com to access your Digital Resources.

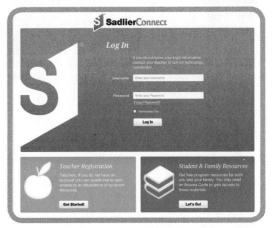

For more detailed instructions see page T3.

LEARNING PROGRESSIONS

In this unit, children will learn to write nonfictional narratives based on their own experiences. The narrative will include sentences and illustrations. In order to learn the skills necessary to craft a nonfictional narrative, children will further develop skills learned in kindergarten. They should be encouraged to retain these skills, as they will continue to build on them in second grade.

Sequencing a Narrative

- By the end of kindergarten, children are able to use a combination of drawing, dictating, and writing to narrate a single event or several closely linked events.

- As first graders, children can write narratives that include two or more sequenced events.

- Proficient second graders can write narratives that include a well-elaborated event or a short sequence of events.

Identifying Details

- Kindergartners provide few details, other than those that tell about the order of events.

- First graders include some details about what happened when writing nonfictional narratives about experiences.

- By the end of second grade, children include details that describe actions, thoughts, and feelings and they use temporal words to signal event order.

Providing a Sense of Closure

- By the end of kindergarten, children end their narratives with a reaction to what happened.

- Proficient first graders are expected to provide some sense of closure when recounting sequenced events in a nonfictional narrative.

- This expectation continues for second graders who should provide a true sense of closure at the end of nonfictional narratives.

Text Types and Purposes: Write Nonfictional Narratives

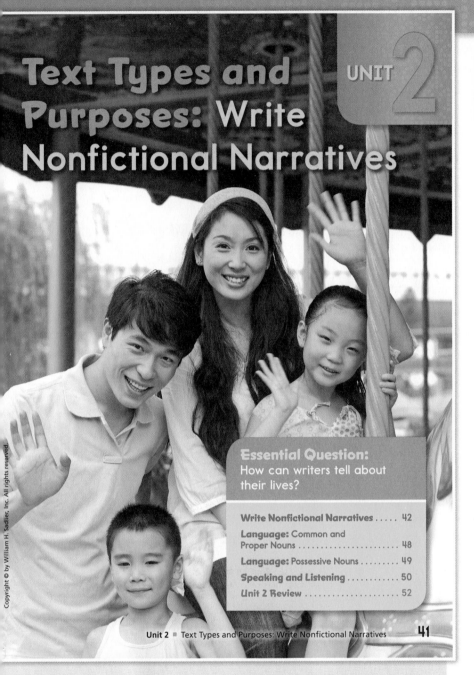

Essential Question:
How can writers tell about their lives?

Unit 2 ■ Text Types and Purposes: Write Nonfictional Narratives **41**

Essential Question:
How can writers tell about their lives?

Children will identify a personal experience to write about, use details and time-order words to explain the experience, and compose a strong ending for their narrative.

Theme: All About Me

Children will continue the journey of self-discovery they began in Unit 1 by writing about true experiences in their own lives.

Curriculum Connection: Social Studies

As children recall and write about interesting experiences in their lives, they learn how they connect with the world around them.

Connect Reading to Writing

Remind children that in Unit 1, they read stories about characters' experiences. These experiences helped characters discover something about themselves. Now children will have an opportunity to write about interesting experiences in their lives. Their nonfictional narratives may help them discover personal characteristics, such as courage or persistence.

Writing Handbook

To assist children in writing a nonfictional narrative, use the *Writing Handbook* on pages 263–268 to guide children in the writing process. The *Writing Handbook* gives children detailed instruction on planning, drafting, revising, and editing their writing, as well as providing tips on Producing and Publishing.

Have children turn to page 263 and review all the parts of the *Writing Handbook*. Then lead them through the suggestions on page 264 on selecting a topic and organizing information. Once children get started on writing their narrative, return to the *Writing Handbook* for information on each part of the writing process.

OBJECTIVE

Write a narrative about a true experience that will interest readers, stating the topic at the beginning, using time-order words and details to describe the experience, and including a strong ending.

Introduce: Organizational Structure

Remind children that a nonfictional narrative tells a true story about something that happened in their own lives. A clear sequence of events and some interesting details make these narratives enjoyable to read.

Analyze a Student Model

Time-Order Words: Explain that writers use time-order words to help readers understand the order in which things happen. Read aloud the first sentence of paragraph 2. Ask: *Which word in this sentence helps you understand the order of events?* (First) *There is one more time-order word in this paragraph. What is it?* (Then)

Write Nonfictional Narratives

Read a Student Model

Henry wrote a nonfictional narrative about a special event. As you read, think about the words Henry uses to show the order of events.

I Can Ride a Bike!

I can ride my bike all by myself! I learned how on Sunday. It was a lot of fun.

Dad helped me.

First, Dad got my bike out. He took the little wheels off the back. I sat on my bike and put one foot on one pedal. Then, I put the other foot on the other pedal. Dad held my bike so I wouldn't fall.

Teacher Talk: Use Time-Order Words

Tell children that they can use time-order words such as *first, then,* and *next* to tell about events, or things that happened. Ask: *The second paragraph begins with a time-order word, First. What other time-order word do you see in paragraph 2 of Henry's narrative? What other time-order words does he use?* Have children underline the time-order words.

Genre: Nonfictional Narratives

Emphasize to children that a nonfictional narrative is based on a real experience in the writer's life. All the facts in the narrative are true, not made up.

Point out the importance of choosing an experience that will be interesting to readers. Explain that simple facts about an experience might not interest readers. However, including details about the writer's actions and feelings makes narratives much more interesting to read.

Next, I started to move. I was very wobbly! I was (scared,) too. Dad did not let go. He said he would not let me fall.

I rode my *bike* down the street. Dad took his hands off my *bike*. Finally, I was riding all by myself! I felt excited. Now I want to ride my *bike* all the time.

I was scared, but I did it!

Teacher Talk: Find Details and Ending

Explain that a nonfictional narrative tells the writer's feelings. Ask: *How did Henry feel when he started to move?* Have children circle the word. Explain that an ending can tell readers the last event and what may happen next. Have children underline the ending of this narrative.

Unit 2 ■ Text Types and Purposes: Write Nonfictional Narratives **43**

Analyze a Student Model

Details: Remind children that nonfictional narratives include details about an experience. Say: *One detail is that Henry was very wobbly. What detail tells how Henry was feeling about the experience?* (He was scared.)

Ending: Explain that Henry ends his narrative by writing about the last event in his experience. Ask: *What was the last thing that Henry did?* (rode all by himself) *What time-order word does Henry use to explain when he rode all by himself?* (Finally) Point out that an ending may also give the reader a clue about something that may happen next. Ask: *What sentence tells what Henry may do next?* ("Now I want to ride my bike all the time.")

Visual Literacy

Pictures and Captions: Tell children that details in pictures sometimes give readers information that is not included in the text. Guide children to identify details in the photograph that are not offered in the words of the narrative. (Henry is about six years old. He is wearing a helmet. He is smiling.) Read the captions under both photographs. Point out that the captions repeat important details in the narrative.

Support English Language Learners

If possible, display a real bicycle to pre-teach children the words *bike, wheels, pedal, foot,* and *wobbly.* Explain that training wheels are small wheels on the back of the bike that help riders balance on the bike. These extra wheels are removed when a rider is ready to learn to ride without them. Point out the pedals of the bike. While holding the bike steady, have children take turns placing their feet on the pedals. Then slightly jiggle the bike to demonstrate the meaning of *wobbly.*

If it is not possible to display a bike, show pictures of bikes, with and without training wheels. Guide children to point out the wheels and the pedals in the pictures. Act out the word *wobbly.*

Model: Organizational Structure

Explain that well-written nonfictional narratives begin with good planning. Emphasize that it is important to choose a true experience that will interest readers. When planning the narrative, the writer should present the events of the experience in order and include details that will make the narrative interesting to readers. Point out that details about feelings are often interesting.

Discuss the chart that Henry used to plan his narrative. Say: *It's important to write the events in the order they happened. Notice that Henry listed each event in the order that it happened. Then he added details about his actions or his feelings. When Henry started writing his narrative, he used the chart to write the events and details in order so readers could understand his experience of learning to ride a bike.*

Heterogeneous Pairs

Pair children appropriately so that one can help the other compare the annotated chart to the Student Model. Using different colored highlighters, have children work together to color the events and details in the chart the same color as the corresponding text in Henry's narrative. For example, they might shade the information in the first box with a yellow highlighter. Then they would highlight the corresponding sentences "(First, Dad got my bike out. He took the little wheels off the back.") with the same yellow highlighter.

Write Nonfictional Narratives

Henry used this chart to plan his nonfictional narrative. He listed the important events in order. Then he added details about his actions, thoughts, and feelings.

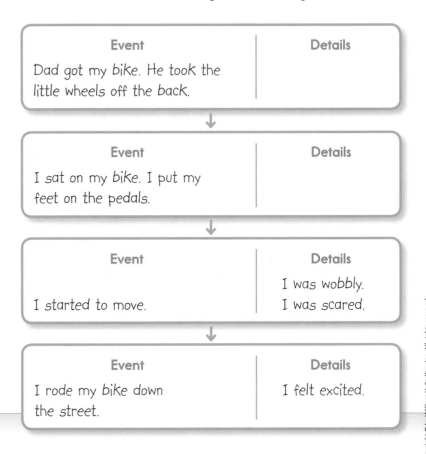

Event	Details
Dad got my bike. He took the little wheels off the back.	
I sat on my bike. I put my feet on the pedals.	
I started to move.	I was wobbly. I was scared.
I rode my bike down the street.	I felt excited.

Review: Understanding Key Details

Children learned about asking and answering questions to understand key details in a text in Unit 1. Remind children that stopping to ask and answer questions about what they read will help them to understand and remember key details. Pair children and have them take turns asking and answering questions about important details in *I Can Ride a Bike!*

In Unit 1, children also made connections between themselves, the text, and the world around them. Guide them to make connections between their own experiences of learning something new and Henry's experience.

Plan Your Nonfictional Narrative

Use a chart like Henry's to plan your nonfictional narrative. Remember to include the events in the order they happened. Add your feelings and thoughts about what happened.

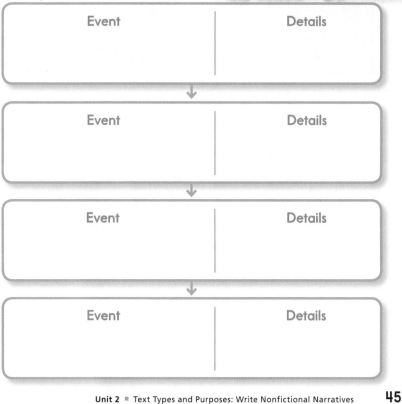

Event	Details

↓

Event	Details

↓

Event	Details

↓

Event	Details

Unit 2 ■ Text Types and Purposes: Write Nonfictional Narratives **45**

OBJECTIVE
Plan a nonfictional narrative about a true experience, putting the events in time order and adding details that express feelings about the experience.

Introduce the Writing Process

Explain that writing is a process with several steps. The first step is planning. The chart that Henry filled out helped him plan his nonfictional narrative. Tell children that they will fill out a chart before writing their narratives.

Plan a Nonfictional Narrative

Think About Organization

Remind children of how Henry organized his narrative. He wrote about events in the order they happened and included details about his actions and feelings. The ending explained how he felt about the experience. Children should follow this organization for their narratives.

Plan

Explain to children that they will use the chart to plan their own narratives. Give them time to think about experiences to write about. Remind them that the experience needs to have at least two events and it needs to be interesting to readers. Circulate to provide individual support as needed.

Peer Collaboration

List these questions on the board and read them aloud: *What are you going to write about? What happened first? How did you feel about that? What happened next? How did that make you feel? Did anything happen after that?* Have one partner ask these questions. Have the other partner use his or her notes in the graphic organizer to answer the questions. Then have partners switch roles.

Circulate to guide children to make suggestions and to help them add details that will strengthen their narratives.

OBJECTIVE
Draw pictures, complete sentence starters, and compose text about a memorable experience.

Draft a Nonfictional Narrative

Tell children that they will now use the ideas from their graphic organizers to write a draft. Emphasize that a draft is not a finished product and that they will have a chance to make changes and correct their work later.

Point out the areas provided for children to create their narratives: the two boxes for illustrations, the sentence starters, and the write-on lines. Remind children to refer to their planning charts as they create their drafts. Ask: *What events are you going to write about in your narrative? Which two events are you going to draw pictures of?* Guide children to complete the first sentence starter. Tell them that it should tell the topic of the experience. Tell children to write their narratives on the lines on page 47. Remind them to use time-order words.

As children write their drafts, observe their ability to print upper- and lowercase letters. Note any letters children have difficulty forming and provide additional instruction and practice as necessary.

Write Nonfictional Narratives

Create Your Nonfictional Narrative

In the boxes on pages 46–47, draw pictures to help tell about your special event.

Use your chart on page 45 to help you as you write. Start by completing the sentences below.

When I was <u>four years old, my sister was born</u>

_____.

First, <u>my mom and dad told me our family was growing</u>

_____.

Differentiate Instruction

As children draft their narratives, circulate and provide support for individuals who have not achieved independent literacy.

Developing: Depending on the number of events children have entered in their charts, provide additional sentence starters for them to use. Begin the sentence starters with the words *then, after that, next,* or *finally.* Have children write their sentences on the lines on page 47.

MORE ONLINE sadlierconnect.com

Answers will vary. The nonfictional narratives should

include at least two events, use time-order words to show

the sequence of the events, and include details. The

narratives should also have a strong ending.

Revise and Edit: Peer Collaboration

Once children have completed their drafts, have them work in pairs to read their drafts and suggest revisions. Have children begin by saying one thing they like about their partner's narrative. Then have them ask a question to clarify something or make a suggestion that would improve the narrative. Role-play these kinds of statements and questions before beginning the collaboration process.

Partners can then read each other's revisions and then make suggestions for ways to improve their drafts.

Nonfictional Narrative Rubric

4	The narrative includes at least two correctly sequenced events and includes details about the writer's actions, thoughts, or feelings.
3	The narrative has the elements listed under "4" above, though they are executed less successfully.
2	The narrative does not correctly sequence events or does not include any details about the events.
1	The narrative is unfinished or shows a minimal understanding of required elements.

Assess and Respond

If children have difficulty identifying events to record in the graphic organizer . . .

Then have children dictate the events in their experience. Write a sentence about each event in the chart. Then have children read the sentences you wrote.

Digital Connection

As children create a final draft of their nonfictional narratives, have them use a word processing program to publish their writing. Show children how to use bold type to emphasize specific words in their narratives. For example, a child might boldface the word *scared* in the sentence "I was **scared**!" They might also boldface exclamatory words such as **Wow** or onomatopoeias such as **Buzz** or **Pop**. Remind children to use bold type sparingly, explaining that if too many words are made bold, the emphasis on these words can be lost.

OBJECTIVE
Correctly identify common and proper nouns.

Guided Instruction

Explain that there are two kinds of nouns. A common noun names a person, place, or thing. A proper noun names a special person, place, or thing and begins with a capital letter. Tell children that today they are going to identify nouns as either common nouns or proper nouns.

Read aloud the definition of a common noun. Then read the five nouns under the definition. Ask children to identify each one as a person, place, or thing. Read the definition of a proper noun and the proper names listed. Have children name the capitalized letters in each one. Guide children to name proper nouns, such as names of people who work in the school and the names of special buildings or places in your town. Write their responses on the board and circle the capitalized letters.

Guided and Independent Practice

Remind children that common nouns name people, places, and things. Proper nouns name special people, places, or things and they are capitalized. As children read the words and sentences, they should look for capital letters to decide if a noun is a common noun or a proper noun.

Common and Proper Nouns

Guided Instruction Here are two kinds of nouns.

- A **common noun** names a person, place, or thing.

  girl   park   book   man   store

- A **proper noun** names a special person, place, or thing. A proper noun begins with a capital letter.

  Ben   Jones Beach   White House   Maria

Guided and Independent Practice Write C for common noun. Write P for proper noun.

1. shoe _____ C _____

2. Sam Chan _____ P _____

3. Dewey School _____ P _____

4. home _____ C _____

Read the sentences. Underline the common nouns. Circle the proper nouns.

5. My favorite month is (June).

6. (Jason) sailed his boat on (Big Lake).

Differentiate Instruction

To provide children with additional practice in identifying common and proper nouns, write the following sentences. Have children underline the common noun and circle the proper noun in each sentence.

Our school is (Willard School.)

Our town is (Ridgewood)

The park is (Oak Park.)

The lake is (Greenwood Lake.)

Possessive Nouns

Guided Instruction You can use an apostrophe and the letter *s* to show that a noun belongs to someone. Here are two ways to write the same thing:

The cat **belongs to May**.   The cat is **May's**.

We write *May's* to show that the cat belongs to May. *May's* is a **possessive noun**. Notice the apostrophe and *s* added to *May*.

Guided and Independent Practice Circle the possessive noun.

1. (Rick's) hat is blue.

2. (Mom's) pie is ready.

3. The (tree's) leaves are brown.

Complete each sentence with a word from the box.

plant's   dog's   sister's

4. The _____ dog's _____ paws are muddy.

5. The _____ plant's _____ leaves are green.

6. I got my _____ sister's _____ old room.

Unit 2 ■ Text Types and Purposes: Write Nonfictional Narratives **49**

OBJECTIVE
Correctly identify and write possessive nouns.

Guided Instruction

Explain that a possessive noun shows that something belongs to someone. Point to items in the classroom and say sentences such as *This desk belongs to Tom*. Then ask: *Whose desk is this?* (It is Tom's desk.)

Read aloud the introduction to possessive nouns. Write *The cat is May's.* on the board. Identify the apostrophe and circle it. Write additional sentences such as *The pencil belongs to Juan*. Ask: *What is another way we can write this?* Guide children to say *That is Juan's pencil*. Write their responses on the board.

Guided and Independent Practice

Work with children to help them complete items 1–3. Then tell children to read the sentences for items 4–6 and write the possessive noun that makes the most sense in the sentence.

As children complete the activity, observe their ability to print lowercase letters. Note any letters children have difficulty forming and provide additional instruction and practice as necessary.

Assess and Respond

If children have difficulty forming possessive nouns . . .

Then prepare this activity. Write 8–10 sentences such as this one on an index card: *This ball belongs to Sam*. Have children take turns choosing a card. Display the card and ask each child to write the corresponding sentence using a possessive noun. (It is Sam's ball.)

Support English Language Learners

Many English language learners may be unfamiliar with the practice of adding an apostrophe and an *s* to nouns to show possession. Use this activity to provide additional practice. On slips of paper, write the possessive form of the names of children in the group, such as *Roberto's* and *Lin's*. Place the slips facedown in a pile. Have children take turns reading a possessive noun and then saying a true sentence that includes the possessive noun. An example might be *This is Roberto's shirt*. After a child offers a sentence, write the sentence on the board, omitting the possessive noun. Have the child write the possessive noun to complete the sentence.

OBJECTIVE
Orally present a nonfictional narrative, speaking clearly and loudly and answering questions after the presentation.

Share Your Writing

Tell children that they will share their nonfictional narratives by reading them aloud. Suggest that children give a little background information about the experiences they chose to write about. Provide a few sentence starters for children to use: *I wrote about this because* _____.

Remind children not to be anxious about sharing their narratives. Point out that they chose the topics of their narratives because they thought it would be interesting to readers or listeners.

Get Ready

Remind children to read their narratives several times to themselves before they read them aloud. Then have children practice reading their narratives to partners. Guide children to speak clearly and loudly as they read.

Present

Have children share their narratives in small groups. Point out the illustration on page 50. Tell children they want their listeners to say the same thing about their presentations—that they did a great job making their voices heard.

Speaking and Listening

Share Your Writing

You will present your narrative. Remember the rules for speaking and listening. Speak clearly and loudly. You want everyone to hear you. Look at your listeners when you speak.

Be ready to answer questions your listeners might have.

Discussion Skills

After you listen to a child's narrative, ask these questions that require him or her to answer in complete sentences:

I'd like to hear more about _____. What else can you tell me about that?

Tell me more about how you felt when _____.

Be a Good Listener

Remember the rules for speaking and listening. As a listener, do not talk while the speaker is talking. Instead, keep your eyes on the speaker and listen. If you want to say something or ask a question, wait until others are finished before taking your turn to talk.

Sometimes more than one person wants to say something or ask a question. Good listeners raise their hand and wait their turn before speaking.

I'm glad that you are raising your hand. You are very patient!

Return to the Essential Question

How can writers tell about their lives?

Think about these questions before the class discussion:

• Why might we want to tell about a special event?
• How can we tell about a special event?

OBJECTIVE
Participate respectfully in presentations as an active listener who waits his or her turn and joins in the discussion.

Be a Good Listener

Remind children that good listeners pay attention to the speaker. They don't interrupt to ask questions or to make comments. Instead, they wait until the speaker is finished, then they ask questions about points they did not understand. Add that good listeners also ask the speaker to give more details about something that was interesting in the narrative.

Point to the illustration and the text in the speech balloon on page 51. Remind children that good listeners raise their hands and wait their turn before speaking.

Return to the Essential Question

Give children time to think about the questions before the discussion. After discussing the questions, have children suggest other ways that they might share their experiences.

Support English Language Learners

Developing English language learners may have difficulty phrasing questions to ask speakers. List the 5 *W* words—*who, what, when, where, why*—on the board. Read them aloud and have children repeat them. Explain that most questions begin with these words. As children share their narratives, guide listeners to ask questions that begin with these words.

Introduce the Review

Explain to children that this review will give them a chance to use the language skills that they studied and practiced in this unit. It will also give them a chance to share what they have learned about being a good speaker or listener.

Language Skills Summary

Tell children that they are going to use what they learned about common, proper, and possessive nouns. Briefly review the main concepts they learned.

- *A common noun names a person, place, or thing. A proper noun names a special person, place, or thing. How can you tell the difference between proper nouns and common nouns?* (Proper nouns begin with capital letters.)

- *A possessive noun shows that a noun belongs to someone. How do you make a possessive noun?* (Add an apostrophe and an *s*.)

Answer Explanations

1. Suggest that children study the answer choices to see how they differ. Identifying the differences will help them recall how possessive nouns are formed.

2. Suggest that children first identify the nouns in the sentence. Then tell them to see how the nouns *Sam* and *yard* differ.

3–5. Tell children to study each underlined word and the answer choices. Tell them to think about whether the word is or is not a common, proper, or possessive noun.

Self Assessment: Progress Check

Have children revisit the Progress Check on page 39 and compare their answers now with the answers they gave before completing Unit 2.

Unit 2 Review

Choose the correct answer. Fill in the circle.

1. Which is the correct way to write a possessive noun?

○ Pacos scarf   ○ Pacos' scarf   ● Paco's scarf

2. Read the sentence. Which word is a common noun?

Sam plays in the yard.

○ Sam   ○ plays   ● yard

Circle the kind of noun each underlined word is.

3. We took <u>Scooter</u> to the vet.

common   (proper)   possessive

4. My dog ate my <u>cookie!</u>

(common)   proper   possessive

5. I slept over at <u>Mark's</u> house.

common   proper   (possessive)

Think about speaking and listening.

6. What can good listeners do to be sure everyone can ask a question?

Sample answer: Good listeners wait their turn

to ask a question.

Test-Taking Tips

Tell children that wherever bubble choices appear on a test, as in items 1 and 2 of this test, they must be sure to completely fill in the whole circle.

Also, tell children to read test directions very carefully to see how answers are to be indicated. Point out that the directions for items 3, 4, and 5 instruct test-takers to circle the type of noun. Emphasize that circling the answer is different from underlining the answer choice or marking it in any other way.

Introducing UNIT 3

This unit is all about living things. As you read, you will ask and answer questions and look for the main idea, or what the selection is mostly about. You will also retell key details, or facts, in your own words and look for ways those details are connected to one another. All of these skills will help you become a better reader!

 Before Unit 3   After Unit 3

Progress Check Can I?

- ☐ Ask and answer questions about a text. ☐
- ☐ Find the main idea and retell key details of a text. ☐
- ☐ Describe how two ideas in a text are connected. ☐
- ☐ Use what I learn to read new words. ☐
- ☐ Read naming words and their plurals that are formed by adding s. ☐

Unit 3 ■ Reading Informational Text: Key Ideas and Details

Student Page 53

HOME ◆ CONNECT...

The Home Connect feature is a way to keep parents or other adult family members apprised of what their children are learning. The key learning objectives are listed, and some ideas for related activities and discussions are included.

Explain to children that they can share the Home Connect page with their parents or other adult family members in their home. Let children know how much time the class will be spending on this unit so they can plan their time accordingly at home.

Encourage children and their parents or other adult family members to share their experiences using the suggestions on the Home Connect page. You may wish to make a place to post some of this work.

Progress Check

The Progress Check is a self-assessment feature that children can use to gauge their own progress. Research shows that when children take accountability for their own learning, their motivation increases.

Before children begin work on Unit 3, have them check the boxes next to any item that they feel they can do well. Explain that it is fine if they don't check any of the boxes. Tell them that they will have an opportunity to learn about and practice all of these items while studying the unit. Let them know that near the end of the unit they will have a chance to reconsider how well they can do each item on this list.

Before children begin their Unit 3 Review on page 81, have them revisit this page. You can use this information to work with children on any items they don't understand before they tackle the Review.

HOME ◆ CONNECT...

It is easy to **ask and answer questions** about informational texts because they are full of facts. Asking questions helps readers better understand and remember what they read. Read an article of interest with your child. Ask each other questions about details in the article.

When readers identify the **main topic**, or main idea, and **retell key details** from a text, they show they understand what they've read. As you read together, have your child name the topic and retell at least two details about it.

As you read, help your child **describe connections** between two ideas in the text. Ask questions such as "Why did that happen?" or "Why does a bird build a nest?" This helps the child see how two ideas or pieces of information are connected.

Finally, help your child **compare texts**. Read about two animals' life cycles together. Compare the two texts. For example, how are the two animals' life cycles alike and different?

Activity: Help your child review his or her own life cycle thus far! Together, look at family pictures that show your child from birth on, or use your own baby or childhood photos. Talk about the changes that occur as a baby grows and learns to walk, ride a bike, and so on. Invite your child to draw a picture of how he or she might look at your age!

IN THIS UNIT, YOUR CHILD WILL...

- Ask and answer questions about a text he or she has read.
- Find the main idea of a text.
- Retell the key details of a text.
- Describe how two ideas in a text are connected.
- Identify words with two letters that make one sound, such as *ch* (church), *sh* (trash), *th* (then), and *wh* (why).
- Identify plurals made by adding *s* to a noun (duck, ducks).
- Compare and contrast different texts on the same topic.

WAYS TO HELP YOUR CHILD

When you read with your child, you help him or her succeed in school and in life. When your child sees you reading "for fun," he or she learns that you value reading. In turn, that influences your child to value reading as well. So grab a book or a magazine or head to the Internet and read, read, read with, and in front of, your child! The results may surprise you.

ONLINE
For more Home Connect activities, continue online at sadlierconnect.com

54 Unit 3 ■ Reading Informational Text: Key Ideas and Details

Student Page 54

UNIT PLANNER

Theme: Cycles of Life	Focus
READ ALOUD *pp. 56–57*	*What Is a Seed?* **GENRE:** Magazine Article
ASKING AND ANSWERING QUESTIONS *pp. 58–61*	*From Tadpole to Frog* **GENRE:** Journal Entry **LEXILE®:** *270L* **WORDS TO KNOW:** air, clear, gently, gills, lungs, tadpole
IDENTIFYING MAIN IDEA AND DETAILS *pp. 62–65*	*A Tree Grows* **GENRE:** Informational Text **LEXILE®:** *290L* **WORDS TO KNOW:** appear, buds, rot, soil
DESCRIBING CONNECTIONS *pp. 66–69*	*Butterflies!* **GENRE:** Informational Text **LEXILE®:** *230L* **WORDS TO KNOW:** cover, pupa *Grow a Butterfly Garden* **GENRE:** Procedural Text **LEXILE®:** *350L* **WORDS TO KNOW:** bloom, list
FOUNDATIONAL SKILLS READ TOGETHER *p. 70*	*The Garter Snake* **GENRE:** Informational Text
FOUNDATIONAL SKILLS READER 1 *pp. 71–72*	*Penguins Grow and Change* **GENRE:** Informational Text
FOUNDATIONAL SKILLS READER 2 *pp. 73–74*	*What Will I Be?* **GENRE:** Informational Text
CLOSE READING *pp. 75–78*	*Sea Turtles* **GENRE:** Informational Text **LEXILE®:** *250L*
CONNECT ACROSS TEXTS *p. 79*	Compare and Contrast Texts
LANGUAGE *p. 80*	Plurals
UNIT 3 REVIEW *pp. 81–82*	*Watch Baby Animals* **GENRE:** Procedural Text **LEXILE®:** *280L*

Objective(s)	Unit Assessment

Objective(s)

- Ask and answer questions about key details in a text.
- Identify the main topic and key details of a text.
- Describe the connection between two ideas in a text.

Ask and answer questions about key details in a text.

Identify the main topic and key details of a text.

Describe the connection between two ideas in a text.

Read decodable text featuring consonant digraphs *th, ch, sh,* and *wh.*

Read decodable text featuring consonant digraphs *th* and *ch.*

Read decodable text featuring consonant digraphs *sh* and *wh.*

Same objectives as pages 58–61; pages 62–65; pages 66–69

Identify and write plural forms of nouns.

Unit Assessment

- Unit 3 Review, *pp. 81–82*
- Unit 3 Performance Task (ONLINE)

Additional Assessment Options

- Performance Task 1 *pp. 141–144*
  (ALSO ONLINE)
- Performance Task 2 *pp. 259–262*
  (ALSO ONLINE)

Optional Purchase:

- iProgress Monitor (ONLINE)
- Progress Monitor Student Benchmark Assessment Booklet

(ONLINE) Digital Resources

- Home Connect Activities
- Unit Performance Task
- Additional Practice
- Full-Length Reading Selections
- Foundational Skills Practice
- Teacher Resources
- iProgress Monitor (optional purchase)

Go to SadlierConnect.com to access your Digital Resources.

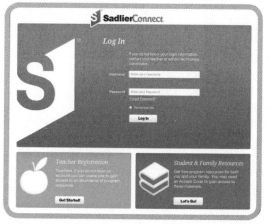

For more detailed instructions see page T3.

LEARNING PROGRESSIONS

In this unit, children will learn to identify main ideas and details. They will practice asking and answering questions independently and gain proficiency in describing the connections between ideas in a text. In order to learn the skills in this unit, children will further develop skills learned in kindergarten. They should be encouraged to retain these skills, as they will continue to build on them in second grade.

Asking and Answering Questions

- Proficient kindergartners will be able to ask and answer questions about key details in a text, with prompting and support.

- In first grade, children learn to ask and answer questions about the text independently, without support or prompting.

- This skill prepares children to demonstrate an understanding of key details in a text in second grade by asking and answering questions such as *Who? What? Where? When? Why?* and *How?*

Identifying Main Idea and Details

- Kindergarten children are expected to identify the main topic and retell key details of a text with prompting and support.

- By the end of first grade, children are able to identify the main topic and retell key details of a text independently, without support or prompting.

- In grade 2, children will identify the focus of specific paragraphs in addition to the main topic of a text.

Describing Connections

- When prompted, kindergarten children can describe the connection between two individuals, events, ideas, or pieces of information in a text.

- In first grade, children learn to independently describe connections between individuals, events, ideas, or pieces of information in a text.

- With this background, second-grade children are able to apply the skill to historical, scientific, and technical texts.

Reading Informational Text: Key Ideas and Details

UNIT 3

Essential Question:
What are the parts of an informational text?

Essential Question:
What are the parts of an informational text?

In this unit, children will learn how to engage effectively with informational texts. They will learn to ask and answer questions, identify the main ideas and important details in a text, and make connections between ideas.

Theme: Cycles of Life

Children will read about different life cycles in the plant and animal worlds. They will read about bean plants and apple trees growing from seeds to produce new seeds and renew the cycle. Additionally, they will read about the varied life cycles of frogs, butterflies, garter snakes, penguins, and sea turtles. They will see many examples of life cycles, from seed to adult plant and from egg to butterfly.

Curriculum Connection: Science

As children enjoy the selections in this unit, they will learn key details and facts about life cycles. They will be well prepared to observe, describe, and record the life cycles of plants and animals.

Vocabulary Overview

air 60, appear 64, bloom 68, buds 64, clear 58, cover 67, gently 58, gills 59, list 68, lungs 60, pupa 67, rot 62, soil 63, tadpole 58

OBJECTIVES

- **Ask and answer questions about key details in a text.**
- **Identify the main topic and key details of a text.**
- **Describe the connection between two ideas in a text.**

Using the Read Aloud

Tell children that you will read a text aloud (see right) as they look at the pictures in their books. Read the text, pausing at the numbers to pose the questions below.

Picture

What are some examples of plants? (sunflowers, trees, bushes) Read caption 1 together.

Picture

How do plants begin? (as seeds) *What do seeds look like?* (big or small, flat or round; some are green) Read caption 2 together.

Picture

How does a seed change into a plant? (A seed grows roots, leaves, and a stem.) Read caption 3 together.

Picture

Why do you think a wet paper towel goes in the bag? (The plant needs water.) Read caption 4 together.

Turn and Talk

Have pairs discuss: How do a plant's different parts help the plant get what it needs?

What Is a Seed?

When you walk outside, what living things do you see? You may see many different kinds of plants growing. You may see trees, bushes, and flowers. All of these plants need water, air, space, and sunlight to help them grow. Plants are living things, which means they have a life cycle. They begin life, they grow and change, and then they make new living things that look like them. The cycle begins all over again. **1**

Most plants begin as seeds. Seeds may be big or small. They may be flat or round. But all seeds are alike in one way: Inside each seed is the food it needs to grow. **2**

If a seed is planted in the ground and gets sunlight and water, roots soon grow down into the soil. Then a tiny plant pushes up through the soil. Leaves grow, and the tiny plant becomes a seedling. The roots and leaves help the seedling get the light and water it needs. It grows taller and bigger. When the plant becomes an adult plant, it begins to make its own seeds. If those seeds get the things they need to grow, they will become new plants. You can see this for yourself. You can plant a bean seed and watch it grow and change. **3**

What You Need

- Dried kidney or lima beans
- Paper towel
- Plastic sandwich bag
- Water
- Tape

What to Do

1. Soak the beans in water overnight to make them soft.
2. Fold a paper towel to fit in the plastic bag.
3. Wet the paper towel and put it inside the bag.
4. Place 3 to 5 beans on the towel.
5. Zip the bag closed.
6. Tape the bag to a window so that it can get sunlight.
7. Check the seed every day. Soon you will see roots, a stalk, and leaves!
8. Get the paper towel wet again if it gets too dry.

Read Aloud

Listen to the selection as your teacher reads. Note important details. Think about the main topic. Think about how ideas are connected.

As you listen, ask yourself questions about the selection. Listen for the answers.

What Is a Seed?

1 These are plants.

2 Plants begin as seeds.

56   Unit 3 ■ Reading Informational Text: Key Ideas and Details

---

Key Ideas and Details

leaf
flower
seed pod
seedling
seed   tiny plant   roots   stem

3 A seed can become a plant.

4 You can see a bean seed grow and change.

Unit 3 ■ Reading Informational Text: Key Ideas and Details   **57**

Preview the Focus Skills

Do a second reading of the Read Aloud as children look at the pictures. As you read, pause briefly where indicated below. Use the suggested think-alouds to preview the unit's targeted reading skills and model how children might use the skills independently during shared reading.

- Pause after reading the first paragraph. Say: *The first sentence asks a question about what living things I see outside. I might learn something if I stop and think about the answer to this question. I see birds, squirrels, and bugs. The next sentence brings my attention to plants. That reminds me that plants are living things and focuses my attention on the plants I see outside, such as the trees, grass, and ivy around my house.*

- Pause after reading the second paragraph. Say: *This paragraph is mostly about seeds. The picture shows seeds, too. I ask myself, what is the main idea of this paragraph? What is it saying about seeds? The first sentence says that most plants begin as seeds. That is the main idea. The other sentences give details. They compare different kinds of seeds.*

- Pause after reading the procedural text. Say: *I want to understand the connection between the pictures and the text. The main idea of paragraph 3 is how a seed changes into a plant. I see the same changes shown in the picture that I heard about in the text.*

Digital Connection

Search online for time-lapse videos of seeds sprouting. Try a search with the keywords *time lapse video mung beans,* for example. You may wish to look for videos of different types of seeds growing, such as corn, acorns, pumpkins, and sunflowers, so that children can compare the way the different kinds of plants grow.

Guided Instruction

OBJECTIVE
Ask and answer questions about key details in a text.

Genre: Journal Entry
Tell children that a journal is like a diary. The writer records events that happen at a certain time. The special purpose of this journal is to take notes about how a tadpole grows into a frog.

Set the Purpose
Help children understand the purpose for asking and answering questions about key details. Ask: *How can we understand what happens in an informational text?*

Model and Teach
Read the text aloud as children follow along in their books.

Teacher Talk: Find Evidence
Tell children that key details are important ideas in the text. Readers can ask and answer questions to help them figure out what the text is about. Reread paragraph 2 with children. Say: *This paragraph begins with "I see frog eggs!" so I know it will tell me about frog eggs. I ask myself "What are frog eggs like?" I'll read the paragraph carefully to find details about frog eggs.*

After I have answered one question, I ask another: "What are the tiny dots in the eggs?" Ask children to answer this question and to respond in a complete sentence.

Asking and Answering Questions

Words to Know

clear
gently
gills
tadpole

From Tadpole to Frog
(Genre: Journal Entry)

1   My backyard has a small pond. Last year we had lots of frogs! This year I'm going to watch them. I will see how the frogs grow and change.

One Day

2   I see frog eggs! They float on the top of the pond. Mom gets a net. We scoop them up. The eggs are very **clear**. I see tiny black dots inside.

3   We look closely at the dots. They are moving. Each dot is a tiny **tadpole!**

4   I **gently** put the net back into the water. We want to take care of the eggs. Mom says the eggs will hatch in three weeks. I cannot wait!

Guided Instruction

Teacher Talk: Find Evidence
Tell children they can ask and answer questions to find key details in informational texts. Suppose they ask: *What do frog eggs look like?* They can look for details to answer the question. Have them underline the fifth and sixth sentences in paragraph 2 to answer the question.

58   Unit 3 ■ Reading Informational Text: Key Ideas and Details

---

Words to Know

clear (*adjective*): see-through
gently (*adverb*): carefully, trying not to hurt anything
gills (*noun*): body part that lets underwater animals breathe in the water
tadpole (*noun*): a stage in a frog's life when it is like a fish

Working with Word Meaning Pair children for practice using each of these words in a complete sentence.

Three Weeks

5   I see tadpoles! There are tadpoles everywhere! They are all black. They all have tiny tails. They swim in the water. This pond is their home.

6   Mom says the tadpoles cannot come out of the water yet. They can breathe because they have **gills.**

7   Some tadpoles stay under the plants. They are not moving. I wonder why. I put my hand in the water. They swim away very fast!

8   Mom says birds and snakes eat tadpoles. The lily pads are good places to hide!

Tadpoles are more like fish than frogs.

Teacher Talk: Find Evidence
Remind children that asking questions helps them to understand the ideas in the key details. Tell them that on this page they might ask: *How can tadpoles breathe in the pond?* Have children underline a key detail in paragraph 6 that answers this question.

Guided Instruction

Unit 3 ■ Reading Informational Text: Key Ideas and Details   **59**

Guided Instruction

Teacher Talk: Find Evidence

Remind children that asking questions about an informational text helps them understand it. Explain that as they read, they can use key details to learn about the topic. Then say: *When I know what the topic is, I can ask questions to help me understand more about it. I know that the topic of this journal is the changes frogs go through as they grow up. I read that tadpoles cannot come out of the water because they can't breathe air. I ask myself, "How can tadpoles breathe in the pond?" I will look for details in the text that answer this question.*

I can also ask and answer other questions about frogs and tadpoles. Now I ask, "How do tadpoles stay safe?" Let's keep reading and look for an answer. Pause after paragraph 8 and give children an opportunity to answer the question. (They hide under plants.)

Use Visuals

To help children retell key ideas from information presented in visuals, have them look at the visuals on pages 58–59. Ask them to tell which part of "From Tadpole to Frog" each visual explains. Ask children to use a complete sentence to tell the key idea shown by the visual.

Support English Language Learners

Search online with the keywords *time lapse video tadpole to frog.* Many educational sites have videos that show this life cycle. Stop the video as needed to preteach the words children will encounter in the selection: *egg, lay, hatch, tadpole, tail, frog, pond.*

Read and Practice

Remind children that asking questions about what they are reading will help them understand and remember what they have read. Read the first paragraph aloud. Then have heterogeneous partners take turns rereading the paragraph as you circulate to provide support.

Teacher Talk: Find Evidence

Have children preview page 61. Say: *I will read paragraph 11 and think about what question the details in this paragraph answer. This paragraph tells me that the tadpole is now a little frog. It is not a big frog yet because it has a tiny tail. So, this paragraph tells me what the little frog looks like. One question I can ask is "How is a little frog different from an adult frog?"*

Turn and Talk

Have children turn to a partner and answer the question "What does the diagram show?" Have volunteers share their answers with the class. Prompt them to use complete sentences when they share the results.

Asking and Answering Questions

Words to Know

air

lungs

Five Weeks

9   The tadpoles are really changing now. They are growing legs. After five weeks, they look more like frogs. Their tails are short, too.

10   Mom says the tadpoles are growing **lungs.** I cannot see them. They are inside the tadpoles. Lungs help them breathe **air.**

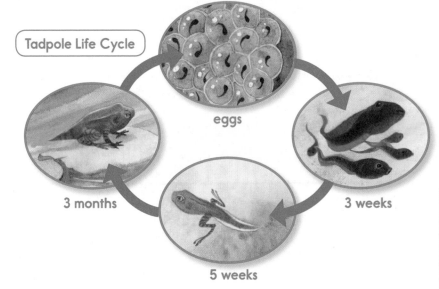

Tadpole Life Cycle

eggs

3 months

5 weeks

3 weeks

Guided Practice

Teacher Talk: Find Evidence
Review how asking and answering questions helps readers understand important facts, or key details, in a text. Have children put a box around paragraph 11. Lead them to ask questions that the paragraph answers, such as "What does a tadpole look like as a little frog?"

60   Unit 3 ■ Reading Informational Text: Key Ideas and Details

---

Words to Know

air (*noun*): the gas that helps things live
lungs (*noun*): body parts used to breathe air

Working with Word Meaning Have children place one hand on their chest as they take deep breaths and place the other hand in front of their mouth. Explain that *air* is moving in and out of their body and that they can feel the *lungs* in their chest fill up with and then release air.

Key Ideas and Details

Three Months

11 Now the tadpole is a little frog. It is not a big frog yet, though. It still has a tiny tail.

Four Months

12 I see frogs in the pond! They are really big. Their tails are gone. They are adult frogs!

A frog is fully grown when it has no tail.

Comprehension Check

MORE ONLINE sadlierconnect.com

1. Read this key detail from paragraph 9: "After five weeks, they look more like frogs." Which question does the key detail answer?

   a. What do frogs look like?

   b. How long does it take before tadpoles begin to look like frogs?

   c. Do tadpoles have legs?

2. The tadpoles hide under lily pads. Why do they do this?

   Birds and snakes eat them. They are hiding from them.

Teacher Talk: Find Evidence
Have children read paragraph 12 to look for key details. Have them ask questions that the details explain, such as "What does an adult frog look like?" Have children circle the details in paragraph 12.

Independent Practice

Unit 3 ■ Reading Informational Text: Key Ideas and Details **61**

Foundational Skills Review: Fluency Practice

Remind children that paying attention to punctuation helps them to read accurately. Have children find all of the punctuation marks in paragraph 11. Model a fluent reading of the paragraph, briefly pausing for the comma and coming to a full pause at each period. Then go back to the beginning of the paragraph and have children chorally read the paragraph. Have them work in groups of three to continue practicing with paragraph 12. Circulate and help children who are struggling to "show" the exclamation point with their voice. Additional fluency passages and activities can be found at **sadlierconnect.com**.

Independent Practice

Read and Apply

Have children read paragraphs 11 and 12 on page 61 independently as you circulate. Provide extra support to struggling readers by choral reading with them.

Teacher Talk: Find Evidence

Say: *Since there's not a subheading that says "Adult Frogs," you'll have to read the text to find out if frogs are adults at three months or four months. Once you've found the right section, look for details about what adult frogs look like.*

Comprehension Check

Answer Explanations:

1. Answer choice **B** contains the phrase "How long," which corresponds to "After five weeks."

2. Children should use paragraph 8 to answer the question.

Critical Comprehension

Use the following question to help children think more deeply about the selection. Children should support their answers with evidence from the text.

Why does the diagram on page 60 show the life cycle as a circle? (Because a frog grows from an egg, and then lays its own eggs, starting the cycle over for new frogs.)

Assess and Respond
If children have difficulty answering the questions in the Comprehension Check . . .
Then pair each child with a partner of greater ability. Have partners work together to answer the questions while you circulate to provide support.

Unit 3 ■ Reading Informational Text: Key Ideas and Details **61**

Guided Instruction

OBJECTIVES
- **Identify the main topic and key details of a text.**
- **Answer questions about key details in a text read aloud.**

Genre: Informational Text

Tell children that informational text presents facts. People read informational texts to learn something about a topic.

Set the Purpose

Help children understand the purpose for learning to identify a main topic and retell key details. Ask: *How can you find out what a text is mostly about? How do you know which ideas are the most important?*

Model and Teach

Read the text aloud as children follow along in their books.

Teacher Talk: Find Evidence

Explain to children that the main topic of a text is what the text is mostly about. Readers can often find a clue to the main topic in the text's title. Say: *I think the title of this informational text, "A Tree Grows," will help me figure out the main topic. I think I will read about how a tree grows from seed to tree. What will this text mostly be about?* Encourage children to respond in complete sentences as appropriate.

Identifying Main Idea and Details

Words to Know

rot

soil

A Tree Grows
(Genre: Informational Text)

1 Do you like apples? Most people do.

2 Cut open an apple. You can see seeds inside. One day the seeds may make new apple trees.

3 In the fall, apples get ripe. A child might pick one to eat.

4 Some apples do not get eaten. They fall to the ground and **rot.** The small seeds rest on the ground. Later, leaves cover up the seeds.

5 In the winter, snow covers the seeds. The air gets cold. Apple seeds need cold air to grow.

Guided Instruction

Teacher Talk: Find Evidence

Explain to children that the main topic, or main idea, is what a text is mostly about. Authors often tell the main idea in the title. Have children circle the words in the title that tell the main topic: A Tree Grows. Ask: *What is the main idea of this text?*

62 Unit 3 ■ Reading Informational Text: Key Ideas and Details

---

Words to Know

rot (*verb*): to fall apart
soil (*noun*): dirt; ground

Working with Word Meaning Talk about *soil* and *rot* as a class. Ask children what they have used *soil* for (gardening, playing) and what happens when it gets wet (mud forms). Ask children to name objects or substances that they have seen *rot*—for instance, a banana turning brown or leaves left in the yard. If possible, show children a decomposing banana or other fruit.

6　　In the spring, the snow melts. Rain gives the seeds a bath. The sun warms the seeds. <u>Roots may burst out of some seeds.</u> They push down into the **soil.** They take in water. They bring water to the seeds.

7　　<u>Stems may grow from the seeds.</u> They come out of the soil. Leaves grow on the stems. They reach for the sun. They make food for the new plants. The plants get bigger and bigger. The stems grow taller. The stems will one day become trunks of apple trees.

An apple tree can grow three feet in one year.

Teacher Talk: Find Evidence
Tell children that authors include details to tell about the main idea of a text. Say: *The main idea of this text is how a tree grows from a seed. Let's underline two details that tell how a seed grows into a tree.* Ask: *What details can you retell about the main idea?*

Guided Instruction

Unit 3 ■ Reading Informational Text: Key Ideas and Details　**63**

Teacher Talk: Find Evidence

Explain that the main idea of this text is how a tree grows from a seed. Details tell the reader more about the main idea. Say: *Once I know the main idea of a text, I get curious about the details—the smaller pieces of information that help me understand the main idea. What will this author tell me about how a tree grows? Paragraph 1 tells me that the tree I will learn about is an apple tree. That is a detail. Paragraph 2 tells me another detail—about the seeds inside an apple. Paragraph 3 tells me that apples get ripe in the fall, and that some apples get eaten. These facts are all details.*

Now I will look for the details that show me exactly how a seed starts growing to turn into a tree.

Review: Asking and Answering Questions

Remind children that when they ask themselves questions as they read, they will pay better attention, be more engaged, and understand the text better. Ask: *What questions do you have about how an apple seed grows into a tree?* (Sample answer: How long does it take before an apple grows?)

Differentiate Instruction

To help children understand main idea and details, ask a volunteer to explain how to do a simple thing, such as walk to the front office of the school from the classroom. Use the explanation to point out that the main idea is *how to get to the front office* and the details are all the steps along the way, such as leaving the classroom, walking down the hall, and so on. Do this several times with children, having them explain simple actions such as opening a window, or learning to ride a bike. Have them identify main ideas and details with less support from you.

Guided Practice

Read and Practice

Remind children to look for details as they read and think about how the details help them understand the main idea of the text. Have heterogeneous partners take turns rereading page 64 as you circulate to provide support.

Teacher Talk: Find Evidence

Explain that each paragraph can have its own main idea, in addition to the main idea of a text. Tell children that the main idea of paragraph 8 is how apple trees change from fall to spring. Then give them time to underline supporting details. Say: *Now that I've looked over paragraph 8, I know that the main idea is how apple trees change from fall to spring. Now I'll look back at the paragraph again to find details about how the trees change.*

Have volunteers help you determine the main idea of paragraph 9 (how apples are formed) before the class moves on to circle the details about when apples are ripe. Have volunteers retell the details in their own words. Ask: *When do apples get ripe?* (in the fall)

Team Jigsaw

Place children in groups of five, and assign each child in the group one stage of an apple tree's life cycle. Each child must describe what happens during that stage. Then the group should put the five sentences together to be shared with the rest of the class.

Identifying Main Idea and Details

Words to Know

appear
buds

8 When fall comes, the leaves fall off the trees. Winter passes. Spring comes, and **buds appear** on the trees. The trees grow and grow.

9 In three years, the apple trees grow flowers. The flowers fall to the ground. Then tiny apples appear! The apples grow all summer. In fall, the apples are big. Each apple is fresh and ripe!

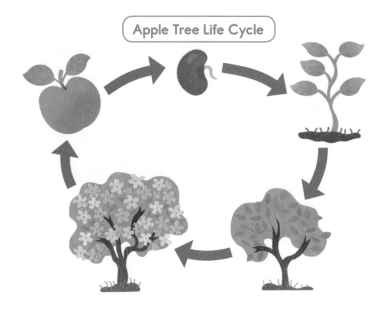

Apple Tree Life Cycle

Guided Practice

Teacher Talk: Find Evidence

Explain that the main idea in paragraph 8 is how apple trees change from fall to spring. Have children underline the details that support this main idea. In paragraph 9 have children circle the details about when apples are ripe. Have them retell the details in their own words.

Words to Know

appear (*verb*): to show up
bud (*noun*): unopened flower

Working with Word Meaning Show children images of flower buds on different kinds of plants. Then have children draw a comic strip with four panels that show a tree branch, a small *bud,* a larger bud, and a flower. Discuss with children in which panel the flower buds *appear.*

Key Ideas and Details

10 (More apples fall to the ground.)(They rot. Then leaves cover the)(seeds.) Soon more apple trees grow!

Comprehension Check

MORE ONLINE
sadlierconnect.com

1. What is the main idea of "A Tree Grows"?

   (a.) An apple tree grows from a seed.

   b. People eat apples.

   c. Apple seeds need snow.

2. How can an apple seed get from a tree to the ground?

   Sample answer: An apple might fall off the tree and rot.

   The seeds rest on the ground.

   _____

   _____

   _____

Teacher Talk: Find Evidence
Tell children that the author explains the life cycle of apple trees from fruit to new trees again. Have children circle the details on this page about the fruit and seeds. Have them take turns retelling details from the text that give information about an apple tree's life cycle.

Independent Practice

Unit 3 ■ Reading Informational Text: Key Ideas and Details **65**

Independent Practice

Read and Apply

Have children read paragraph 10 on page 65 independently as you circulate. Provide extra support to struggling readers by choral reading the paragraph with them.

Teacher Talk: Find Evidence

Remind children of the main idea of the text before they look for details on this page. Say: *Look for more details about the tree's life cycle on this page. Then look back over the text and think about the whole life cycle of an apple tree.*

Comprehension Check

Answer Explanations:

1. Only answer choice **A** is a main idea of "A Tree Grows." The other answer choices are details from the text.

2. Answers should show an understanding that apples fall to the ground, decompose, and release seeds.

Critical Comprehension

Use the following question to help children think critically about the selection. Children should support their answers with evidence from the text.

- *What did you learn about apple seeds from reading "A Tree Grows"?* (Sample answer: Apple seeds need cold air to grow.)

Assess and Respond
If children have difficulty answering the questions in the Comprehension Check . . .
Then work together on a chart that shows main ideas from the selection and the details that support them.

Team Jigsaw

Organize the class into groups of three. Each child in a group will become an expert on one of the three pages they have read: 62, 63, and 64. Have groups work together, each child bringing his or her knowledge of the assigned page to label the diagram on page 64.

If groups need support, let them know there are many ways to complete the task. Give the example of an identifying label such as *seed*. They may also use informative labels such as *spring*. Or they may choose descriptive labels, such as *flowery*.

After groups complete their labels, they will share their ideas with other teams, and answer questions.

Guided Instruction

OBJECTIVES

- **Describe the connection between two ideas in a text.**
- **Answer questions about key details in a text read aloud.**

Genre: Procedural Text

Tell children that they will read a procedural text (starting on page 67) that tells how to do something. Point out that a procedural text, such as a recipe, usually includes a list of needed materials and instructions.

Set the Purpose

Help children understand the purpose for describing connections between two pieces of information. Ask: *How do details connect to a main idea? How do details connect to one another?*

Model and Teach

Read the text aloud as children follow along in their books.

Teacher Talk: Find Evidence

Explain that this text is about the life cycle of a butterfly. Say: *I want to learn about the butterfly's life cycle. First, I'll find out how it begins. I'll look for a detail that tells me. The caterpillar stage is next. I'll look for details about how the butterfly moves into that stage. How is the egg connected to the caterpillar?* Encourage children to respond in complete sentences, as appropriate.

Words to Know
cover
pupa

Butterflies!

(Genre: Informational Text)

1   Butterflies are such fun to watch. You see them in the summer. They love flowers!

2   A butterfly begins as a tiny (egg.) Look in a garden. You may see eggs on leaves. Each egg has a caterpillar inside. <u>One day, the caterpillar comes out of the egg.</u> It has tiny hairs. It may be one of many colors.

3   The caterpillar is hungry. It eats lots of leaves. Soon it gets fat. The more it eats, the more it grows.

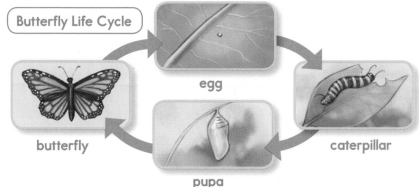

Butterfly Life Cycle

egg

caterpillar

pupa

butterfly

Guided Instruction

Teacher Talk: Find Evidence

Tell children that a life cycle has a beginning, middle, and end. In paragraph 2, have them circle the word that tells how the butterfly's life begins. Then have them underline a sentence that tells about the caterpillar. Ask: *What is the connection between a caterpillar and its egg?*

66   Unit 3 ■ Reading Informational Text: Key Ideas and Details

---

Words to Know

cover (*noun*): wrapping that goes over or around something

pupa (*noun*): stage of a butterfly's life when it turns from a caterpillar into a butterfly

Working with Word Meaning Help children understand these words by acting out the stages of a butterfly life cycle. A volunteer should act out egg and caterpillar. Then wrap a covering such as a blanket over the volunteer; when you remove it, the volunteer should fly like a butterfly. Be sure to use the Words to Know as you act out the stages.

4   One day, the caterpillar makes a **cover.** Inside the cover, it changes again. It becomes a **pupa.** It is growing wings and a body.

5   In the summer, the butterfly comes out of its cover. It is ready to fly!

Grow a Butterfly Garden
(Genre: Procedural Text)

Watching butterflies is fun. You can grow a butterfly garden. Then butterflies will come to you! Read how to make a butterfly garden.

What You Need

- books about butterflies
- flower seeds or plants
- stones
- shovel
- water hose

Teacher Talk: Find Evidence
Explain that this text tells how to grow a butterfly garden. It gives directions for how to do it, and it lists the items needed. Have children underline the title and circle the items in What You Need.
Ask: *What is the connection between the title and the items you circled?*

Guided Instruction

Unit 3 ■ Reading Informational Text: Key Ideas and Details   **67**

Teacher Talk: Find Evidence
Support children in moving into the new selection. Discuss the genre of selection 2. Say: *I remember that a procedural text tells how to do something. I will look at the title to find out what this text will tell me how to do. This text will tell me how to grow a butterfly garden.*

Under the heading "What You Need," I see a list of items. I can think about the connection between this list and the title of the selection. This list tells me what I'll need to grow a butterfly garden.

Review: Identifying Main Idea and Details

Review the skill, using the selection "Butterflies!" Ask children to name the topic of the selection. Ask: *What is the selection mostly about?* If children name the topic *butterflies,* lead them to name the specific main idea, the life cycle of a butterfly. Ask questions such as *Is it about different kinds of butterflies?* to help children narrow the topic to a main idea. Once children have identified the main idea, ask: *What details about the butterfly's life cycle have we read?* (starts life as an egg, becomes a caterpillar and then a pupa, emerges from a cocoon as a butterfly)

Support English Language Learners

When you move on to the procedural text, make sure that English language learners understand the difference between the two texts. Go through the list of materials with children, asking volunteers to illustrate each item on the board or on a large piece of paper to share with the rest of the class. Explain that the text gives readers steps they need to follow, in order. You may choose to have children illustrate each step.

Guided Practice

Read and Practice

Form small groups to read and discuss each step in the process described on page 68. Tell children: *This text describes what to do if you want to plant a garden that will attract butterflies.*

Teacher Talk: Find Evidence

Explain that after a procedural text gives a list of supplies, it gives directions to follow. Say: *This section gives details about how to plant a butterfly garden. The steps are listed in order. To plant this garden, I would have to follow the steps as they are listed. Each step leads into the next.*

Ask: *Why is it important to dig up the garden before seeds are planted? Why would seeds need soft soil? I'll think about what I know about seeds to help me answer.*

Reciprocal Teaching

Place children in groups of four and assign each to be the summarizer, questioner, clarifier, or predictor. After you have read steps 1 and 2, ask the summarizer to sum up the key ideas. The questioner should pose questions, and the clarifier attempt to answer them. The predictor should guess what will happen next. After the discussion, have the children switch roles and continue with steps 3 and 4, 5 and 6, and 7.

Digital Connection

Many time-lapse videos of caterpillars becoming butterflies are available online, as part of educational Web sites. Your class will enjoy seeing this transformation happen before their eyes.

Describing Connections

Words to Know

bloom

list

What to Do

1. Read a book about butterflies. Find out which butterflies live near you.

2. Find the names of the flowers or plants that these butterflies like. Write each name on a **list.**

3. Take the list to a garden shop. Buy seeds that are on the list. You can also buy the plants.

4. In the spring, shovel your garden. <u>Make the soil loose and soft.</u>

5. Plant the flower seeds, or seedlings. Water them every day.

6. Place stones near the flowers. Butterflies like to rest on stones.

7. Watch the flowers **bloom.** Then check your garden. The butterflies will appear!

You can also put plants that caterpillars like to eat in your garden.

Guided Practice

Teacher Talk: Find Evidence

Point out that this text gives steps for how to plant a garden. Call attention to steps 4 and 5. Lead children to talk about how these two steps are connected. Then have them underline the sentence in step 4 that tells what must happen before the seeds in step 5 can be planted.

68 Unit 3 ■ Reading Informational Text: Key Ideas and Details

---

Words to Know

bloom (*verb*): to open into flowers
list (*noun*): names or items written in order; note

Working with Word Meaning Ask children to draw an illustration of a garden filled with plants blooming. Ask them to think about which plants they have seen *bloom*, such as flowers, bushes, some trees, and some vegetables; and those they may have not seen bloom, such as some cacti, most trees, and grasses. Help children make a *list* of each type of plant on the board.

Key Ideas and Details

8. Next spring, look for butterfly eggs. (They may be in your garden.) If so, you will soon have caterpillars, too!

Comprehension Check   MORE ONLINE sadlierconnect.com

1. Think about what you learned in "Butterflies!"
   What new information did you learn from "Grow a Butterfly Garden"?

   (a.) Butterflies like flowers.

   b. Butterflies lay eggs.

   c. A garden is easy to make.

2. Think about how an egg changes into a butterfly.
   Use these words to connect and tell about the changes.

   caterpillar   pupa   egg

   The caterpillar comes out of the egg. The caterpillar

   changes to a pupa. The pupa changes to a butterfly.

   _____

Teacher Talk: Find Evidence
Discuss that step 8 tells what to look for when the butterfly garden is finished. Have children circle the sentence that tells where to look for butterfly eggs in the spring. Have partners discuss the connection between the garden flowers and the appearance of butterflies.

Independent Practice

Extend Thinking: Author Bias

Explain to children that informational texts sometimes have a mix of facts and opinions. Direct children's attention to the first paragraph of each selection. Focus on the author's use of the word *fun* in each paragraph.

Discuss how you know this is an opinion. (It cannot be proved to be right or wrong.) Find out whether there are diverse opinions in the classroom. Lead a discussion about the impact of the author's opinion on the selection. Ask: *Did it make reading the selection more fun? Did you still feel sure about which ideas are facts? If you did not agree with the author, did you feel left out?*

Read and Apply

Tell children that they will read the last step in growing a butterfly garden independently. Circulate to provide support to struggling readers.

Teacher Talk: Find Evidence

Say: *Find the sentence that tells where butterfly eggs might be. Then let's think about why butterfly eggs would be in the garden. Think about what we learned about the butterfly life cycle.*

Comprehension Check

Answer Explanations:

1. Answer choice **A** reflects a key idea in "Grow a Butterfly Garden," but not "Butterflies!"

2. Children should include all three terms—egg, caterpillar, pupa—in their responses and explain that one changes into the other.

Critical Comprehension

Use the following question to help children think more deeply about the selections. Children should support their answers with evidence from the text.

How can a butterfly garden help butterflies to make more butterflies? (Butterflies would lay their eggs on the plants. The caterpillars would eat the plants.)

Assess and Respond
If children have difficulty answering the questions in the Comprehension Check . . .
Then have a class discussion about sequences. Find examples of sequences in children's lives. Then, reexamine sequences in the texts.

OBJECTIVE
Read decodable text featuring consonant digraphs *th*, *ch*, *sh*, and *wh*.

Prepare to Read

Tell children that you will be reading an informational text about garter snakes. As you read, children should look for words that have two consonants together that make just one sound.

Introduce Phonics Skills

After you have read the selection once, read it again, this time focusing on the target foundational skills.

- I *see the word* what *in the very first line. It has a* w *and an* h*, which stand for one sound,* /wh/.

- *In the second line, I see the word* these. *This word has a* t *and an* h*, which stand for one sound,* /th/. *The word* thin *in the next line has the same letters but a little different sound.*

- *The word* fish *has an* s *and an* h *that together stand for one sound,* /sh/.

- *In paragraph 3, the first word is* each. Each *ends with a* c *and an* h *that stand for one sound,* /ch/.

- *The last line of paragraph 2 has the word* small. *The two* ls *at the end of* small *stand for one sound,* /l/.

- Have children look at the first sentence of the selection. Discuss the features of a sentence. Say: *The first word is capitalized, and the sentence ends with a sentence end mark, a question mark. That's how I know where the sentence ends.*

Focus on Fluency

Remind children that reading accurately means paying attention to punctuation. Have children read paragraph 3 aloud to show how they read a period, a comma, and an exclamation point.

Foundational Skills Read Together

As you read along, listen for words with *th*, *ch*, *sh*, and *wh* in the first or last position of a word.

The Garter Snake

1   What lives in the garden? Look closely. You might see a garter snake. These snakes are brown or black. They have a very thin shape. They have long stripes.

2   Garter snakes eat bugs. They also like worms and mice. Some can swim. These snakes eat small fish!

3   Each mother snake can have many babies. Some have between 20 and 40! When the babies grow bigger, they shed their skin. They do this many times.

4   Garter snakes are not dangerous. They do have sharp, tiny teeth, though. They need their teeth to help chew the food they catch.

5   Check your garden. You might see a garter snake!

garter snake

70

Focus on Phonological Awareness

Syllable Awareness

Use words from the selection for a quick syllable awareness warm-up. Say: *I will read a word. Listen for vowel sounds. Count how many vowel sounds you hear. The number of vowel sounds is the same as the number of syllables. After I say the word, tell me how many syllables you hear.*

garter (2)	might (1)	bigger (2)	dangerous (3)
snake (1)	shape (1)	babies (2)	catch (1)
garden (2)	worms (1)	many (2)	check (1)

Foundational Skills Reader 1

DIRECTIONS: Cut and fold the book.

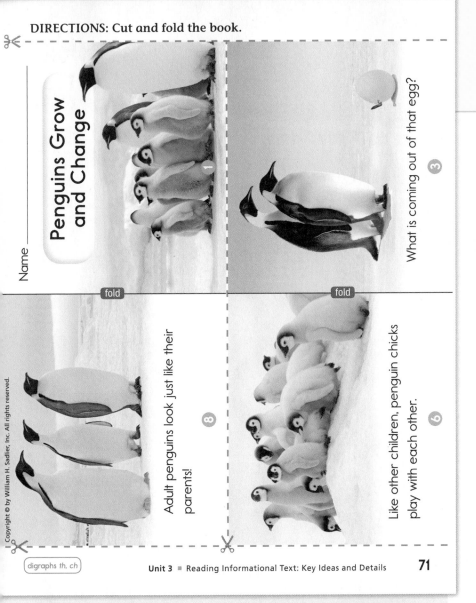

Penguins Grow and Change

Name

1

What is coming out of that egg?

3

fold

fold

Adult penguins look just like their parents!

8

Like other children, penguin chicks play with each other.

6

digraphs th, ch

Unit 3 ■ Reading Informational Text: Key Ideas and Details **71**

OBJECTIVES

- **Read decodable text featuring consonant digraphs *th* and *ch*.**
- **Read along orally, paying special attention to setting a purpose for reading.**

Prepare to Read

Tell children that they will be reading an informational text about the life cycle of a penguin. Tell them they can take the book home to share. Have them follow the directions to cut and fold the book.

Review Phonics Skills

Explain that this book features many words that have one sound spelled with two consonants.

- *Remember that the letters* t *and* h *together stand for one sound, /th/. Find words with* th *in the book.*
- *Remember that the letters* c *and* h *together can stand for the /ch/ sound. Find words with* ch *in the book.*
- *Both /th/ and /ch/ can appear in different places in a word.*
- Direct children to page 3. Ask: *Is this a sentence? How do you know?* (begins with a capital letter and ends with a question mark)

Introduce Reader 1

Divide the class into two groups. Assign each group to even or odd pages. Have each group chorally read its corresponding page of the book as you read each page aloud.

Foundational Skill: Phonics Practice

Write the following words from the Read Together and Foundational Skills Reader 1 on the board or on a chart. Have children practice reading the words.

Read Together words with *th*: the, these, they, thin, teeth, though; **words with *ch*:** each, check

Foundational Skills Reader 1 words with *th*: that, their; **words with *ch*:** change, chick, children, each

Read with a Partner

Select pairs of children to read together. Ask partners to read the text together several times, first chorally, then individually. Once the pairs are comfortable with one of their oral readings, have them record it for playing back later.

Focus on Fluency

Give children examples that demonstrate what it means to read with purpose. Say: *Suppose I am writing a report about penguins. I am reading this book because I want to know facts about penguins. I will use the facts to write my report. Now, suppose I love penguins, and I am reading just to enjoy penguins.* Then explain the special purpose of the Foundational Skills Readers. Say: *I am reading this book to practice reading aloud, and especially to practice reading words with two letters that make one sound (digraphs).*

Reading at Home

Once children are comfortable reading the book, send it home for children to read to family members.

Assess and Respond
If children have difficulty decoding words with the digraph *th* or *ch* . . .
Then have them highlight words with these digraphs in the text. Have children circle each digraph and read the word aloud.

Foundational Skills Reader 1

DIRECTIONS: Cut and fold the book.

4 It is a fuzzy baby chick!

2 A father penguin cares for an egg.

fold

fold

5 The baby does not look like its mother.

7 Penguin chicks grow taller and bigger.

72 Unit 3 ■ Reading Informational Text: Key Ideas and Details

Fluency: Read with purpose and understanding

Foundational Skills: Fluency Practice

Explain to children that reading with purpose will help them get the most out of their reading. Tell children that you are going to read the book to find out about the life cycle of a penguin. Work with children to identify the stages of a penguin's life from the words and pictures as you read. Then lead children in a choral reading of the entire reader. Have children practice; then record them reading aloud. Additional fluency passages and activities can be found at **sadlierconnect.com**.

Foundational Skills Reader 2

DIRECTIONS: Cut and fold the book.

Name ___

What Will I Be?

1

fold

I will be a grown cat!
I can dash this way and that!

3

fold

One day you will get big.
What will you be like?

8

When I am little, I live in a shell.
What will I be like when I get big?

9

digraphs sh, wh

Unit 3 ■ Reading Informational Text: Key Ideas and Details **73**

OBJECTIVES

- **Read decodable text featuring consonant digraphs *sh* and *wh*.**
- **Read along orally, paying special attention to setting a purpose for reading.**

Prepare to Read

Tell children that they will be reading an informational text about young animals becoming adults. Tell them they can take the book home to share. Have them follow the directions to cut and fold the book.

Review Phonics Skills

Explain that this book features many words that have one sound spelled with two consonants. Review words with *sh*, *wh*, and *ll*.

- *Remember that the letters* w *and* h *together stand for one sound, /wh/. Find words with* wh *in the book.*
- *Remember that the letters* s *and* h *together make one sound, /sh/. Find words with* sh *in the book. The /sh/ sound can be found in different parts of a word.*
- *When two* ls *appear together at the end of a word, they make one sound, /l/. Find* ll *words as you read.*

Introduce Reader 2

Help children establish a purpose for reading. Then have the class echo read the book: read a sentence and have children read the sentence after you.

Foundational Skill: Phonics Practice

Write the following words from the Read Together and Foundational Skills Reader 2 on the board or on a chart. Have children practice reading the words.

Read Together words with *wh*: what, when; **words with *sh*:** shape, fish, shed, sharp; **words with *ll*:** small

Foundational Skills Reader 2 words with *wh*: what, when; **words with *sh*:** dash, dish, show, shell; **words with *ll*:** will, ball, shell

Read with a Partner

Have heterogeneous pairs of children take turns reading to each other. Have each pair read the text together several times, then take turns reading page by page. Once the pairs are comfortable with one of their oral readings, have them record it for playing back later.

Focus on Fluency

Review reading for the purposes of entertainment and to gather information. Then add this common purpose: reading to become informed about a topic. Explain that a reader who wants to become informed about a topic will not skip over an idea they do not understand.

Reading at Home

Once children are comfortable reading the book, send it home for children to read to family members.

Assess and Respond
If children have difficulty decoding the digraphs *wh* or *sh* . . .
Then have children list samples of these words on the board. Have one side of the room stand for the side *wh*, and the other side stand for *sh*. Read the rest of the word, pointing at the appropriate side of the room when you encounter the digraphs, and have the children speak it aloud.

Foundational Skills Reader 2

DIRECTIONS: Cut and fold the book.

4
When I am little, I can fit in a dish.
What will I be like when I get big?

2
When I am little, my mother washes me.
What will I be like when I get big?

fold

5
I will be a handsome dog.
I will show you how I catch a ball.

7
I will be bigger and live in a bigger shell!
I will swim with other sea turtles.

fold

74 Unit 3 ■ Reading Informational Text: Key Ideas and Details

Fluency: Read with purpose and understanding

Foundational Skills: Fluency Practice

Remind children that reading with purpose will help them get the most out of their reading. Tell children that you are going to read the book with the purpose of learning about different kinds of young animals and the adults they will become. Read through the text with children, comparing and connecting each young animal with the adult version. Then model reading again with more ease to show how practice improves reading. Finally, choral read the entire reader. Have children practice, then record them reading aloud. Additional fluency passages and activities can be found at **sadlierconnect.com**.

Close Reading

Sea Turtles

(Genre: Informational Text)

1   Sea turtles live in the sea. They like warm waters. They spend all their lives in water.

2   Only a mother sea turtle visits a beach. She goes back to the place where she was born. She finds a place in the sand. Then she digs a hole. She lays her eggs in the hole. She covers them with sand. Weeks later, the eggs hatch. Baby turtles come out!

3   Each baby runs toward the water. Danger is everywhere. Baby sea turtles are black. The sand is white. The turtles are easy to see.

Unit 3 ■ Reading Informational Text: Key Ideas and Details   **75**

OBJECTIVES
- **Ask and answer questions about key details in a text.**
- **Identify the main topic and key details of a text.**
- **Describe the connection between two ideas in a text.**

Genre: Informational Text

Remind children that they have read several informational texts about life cycles in this unit. Instruct children to ask and answer questions as they read this text about sea turtles to better understand the main topic and key details. While reading, they can also look for ways the ideas in the text are connected.

Path Options

You may wish to have children read the text independently and apply the skills learned in this unit. Or, you may wish to do a close reading with children; if so, use the supports provided on these pages. As a third option, set up a buddy system, with some heterogeneous and some homogeneous pairs, to fit the needs of your class. Regardless, children should read the text more than once to facilitate understanding and to be able to answer the Comprehension Check questions correctly.

Support English Language Learners

Preteach some of the verbs children will need to know to successfully read the selection. Make sure children are able to use each word in a sentence.

spend (*verb*): pass the time. *I spend the day at school.*

visit (*verb*): make a brief stay. *I will visit my aunt on Saturday.*

dig (*verb*): take away dirt. *I dig with a shovel.*

hatch (*verb*): come out from an egg. *A chick will hatch from an egg.*

dash (*verb*): to move fast, all at once. *A mouse will dash away from a cat.*

Support First Reading

Circulate to check children's understanding. As needed, use the following comprehension and strategy check-ins to support basic understanding of the selection as children read.

Check-in Questions

• **page 75** *What is this page mostly about?* (Sample answer: baby sea turtles)

• **page 76** *What is the connection between where the turtles live and what they eat?* (Sample answer: The turtles live in the ocean, so they eat food found in the ocean.)

• **page 77** *What are some details about the sea turtle life cycle?* (Sample answers: sea turtles hatch from eggs; sea turtles live in the ocean; some sea turtles live 100 years.)

Review: Asking and Answering Questions

Ask children: *What dangers are there for baby sea turtles?* (Dogs, crabs, and birds try to eat them.) Ask: *How do they stay safe?* (They move fast.) Ask children to tell you where they found the answers to these questions in the text.

Review: Identifying Main Idea and Details

Reread paragraphs 5 and 6 with children. Ask: *What are these paragraphs mostly about?* (They are about how baby sea turtles grow up and become adults.) Make sure children understand that *main idea* refers to what the text is mostly about.

Close Reading

4   Dogs chase them. Crabs dash after them. Birds swoop down to get them. That is why the turtles rush. They do not want to be eaten!

5   The baby turtles live in the ocean. They swim. They eat food like seaweed and fish eggs. They grow and grow. After ten years, they are much bigger. They are as big as dinner plates.

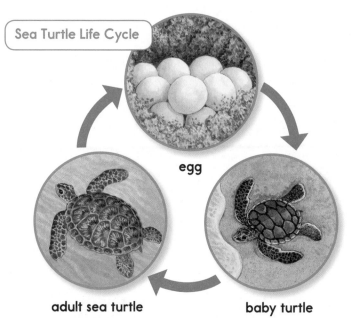

Sea Turtle Life Cycle

egg

adult sea turtle

baby turtle

76   Unit 3 ■ Reading Informational Text: Key Ideas and Details

Differentiate Instruction

To help children who cannot read the text, make a recording that children can listen to and follow along. Then pair these children with proficient readers for choral reading. Ask pairs of children to identify the most difficult parts of the text. Reread and discuss these parts of the text as a class.

6   Sea turtles grow big. Some are as big as a car!
They live a long time, too. Some live 100 years.

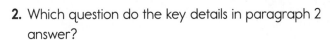

Comprehension Check

1. Read this sentence.
    Sea turtles grow big.
    Which key detail tells more
    about the sentence?

    a. They live in the sea.

    b. They swim.

    (c.) Some are as big as a car.

2. Which question do the key details in paragraph 2
    answer?

    a. How many sea turtles swim in the sea?

    b. Why do sea turtles eat different things?

    (c.) Where do sea turtles lay their eggs?

Unit 3 ■ Reading Informational Text: Key Ideas and Details   **77**

Strategic Reading

Support all readers by reminding them of the value of forming mental images while reading. Explain to children that this is one way to stop and think about what they are reading, and make sure that they understand it. Model the strategy as you read page 75 aloud. After you read paragraph 1, stop and say: *In my mind I can see the blue waters of a warm ocean. I can see sea turtles swimming with their legs. Thinking about the turtles makes me feel curious and excited to learn more. Questions start to form in my mind, such as, "How do they swim when they are so big?" and "What do they eat?"*

Review: Describing Connections

Say: *Describe the connection between what you see in the picture on page 77, and what you have read about the life cycle of a turtle.* (The picture shows big mother sea turtles going back to the beach to lay eggs.)

Multiple Readings for Critical Comprehension

Have children reread this selection, and pose questions that focus on critical comprehension. Remind children that they can mark the text. Tell children they must provide text evidence to support their answers.

• *Do you think this would be a good article to read if you were writing a report about sea turtles? Explain your answer.* (Sample answer: Yes. Because it has a lot of facts.)

• *What is the most dangerous time of life for a sea turtle?* (The journey from the beach to the water after sea turtle eggs hatch.)

Comprehension Check

Score children's understanding of unit skills and texts using the Comprehension Check on this page and the next. Use children's total score to determine their readiness for the Unit 3 Review on page 81.

Multiple-Choice Questions: *1 point each*

1. Only answer choice **C** tells more about the turtles' size.

2. Only answer choice **C** poses a question that can be answered by details in paragraph 2. Specifically, "Only a mother sea turtle visits a beach. She lays her eggs in the hole."

Short-Answer Questions:
3 points each

Item 3 Rubric

3	Children connect the eggs to hatching and the appearance of baby turtles, who run toward the ocean.
2	Children connect the eggs with baby turtles but either do not include their hatching or running for the sea.
1	Children mention baby turtles, but do not connect them to the eggs or to their running for the sea.
0	Children cannot make a connection between hatching and emergence of the sea turtles.

Item 4 Rubric

3	Children connect the food to helping baby sea turtles grow.
2	Children understand that food helps baby turtles grow but do not express the connection well.
1	Children mention food but do not connect it to baby sea turtles' growth.
0	Children do not understand the connection between the food and the turtles' growth.

Theme Wrap-Up

Lead children in a discussion about life cycles. Remind them that they have learned about the life cycles of both plants and animals. Ask them to tell which life cycle they enjoyed reading about the most. Ask them to recall some of the facts they found the most fascinating.

Close Reading

3. A mother sea turtle makes a hole in the sand. She lays eggs there. What happens after a few weeks?

Sample answer: The eggs hatch and the baby sea turtles

come out. Then they run to the sea as fast as they can.

_____

_____

4. Baby sea turtles eat seaweed and fish eggs. They grow and grow. How are these two details connected?

The food they eat helps the baby sea turtles to grow.

_____

_____

_____

_____

Assess and Respond (pages 75–78)

If	Then
Children scored 0–3 points, they are **Developing** their understanding of unit skills …	Provide children with reading support and more intensive modeling of skills.
Children scored 4–6 points, they are **Improving** their understanding of unit skills …	Use children's scores to target areas that are weak and review those specific skills.
Children scored 7–8 points, they are **Proficient** in their understanding of unit skills …	Have these children move on. They are ready for the formal assessment.

Compare and Contrast Texts

Look at the pictures from three texts you have read. How are the main ideas and details in the texts similar? How are they different? Tell how the texts are connected.

From Tadpole to Frog

A Tree Grows

Sea Turtles

Return to the Essential Question

What are the parts of an informational text?

Talk about the main ideas and details in the texts. How are they alike, different, and connected to each other?

Unit 3 ■ Reading Informational Text: Key Ideas and Details   **79**

Compare and Contrast Texts

Read aloud the directions on page 79. Then provide some information about each of the featured texts, to help children as they recall the key ideas.

The selection "From Tadpole to Frog" tells about how frogs are born and grow. Where do frogs live? (a pond) *How do their lives begin?* (as eggs)

The selection "A Tree Grows" is about a certain kind of tree. What kind of tree did you read about? (apple) *How does an apple tree begin?* (as a seed)

The selection "Sea Turtles" has some details about the dangers baby sea turtles face on their way to the ocean. What are these dangers? (Turtles may be chased and eaten by dogs, crabs, and birds.)

What do the life cycles of these living creatures have in common? How do they differ? (Animals and plants are born or sprout as small creatures that grow, have babies, and die. Tadpoles undergo many changes as they become adults. Trees grow from seeds and make fruit to spread their seeds. Turtles hatch from eggs and live for many years.)

Give children time to organize their thoughts about the texts. Remind them to ask questions about any confusion they have about the texts before you begin. Then lead the Essential Question discussion.

Support Essential Question Discussion

Read the Essential Question aloud. Then prompt children to share their ideas about the selections.

- *How did the pictures and diagrams help you understand the texts?*
- *How did subheadings in some of the texts help you understand them?*

Discussion Skills

Find opportunities to ask children to restate someone else's statement. Ask: *Can you repeat what he/she just said in your own words?* Also prompt children to ask the speaker questions to clarify something they do not understand. As needed, remind children of the agreed-upon rules for discussions, especially listening to others with care.

OBJECTIVE
Identify and write plural forms of nouns.

Guided Instruction

Read aloud the Guided Instruction section on page 80. Clarify that the word *dog* stands for one dog. The word *dogs* can stand for two, three, four, or more dogs. Ask: *How can I talk about more than one desk?* (Sample answer: You can use the word *desks*.)

Guided Practice

Have children work in pairs to complete the Guided Practice. Circulate to provide help as needed. When children struggle, focus their attention on the word that appears in both the singular and plural form, and ask: *Which word means "more than one"?*

Independent Practice

Before children begin work in the Independent Practice, read the instructions together as a class. Point out the headings *One* and *More than one*. Give children an opportunity to ask questions. Then circulate and provide support as needed.

Apply to Reading

Have children return to "From Tadpole to Frog." Ask them to turn to page 59. Tell them that there are many examples of plurals on this page. Challenge them to see how many they can find. (tadpoles, tails, gills, plants, birds, snakes, lily pads, places)

Language

Plurals

Guided Instruction Many nouns, or naming words, end in the letter *s* to show more than one.

Read this sentence from "Sea Turtles":

Dogs chase them.

The naming word *dogs* ends in the letter *s*. The letter *s* tells you there is more than one dog.

Guided Practice Read each pair of sentences. Circle each word that means more than one.

1. I see one cat. Pat sees two (cats.)

2. I pick a flower. My garden has many (flowers.)

3. I ate a cookie. Julio ate many (cookies.)

4. I like (hats.) Mom gave me her hat.

Independent Practice Write each naming word again to make it mean more than one.

One	More than one
5. one frog	two ___frogs___
6. one snake	three ___snakes___

Support English Language Learners

Use realia to provide practice for English language learners. Use some objects in the classroom, or bring in some small, familiar objects. For example, show children one cup, and say *one cup*. Then show children two cups and say *two cups*. Repeat with other realia, such as *one pen* and *two pens, one rock* and *two rocks, one book* and *two books* and so on. Invite children to chime in when they are ready. When all children are able to participate, they will be ready to complete the assignment.

Read along with the following selection.

Watch Baby Animals

All baby 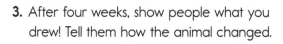change. You can watch them to see how much. Look in a bush or tree. Peek in a pond or garden. You can keep track of what you see.

What to Do

1. Draw and write about the animal. Do not touch it!

2. Draw the animal each time you see it for four weeks.

3. After four weeks, show people what you drew! Tell them how the animal changed.

Fill in the circle of the correct answer.

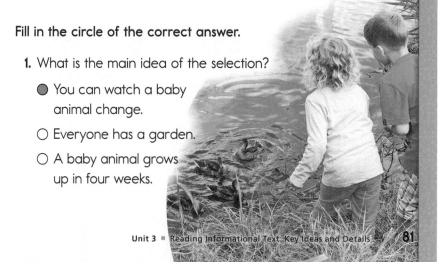

1. What is the main idea of the selection?

   ● You can watch a baby animal change.

   ○ Everyone has a garden.

   ○ A baby animal grows up in four weeks.

Unit 3 ▪ Reading Informational Text: Key Ideas and Details **81**

Self-Assessment: Progress Check

Have children revisit the Progress Check on page 53 and respond to the questions again. Ask them to compare their Before and After responses.

Review children's responses, and give them an opportunity to request additional help with one or more of the unit skills. Form study groups around unit skills. After discussing and helping one another with the skill, groups will work together to ask questions they still have about the skill. Groups will pose up to three questions to the class for class discussion.

Unit Summary

Children have had instruction and practice in reading informational texts that provide facts about the life cycles of different plants and animals. Children have learned that asking and answering questions about what they are reading will help them enjoy, understand, and remember what they read. They have gained experience in identifying a main idea and key details in both a selection and a paragraph. They have practiced describing how two pieces of information are connected. Children have had opportunities to read independently, including reading digraphs aloud and reading plural forms of common nouns. They should be well prepared for the review section.

Introduce the Review

Explain to children that they will read a new passage along with you that is related to the unit's theme and the selections they have already read. Then they will answer the questions on pages 81–82.

Answer Explanations

Scoring: Items 1, 2, 4, 6, 7, and 8 on pages 81–82 are worth 1 point each. Explanations for the correct answers are given below and on the next page. Also see the rubrics on the next page for guidance in scoring the short-answer questions.

1. Only the first answer choice is a good match for the title "Watch Baby Animals" as well as the content of the text.

2. Children should see that the paragraph describes watching baby animals; the list under "What to Do" gives specific steps on how to watch safely and take notes.

Answer Explanations

Item 3 Rubric

2	Child asks a question about a specific detail in the text and answers it.
1	Child asks a question about a detail in the text but does not answer it.
0	Child does not ask or answer a question about the text.

4. Only the word *animals* names more than one animal.

Item 5 Rubric

2	Child identifies the main topic of the text, how to watch baby animals.
1	Child mentions baby animals but does not mention watching them.
0	Child does not provide the main topic of the text.

6. Only *show* begins with the digraph *sh*.

7. Only *what* begins with the *wh* digraph.

8. Only *them* begins with the digraph *th*.

Unit 3 Review

2. How does "What to Do" connect to the paragraph?

- ● It tells how to watch baby animals.
- ○ It tells how to draw a picture.
- ○ It tells how baby animals become big.

3. A key detail in step 1 of "What to Do" is "Do not touch it!" Ask a question about this key detail. Then answer it.

Sample answer: Why did the author say this? Because

he or she does not want to scare the animal.

4. Circle the word in the paragraph that names more than one animal.

5. What is the main topic of this selection?

Sample answer: How to watch baby animals

6. What word in the selection begins like *shell*? show

7. What word in the selection begins like *where*? what

8. What word in the selection begins like *this*? them

Analyze Scores

8–10 pts Strong	Child has a good grasp of the skills and concepts taught in this unit. Point out any mistakes the child has made and explain the correct answers if necessary.
4–7 pts Progressing	Child is struggling with some skills or concepts. Identify the specific skills that are problematic to target a review of instruction.
0–3 pts Emerging	Child has difficulty understanding the skills and concepts taught in this unit. Child may need further instruction with a higher level of support and detailed explanation of the unit's skills and concepts.

Introducing UNIT 4

In this unit, you will write to give information about an animal's life cycle. This type of writing is called informative text. An informative text gives facts about a topic.

Good writers begin an informative text by naming their topic. They add facts and details. They end their text by telling the topic again.

Progress Check Can I?

Before Unit 4		After Unit 4
☐	Name a topic. Write facts about it.	☐
☐	Write an ending for the text.	☐
☐	Use commas in dates and in a list of words.	☐
☐	Begin names of months with a capital letter.	☐
☐	Use verbs that tell about now, the past, and the future.	☐
☐	Make verbs agree with nouns.	☐

Unit 4 ■ Text Types and Purposes: Write Informative Texts

Student Page 83

Progress Check

The Progress Check is a self-assessment feature that children can use to gauge their own progress. Research shows that when children take accountability for their own learning, their motivation increases.

Before children begin work on Unit 4, have them check the boxes next to any item that they feel they can do well. Explain that it is fine if they don't check any of the boxes. Tell them that they will have an opportunity to learn about and practice all of these items while studying the unit. Let them know that near the end of the unit they will have a chance to reconsider how well they can do each item on the list.

Before children begin their Unit 4 Review on page 96, have them revisit this page. You can use this information to work with children on any items they don't understand before they tackle the Review.

HOME ◆ CONNECT...

The Home Connect feature is a way to keep parents or other adult family members apprised of what their children are learning. The key learning objectives are listed, and some ideas for related activities and discussions are included.

Explain to children that they can share the Home Connect page with their parents or other adult family members in their home.

Encourage children and their parents or other adult family members to share their experiences using the suggestions on the Home Connect page.

HOME ◆ CONNECT...

In this unit, your child will learn about writing an **informative text.** An informative text tells facts about a topic. Help your child decide on a topic that he or she would like to learn more about. Then help your child find facts about the topic. Look at different types of informative texts, such as science textbooks, magazine articles, and online encyclopedia articles. Point out facts that the writer includes. If needed, explain to your child the difference between facts and opinions.

Your child will be writing an informative text about the life cycle of a butterfly, or another animal of choice. Discuss with your child where he or she might find facts about butterflies or other animals. Then, discuss how he or she can record these facts to be used when writing. Encourage your child to share facts about the life cycle of a butterfly, or the other animal, in his or her own words.

Activity: A biography is a type of informative text. Encourage your child to interview a friend or family member, such as a grandparent. Help your child develop a list of questions. Then, ask your child to make a scrapbook page about the person, including the facts learned in the interview.

IN THIS UNIT, YOUR CHILD WILL...

- Write an informative text.
- Name a topic for the text.
- Supply facts about the topic.
- Provide a strong ending for closure.
- Learn specific language skills and how to use them in writing informative texts.
  - Use commas to separate dates and words in a series.
  - Capitalize names of months in dates.
  - Use the correct forms of verbs to show the present, the past, and the future.
  - Use the correct forms of verbs for singular and plural nouns.

WAYS TO HELP YOUR CHILD

Help your child to read like a writer. As he or she reads informative texts, point out ways that the writer introduces facts. You can point out features such as boldfaced words, headings, bullets, and text boxes. Explain how these text features help to make the writing clearer.

ONLINE
For more Home Connect activities, continue online at sadlierconnect.com

84 Unit 4 ■ Text Types and Purposes: Write Informative Texts

Student Page 84

UNIT PLANNER

Theme: Cycles of Life Curriculum Connection: Science	Focus
WRITING MODEL pp. 86–87	*A Frog's Life*
WRITING ACTIVITY pp. 88–91	**ORGANIZATIONAL STRUCTURE:** Web
LANGUAGE MINI-LESSONS pp. 92–93	• Commas • Verbs
SPEAKING AND LISTENING pp. 94–95	• Share Your Writing • Be a Good Listener • Return to the Essential Question
UNIT 4 REVIEW p. 96	Language Skills Summary

Objective(s)

Write an informative text, stating the topic at the beginning, supporting the topic throughout with facts, and restating the topic at the end to provide closure.

- Plan an informative text about the life cycle of a butterfly, including facts to support the topic.
- Draw pictures, complete sentence starters, and compose an informative text about the life cycle of a butterfly.

- Use commas in dates and in series of items.
- Capitalize dates and names of people.
- Use verbs that agree with singular and plural nouns.
- Use past, present, and future verb tenses correctly.

- Orally present an informative text, showing drawings during the presentation and answering questions after the presentation.
- Participate respectfully in presentations by listening carefully and joining in the discussion.

Unit Assessment

- Unit 4 Review, *p. 96*

Additional Assessment Options

- Performance Task 1 *pp. 141–144*
  (ALSO ONLINE)
- Performance Task 2 *pp. 259–262*
  (ALSO ONLINE)

Optional Purchase:
- iProgress Monitor (ONLINE)
- Progress Monitor Student Benchmark Assessment Booklet

(ONLINE) Digital Resources

- Home Connect Activities
- Additional Practice
- Teacher Resources
- iProgress Monitor (separate purchase)

Go to SadlierConnect.com to access your Digital Resources.

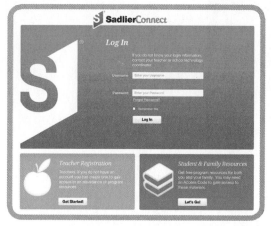

For more detailed instructions see page T3.

LEARNING PROGRESSIONS

In this unit, children will learn to write an informative text about the life cycle of a butterfly. The text will include illustrations and sentences. In order to learn the skills necessary to craft an informative text, children will further develop skills learned in kindergarten. They should be encouraged to retain these skills, as they will continue to build on them in second grade.

Naming the Topic

- Proficient kindergarteners are able to name what they are writing about when composing informative texts by using a combination of drawing, dictating, and writing.

- First graders understand that an informative text has a topic and learn to name the topic as part of the introductions they write.

- In second grade, children learn to create effective openings for the informative texts they write, which includes introducing the topic.

Supplying Facts

- Kindergarteners include some information about a topic when writing informative texts.

- Proficient first graders learn to provide facts about their topics when writing informative texts.

- Second graders add definitions to the facts they supply and learn to use them to develop points clearly in the body of an informative text.

Providing a Sense of Closure

- In kindergarten, children are not expected to provide closure when writing informative texts.

- By the end of first grade, children learn to provide some sense of closure at the end of an informative text.

- As second graders, children should understand that the ending of an informative text should have a concluding statement or section.

Text Types and Purposes: Write Informative Texts

Essential Question:
How do writers organize information?

Unit 4 ■ Text Types and Purposes: Write Informative Texts **85**

Essential Question:
How do writers organize information?

Children will learn the importance of clearly identifying a topic, providing facts about it, and creating a sense of closure when writing an informative text.

Theme: Cycles of Life

Children will carry forward their thinking about life cycles from Unit 3, as they plan and write an informative text on the life cycle of butterflies.

Curriculum Connection: Science

Children use the facts they have learned about life cycles to develop an informative text explaining the life cycle of butterflies.

Connect Reading to Writing

Remind children that in Unit 3, they read several informational texts about life cycles. The texts "From Tadpole to Frog" (Student Book, pages 58–61) and "Butterflies!" (Student Book, pages 66–69) both provide facts about animal life cycles. Now children will have an opportunity to use the facts they learned to write about the life cycles of butterflies.

Writing Handbook

To assist children in writing an informative text, use the *Writing Handbook* on pages 263–268 to guide children through the writing process. The *Writing Handbook* gives children detailed instruction on planning, drafting, revising, and editing their writing, as well as providing tips on producing and publishing.

Have children turn to page 263 and review all of the parts of the *Writing Handbook*. Then lead them through the suggestions on page 264 on selecting a topic and organizing their information. Once children get started on their informative text, return to the *Writing Handbook* for information on each part of the writing process.

OBJECTIVE

Write an informative text, stating the topic at the beginning, supporting the topic throughout with facts, and restating the topic at the end to provide closure.

Introduce: Organizational Structure

Explain that an informative text provides information about a specific topic. The topic is clearly stated at the beginning and at the end of the text. Facts that support the topic are given throughout. As you read the model with children, identify the topic and the supporting facts.

Analyze a Student Model

Topic: Explain that the title of a text often gives clues about its topic. Read the title and the first sentence with children. Ask: *What words are the same in the title and the first sentence?* (frog's life) *What new information does the first sentence provide about the frog's life?* (It has three parts.)

Supporting Facts: Remind children that facts are statements that can be proven true. *Which sentences in the paragraph are facts?* (A frog's life has three parts. The mother frog lays eggs in water. Eggs hatch. Each egg is a tadpole.)

Read a Student Model

Yuki wrote an informative text about the life of a frog. Notice how she tells her topic. Then notice the facts she uses to tell more about a frog's life.

A Frog's Life

(A frog's life has three parts.) First, the mother frog lays eggs in water. The eggs hatch. Now each egg is a tadpole.

This is a tree frog.

Teacher Talk: Find a Topic and Supporting Facts

Tell children that the topic is what the text is about. Ask: *Which sentence tells the topic?* Have children circle it. Explain that facts give more information about a topic. Ask: *Which sentence tells a fact about the eggs after they hatch?* Have children underline the sentence.

86 Unit 4 ■ Text Types and Purposes: Write Informative Texts

Genre: Informative Text

Point out that an informative text gives facts to a reader, so the first step is to gather facts about the topic.

Explain that children know some facts; others can be gathered from many different sources, such as Web sites, books, and magazines. However, writers should make sure that the sources they use are reliable and can be trusted. For example, a museum website would be a trusted source for facts about animal life cycles. Then point out that while some facts may be interesting, they may tell more about another topic. Remind children to write down only the facts about their topics.

This tadpole will grow to be a frog.

Each tadpole grows four legs. Soon, it comes out of the water. Then it loses its tail. It is an adult. The adult frog can live on land. A frog changes a lot in its life!

Teacher Talk: Provide a Conclusion

Explain to children that a conclusion is a clear ending that restates the topic. Say: *Let's find a sentence at the end that tells the topic again.* Have children circle the sentence.

Unit 4 ■ Text Types and Purposes: Write Informative Texts **87**

Analyze a Student Model

Supporting Facts: Tell children that the second paragraph of the text has more information about the life cycle of a frog. Have children refer to the circled topic on page 86. Ask: *Which parts of a frog's life do these facts describe?* (tadpole and adult)

Conclusion: Point out that the text ends with a concluding statement. Remind children that the concluding statement reminds the reader of the topic. It signals to the reader that the text is finished and ties all of the facts together. However, it does not use exactly the same words as the introduction. Ask: *How are the first and last sentences alike?* (They both tell that a frog changes in its life cycle.) *How are they different?* (The concluding sentence does not tell that there are three parts.)

Visual Literacy

Pictures and Captions: Tell children that pictures in informative texts include photographs, diagrams, and drawings. The pictures show what the text talks about. Point out that captions explain what the reader sees in the pictures. Ask: *What do you learn from the pictures and captions in this text?* (You learn what the **tree** frog looks like in two stages—tadpole and adult.)

Support English Language Learners

To support English language learners, first, provide reinforcement for key vocabulary words such as *frog, egg, hatch, tadpole,* and *adult.* Create picture cards for each word and label each picture. As you display each picture, say the word and have children repeat it.

Next, arrange the cards in a circle to model the life cycle. Explain each stage, in order, and then invite children to use the words to explain the life cycle of a frog.

Model: Organizational Structure

Explain to children that strong informative texts have a clearly stated topic followed by facts to tell more about the topic. When writers plan their informative texts, they organize their facts. They only include facts related to the topic. Then they place these facts into groups.

Discuss the chart that Yuki used. Point out the information in the three circles. Say: *Look at the circle labeled 1. Yuki has written "Egg" as the main idea since this is how the frog's life cycle begins. Then she adds a fact about this stage. Notice the arrow that points to the circle labeled 2. This shows the tadpole stage. This is the next step in the frog's development. Notice that the three facts in this circle describe what happens when the frog is a tadpole. Now look at the last circle, labeled "Adult." Yuki has written two facts about adult frogs.*

Think-Pair-Share

Ask children to think about these questions: *Why did Yuki write one word in dark print at the top of each circle? How did this help her to add details to her writing?* Next, pair children to discuss their thoughts and ideas. Then have children share their responses with a larger group or with the whole class.

Write Informative Texts

Yuki used this web to plan her informative text. She showed the parts of a frog's life in order. She included facts about each part.

Frog Life Cycle

1 Egg
The mother frog lays eggs in water.

2 Tadpole
An egg hatches into a tadpole. The tadpole grows legs. It comes out of the water.

3 Adult
The tadpole loses its tail. It is now an adult frog.

Review: Main Topic and Key Details

Remind children that they learned about the main topic and key details in Unit 3. Review that the main topic explains what the passage is mostly about while the key details give more information about that topic. Guide children to understand that Yuki's main topic is that a frog's life cycle has three parts. Each of the facts listed in her text are the key details that support the main topic.

Plan Your Informative Text

Use a web to plan your informative text. Write the topic. Tell a fact about each part in the life cycle of a butterfly or other animal.

Topic: _____

1

_____
_____
_____
_____

2

_____
_____
_____
_____

4

_____
_____
_____
_____

3

_____
_____
_____
_____

Unit 4 ■ Text Types and Purposes: Write Informative Texts **89**

OBJECTIVE

Plan an informative text about the life cycle of a butterfly, including facts to support the topic.

Introduce the Writing Process

Explain that writing is a process with several steps. The first step is planning. The graphic organizer that Yuki filled out helped her to plan her text. Tell children that they will fill out a graphic organizer before writing their informative texts.

Plan an Informative Text

Think About Organization

Remind children of how Yuki organized her informative text. First she stated her topic. Then she described each stage of the frog's life cycle in order, including facts for each stage. Finally, she ended the text with a concluding sentence. Children should follow this organization for their texts.

Plan

Explain to children that they will complete the graphic organizer, using facts they have learned from reading reliable, or trusted, sources. Explain that this will help them plan their writing. Ask leading questions for each box. Encourage children to draw and write notes or complete sentences in the boxes. Ask: *What happens at this stage? How does the butterfly look? How does it change?* Continue with the other boxes. Circulate to provide individual support as children use the boxes to plan their informative texts.

Peer Collaboration

Have pairs use their graphic organizers to talk through their informative texts in preparation for writing. Expanding orally on their ideas should help them generate oral language that will support their writing.

Provide prompts such as the following to guide their discussions as they comment and ask questions.

Did I write one or more facts in each box? What other details can I add?

Can you tell me more about _____?

Can you describe _____?

OBJECTIVE
Draw pictures, complete sentence starters, and compose an informative text about the life cycle of a butterfly.

Draft an Informative Text

Point out the different areas provided for children to create their texts: an area for illustrations, two sentence starters, and then write-on lines. Have children refer to their planning charts. Guide them in completing the first sentence starter. Ask: *How many parts does a butterfly's life cycle have?* (four) Direct the children to find the planning section that lists facts about the first stage of a butterfly's life cycle. Remind them to include facts to describe each stage of a butterfly's life cycle. Guide students to complete the second sentence starter. Say: *Think of Yuki's main topic. How can you finish this sentence? What is the first step in the butterfly's life cycle?* (egg) Explain that the remaining lines are for facts about the other stages.

Create Your Informative Text

In the boxes on pages 90–91, draw pictures to show the life cycle of your animal. Show a fact about each stage.

Then use your web on page 89 to help you as you write. Start by completing the sentences below.

The life cycle of <u>Sample answer: a butterfly has four parts</u>

_____.

First, <u>Sample answer: the mother butterfly lays eggs</u>

_____.

Differentiate Instruction

Children with emergent literacy levels may find it easier to begin writing by drawing labeled diagrams. Encourage them to draw detailed drawings showing each stage of development and to provide labels to explain these stages. For children who are developing literacy, you may provide further sentence starters such as those below.

This is a _____.

It has _____.

It will change into a _____.

Answers will vary. Children should introduce the topic of their

informative texts, add facts about the topic, and write a

conclusion that restates the topic.

Unit 4 ■ Text Types and Purposes: Write Informative Texts **91**

Revise and Edit: Peer Collaboration

Once children have finished their drafts, have them work in pairs to read their drafts to each other and suggest revisions. Explain that they should ask each other questions to make sure everything is clear. Partners might suggest other facts to include, facts to delete that do not relate to the main topic, or descriptions that can be added.

Partners can then read each other's revisions and then make suggestions for ways to improve the draft.

Informative Text Rubric

4	The text includes a topic that is clearly stated at the beginning and end of the text; facts that support the topic are presented in well-developed paragraphs.
3	The text has the elements listed under "4" above, although they are executed less successfully.
2	The text is missing one or more of the required elements.
1	The text is unfinished or shows a minimal understanding of required elements.

Assess and Respond

If children have difficulty creating a text from the planning chart . . .

Then tell them to write a heading for each section of the chart. Then have them write sentences to tell more about each heading.

Digital Connection

Children may wish to use a computer to create a final draft of their informative text. Provide support for children as they type their drafts. Model for children how to use the features in the word processing program to add boldface or otherwise highlight important terms and headings. Demonstrate how to leave space for adding images.

OBJECTIVES

- **Use commas in dates and in series of items.**
- **Capitalize dates and names of people.**

Guided Instruction

Point out a comma in text, or draw one on the board. Explain that writers use commas to separate ideas when they write. Read aloud the introduction and the first bulleted item, pausing at each comma. Read the sentence again, asking the children to point to the commas as you read. Explain that the commas separate the three items, the vegetables. Read the second bulleted text. Point out that the comma is used to separate the day from the year. Remind children that the names of people, places, and things begin with capital letters. *February* is the name of a month, so it begins with a capital letter.

Guided and Independent Practice

Point out that for items 1 through 4, children will look for places to add a comma or capitalize the name of a month. Remind them that they may make more than one change in a sentence. For children who need more support, have them read the sentence twice. On the first read, they should look for places needing commas. On the second read, they should look for words that need to be capitalized.

For items 5 and 6, the children should complete the sentences using commas and capital letters.

Commas

Guided Instruction Sometimes we use **commas** when we write.

- Commas separate words in a list.

  I like carrots, peas, and beans.

- Commas also separate the month and day from the year. The name of the month begins with a capital letter.

  February 14, 2013

Guided and Independent Practice Add commas. Circle each letter that should be a capital.

1. She was born ⓐugust 8, 2003.

2. The zoo has zebras, lions, and seals.

3. He owns cats, dogs, and birds.

4. People landed on the moon on ⓙuly 20, 1969.

Complete the sentences.

5. Today's date is <u>Sample answer: Sentence should have</u> <u>capitalized month and a comma between day and year</u>.

6. Three fruits I like are <u>Sample answer: grapes, apples,</u> <u>and pears</u>

92 Unit 4 ■ Text Types and Purposes: Write Informative Texts

Differentiate Instruction

Children may be ready to explore other uses of the comma, such as to separate a city and state or to separate the greeting from the body of a letter. Create an anchor chart about comma usage. Record the two rules on the page along with the examples. Encourage the children to look for other examples of comma use in their reading. As they find examples, add a new rule to the anchor chart and provide an example. Children may then reference the chart during their writing.

Verbs

Guided Instruction A **verb** tells about an action.

- Some verbs tell about **now**. Some verbs tell about the **past**. Some verbs tell about an action that will happen in the **future**.

  Now   I **walk** home.

  Past   I **walked** home.

  Future   I **will walk** home.

- In the two sentences below, the verbs agree with the nouns. This means that when the noun names only one thing, an *s* is added to the verb.

  One frog **hops**.   Two frogs **hop**.

Guided and Independent Practice Circle the correct verb.

1. Yesterday, Beth (will share, (shared)) her pet frog.

2. Tomorrow, I (bring, (will bring)) my hamster.

3. Mrs. Ling (tell, (tells)) us about her pet.

4. Two boys ((bring), brings) their pets.

Write a sentence that tells about now.

5. _Sentence should include a verb in the present tense_ .

OBJECTIVES
- **Use verbs that agree with singular and plural nouns.**
- **Use past, present, and future verb tenses correctly.**

Guided Instruction
Read aloud the introduction and the first bulleted item. Have children identify the verb in dark print and notice how it changes. Give another example of a verb in each tense. Read the second bullet. Point out how the verb changes when matched with a plural noun. Provide another example such as *A dog runs.*

Guided and Independent Practice
Point out that for items 1 through 4, children will circle the correct verb. For item 5, children should write a sentence in the present tense.

Assess and Respond
If children have difficulty identifying the correct verb . . .
Then say the sentence with each form of the verb, and ask children to listen for which sounds correct. Correct or reinforce their choices as necessary.

Support English Language Learners

Verb tenses can be difficult for English language learners, as their native language may have varying tenses. For example, present perfect is used for actions that were true in the past and continue to be true now. However, in Spanish, this tense is also used for events that were recently true. When possible, point out the differences in tenses, then model the correct tense and have the children echo the sentence after you.

OBJECTIVE
Orally present an informative text, showing drawings during the presentation and answering questions after the presentation.

Share Your Writing

Tell children they will present their informative texts by reading them aloud. Remind children that since their drawings help to describe the life cycle, it is important to show their drawings as they read.

Review that as they share, children should speak clearly and look at their listeners. They should be ready to answer questions about their topics.

Get Ready

Children can practice their presentations in pairs. Guide them to apply the speaking skills they have learned: speak clearly, use complete sentences, look at your listeners, show your drawings, and be ready to answer questions.

Present

Have children give their presentations in small groups. Monitor to be sure children are applying the listening skills they have learned: wait their turn, listen carefully, ask a question, build on what others say, and tell if they agree or disagree.

Speaking and Listening

Share Your Writing

You will present your text. Speak clearly and in complete sentences. Look at your listeners.

Show your drawings as you talk.

The butterfly begins life as an egg.

Be ready to answer questions about your writing.

Discussion Skills

As you monitor the small group presentations, encourage the children to engage in multiple exchanges after each speaker presents. As they speak, encourage them to incorporate the vocabulary they have learned about butterfly life cycles. The following questions can support their discussions.

• Why did you include _____?

• Can you tell me more about _____?

Be a Good Listener

When you listen, look at the speaker. Think about what the speaker is saying. Be sure to sit still. Be quiet so that everyone can hear the speaker.

Wow! I never knew that!

After the speaker talks, you will ask questions and discuss ideas. Listen carefully to what others say.

Return to the Essential Question

How do writers organize information?

Think about these questions before the class discussion:

• What are facts?
• How can we organize our facts so readers can understand our topic?

OBJECTIVE
Participate respectfully in presentations by listening carefully and joining in the discussion.

Be a Good Listener
Remind children that being a good listener involves using their ears, eyes, mouth, body, and brain appropriately. Good listeners pay attention to what the speaker is saying. They look at the speaker so that they can see any motions, such as gestures, that the speaker uses. Good listeners keep their hands and feet still so they don't distract others. Good listeners are quiet when the speaker is speaking. Finally, good listeners think about what the speaker is saying. They think about questions and ideas they would like to share.

Return to the Essential Question
Give children time to think about the questions before the discussion. After discussing those questions, have children suggest other ways to organize facts.

Support English Language Learners

English language learners may profit from the support of prompts or sentence frames such as the ones listed below.

I thought that _____ was interesting.

I liked hearing about _____.

I wrote about _____ too!

Can you tell me about _____?

Introduce the Review

Explain to children that this review will give them a chance to use the language skills that they have studied and practiced in this unit. It will also give them a chance to share what they have learned about being a good speaker or listener.

Language Skills Summary

Let children know that they are going to use what they learned about commas, capital letters, and verbs. Briefly review the main concepts they learned. Ask:

- *When should you use a comma?* (to separate items in a list and to separate the day and year)
- *What words should be capitalized?* (names of months)
- *What must you pay attention to when you choose which verb to use?* (the subject and when the action happened)

Answer Explanations

1–2. Remind children that commas are often used to separate things. Ask them to think about what should be separated.

3–4. Write the key words *Yesterday,* *Today,* and *Tomorrow* on the board. Remind children that the verb must show when the action happened.

5. To help children decide which verb form is correct, have them use each choice to read the sentence to themselves,

Self-Assessment: Progress Check

Have children revisit the Progress Check on page 83 and compare their answers now with the answers they gave before completing Unit 4.

Unit 4 Review

Choose the correct answer. Fill in the circle.

1. Which date is written correctly?
   - ● We took a trip on May 3, 2013.
   - ○ We took a trip on May, 3 2013.
   - ○ We took a trip on may 3 2013.

2. Which sentence is written correctly?
   - ○ Ron Kim and Meg went to the store.
   - ● Ron, Kim, and Meg went to the store.
   - ○ Ron Kim and Meg, went to the store.

Circle the correct verb.

3. Yesterday, we (jumps, (jumped)) rope.

4. Tomorrow, we (jumped, (will jump)) rope.

5. Diana (jump, (jumps)) rope with us.

Think about speaking and listening.

6. Write a sentence that tells why a good listener listens with care.

   Sample answer: A good listener wants to understand

   what the speaker is saying.

Test-Taking Tip

Point out to children that sometimes it helps to quietly read the sentences and answers aloud. For items 3–5, children may wish to quietly read aloud the sentences, trying each answer choice to see which answer sounds correct.

Introducing UNIT 5

In this unit, you will read different kinds of texts about families. Some of the texts give information. Some tell stories. When you read the stories, you will decide who is telling them.

Authors use words about feelings and words about our senses. You will look for these words as you read.

Progress Check Can I?

Before Unit 5 / After Unit 5

☐ Find words that tell about feelings or how things look, feel, sound, smell, or taste. ☐

☐ Tell the difference between made-up stories and texts that give information. ☐

☐ Name who is telling a story. ☐

☐ Use what I learn to read new words. ☐

☐ Make new words by adding the endings *s*, *ed*, and *ing* to verbs. ☐

Unit 5 ■ Reading Literature: Craft and Structure

Student Page 97

HOME◆CONNECT...

The Home Connect feature is a way to keep parents or other adult family members apprised of what their children are learning. The key learning objectives are listed, and some ideas for related activities and discussions are included.

Explain to children that they can share the Home Connect page with their parents or other adult family members in their home. Let children know how much time the class will be spending on this unit so they can plan their time accordingly at home.

Encourage children and their parents or other adult family members to share their experiences using the suggestions on the Home Connect page.

Progress Check

The Progress Check is a self-assessment feature that children can use to gauge their own progress. Research shows that when children take accountability for their own learning, their motivation increases.

Before children begin work on Unit 5, have them check the boxes next to any item that they feel they can do well. Explain that it is fine if they don't check any of the boxes. Tell them that they will have an opportunity to learn about and practice all of these items while studying the unit. Let them know that near the end of the unit, they will have a chance to reconsider how well they can do each item on this list.

Before children begin their Unit 5 Review on page 125, have them revisit this page. You can use this information to work with children on any items they don't understand before they tackle the Review.

HOME◆CONNECT...

I n this unit, your child will learn that authors of stories use different kinds of language. The language makes the writing more interesting. Your child will learn to recognize **words that suggest feelings** and **words that appeal to the senses** of hearing, taste, smell, touch, and sight. When reading with your child, have your child identify these types of words.

Your child will also learn to **recognize informational texts** (nonfiction) and **made-up stories** (fiction). As you read with your child, talk about whether the text is a made-up story or one that gives information. Ask your child to explain how he or she knows.

Every story has at least one narrator—the person who is telling the story. Your child will **learn to identify the narrator** by looking for clues on the pages. When reading stories, have children look for the words *I* or *me*. Then have children look for the name of the character who is the *I* or *me* in the story.

IN THIS UNIT, YOUR CHILD WILL...

- Recognize words that suggest feelings, such as *happy* and *angry*.
- Recognize words that appeal to the senses, such as *rough* and *salty*.
- Tell the difference between fiction and nonfiction.
- Identify who is telling a story.
- Read words with regular spellings, such as *mat* and *plane*.
- Identify verbs and their forms ending in *s*, *ed*, or *ing*.
- Compare and contrast three different texts on the same topic.

WAYS TO HELP YOUR CHILD

Trips to the library help you discover your child's interests. Does your child choose nonfiction books? Are the books always on the same topic? Or does your child like fiction? If so, what types of fiction? Encourage your child to broaden his or her interests. Make suggestions for new kinds of books to read.

👫 **Activity:** On your next walk with your child, invite your child to observe the world around you. Ask: *What do you see? What do you smell? What do you hear or feel? What might you taste? What words can describe the world around you?* Try to go out at different times of the day and discuss if things are the same or different.

ONLINE
For more Home Connect activities, continue online at sadlierconnect.com

98 Unit 5 ■ Reading Literature: Craft and Structure

Student Page 98

UNIT PLANNER

Theme: All in a Family	Focus
READ ALOUD *pp. 100–101*	*Bunk Bed Brothers* **GENRE:** Realistic Fiction
IDENTIFYING SENSORY WORDS *pp. 102–105*	*Ice Cream Music* **GENRE:** Narrative Poem **LEXILE®:** N/A **WORDS TO KNOW:** blaze, mine, spin, sting, treat
IDENTIFYING FICTION AND NONFICTION *pp. 106–109*	*Black Bear, Brown Bear* **GENRE:** Informational Text **LEXILE®:** 260L **WORDS TO KNOW:** silver, weigh *Lunch with the Bears* **GENRE:** Fantasy **LEXILE®:** 250L **WORDS TO KNOW:** dash, strange
IDENTIFYING THE NARRATOR *pp. 110–113*	*Max's Monster* **GENRE:** Adventure Story **LEXILE®:** 170L **WORDS TO KNOW:** check, scary, shone, sudden
FOUNDATIONAL SKILLS READ TOGETHER *p. 114*	*Scat, Cat!* **GENRE:** Realistic Fiction
FOUNDATIONAL SKILLS READER 1 *pp. 115–116*	*Fred's Trip* **GENRE:** Realistic Fiction
FOUNDATIONAL SKILLS READER 2 *pp. 117–118*	*Big Waves, Big Prizes* **GENRE:** Realistic Fiction
CLOSE READING *pp. 119–122*	*Blue Flube* **GENRE:** Fantasy **LEXILE®:** 170L
CONNECT ACROSS TEXTS *p. 123*	Compare and Contrast Texts
LANGUAGE *p. 124*	Verb Endings *s, ed, ing*
UNIT 5 REVIEW *pp. 125–126*	*A Cooking Tip* **GENRE:** Realistic Fiction **LEXILE®:** 270L

Objective(s)

- Identify sensory and feeling words.
- Contrast the features of fictional and informational text.
- Determine the narrator of a story.

Identify sensory and feeling words.

Contrast the features of fictional and informational text.

Determine the narrator of a story.

Read decodable text featuring one-syllable CVC, CCVC, CVCe, and CCVCe words.

Read decodable text featuring one-syllable CVC and CCVC words.

Read decodable text featuring one-syllable CVCe and CCVCe words.

Same objectives as pages 102–105; 106–109; 110–113

Identify verbs and their inflected forms.

Unit Assessment

- Unit 5 Review, *pp. 125–126*
- Unit 5 Performance Task (ONLINE)

Additional Assessment Options

- Performance Task 1, *pp. 141–144*
  (ALSO ONLINE)
- Performance Task 2, *pp. 259–262*
  (ALSO ONLINE)

Optional Purchase:

- iProgress Monitor (ONLINE)
- Progress Monitor Student Benchmark Assessment Booklet

(ONLINE) Digital Resources

- Home Connect Activities
- Unit Performance Task
- Additional Practice
- Full-Length Reading Selections
- Foundational Skills Practice
- Teacher Resources
- iProgress Monitor (optional purchase)

Go to SadlierConnect.com to access your Digital Resources.

For more detailed instructions see page T3.

99B

LEARNING PROGRESSIONS

In this unit, children will learn about genre, and analyze point of view as well as language in fiction. In order to learn the skills in this unit, children will further develop skills learned in kindergarten. They should be encouraged to retain these skills, as they will continue to build on them in second grade.

Identifying Sensory Words

- In kindergarten, children learn to ask and answer questions about unknown words they encounter in their reading.

- By the end of first grade, children will be able to identify words and phrases that suggest feelings or appeal to the senses.

- Second-grade children will learn how to describe how words and phrases supply rhythm and meaning in a story, poem, or song.

Identifying Fiction and Nonfiction

- Kindergarten instruction introduces new readers to common types of texts.

- In first grade, children focus on explaining the major differences between books that tell stories and books that give information, across a wide range of text types.

- By the end of second grade, children will be able to describe the overall structure of a story, including describing how the story is introduced in the beginning and concluded at the end.

Identifying the Narrator

- With support, proficient kindergarten children can name the author and illustrator of a story and define the role of each in telling the story.

- In grade 1, children learn to identify the narrator of a story as distinct from the author.

- Then, in grade 2, children acknowledge differences in the points of view of characters, including speaking in a different voice for each character when reading dialogue aloud.

Reading Literature: Craft and Structure

UNIT 5

Essential Question:
How can readers recognize different kinds of texts?

Unit 5 ■ Reading Literature: Craft and Structure **99**

Vocabulary Overview

blaze 102, check 110, dash 108, mine 104, scary 113, shone 112, silver 106, spin 104, sting 102, strange 109, sudden 110, treat 105, weigh 106

Essential Question:
How can readers recognize different kinds of texts?

In this unit, children will learn to distinguish between fiction and nonfiction. They will identify sensory language and learn that it adds detail to a text. They will learn to identify the narrator of a story in which there are multiple characters and dialogue.

Theme: All in a Family

Children will read across a wide range of genres (realistic fiction, narrative poetry, adventure fiction, and fantasy) and will meet many kinds of relations, and even a few unusual pets. They will read about brothers in conflict, and how they resolve their differences. They will read about a family that makes ice cream together and the fun they have. They will read about a family of bears taking a picnic. Throughout the unit there will be opportunities to explore what makes families different and what families have in common.

Curriculum Connection: Social Studies

As children enjoy the selections in this unit, they will be exposed to the social group called the family. They will question the idea that there is only one kind of family.

OBJECTIVES

- **Identify sensory and feeling words.**
- **Contrast the features of fictional and informational text.**
- **Determine the narrator of a story.**

Using the Read Aloud

Tell children that you will read a text aloud (see right) as they look at the pictures in their books. Read the text, pausing at the numbers to pose the questions below. Discuss the images with children as you move from one photo to another.

Picture

Which character is James? Point to Mark. How can you tell which character is which in the picture? (Mark has fuzzy bear slippers. James is making snow.)

Picture

How is the picture a clue that this is a story? (The story has illustrations, not photos.)

Picture

Look at the faces in picture 3. What are some words you could use to tell how the characters are feeling? (angry, annoyed, worried)

Picture

Look at the faces in picture 4. What are some words you could use to tell how the characters are feeling? (happy, cheerful)

Turn and Talk

Have pairs discuss: *How do the pictures show that Mark and James change in this story?*

Bunk Bed Brothers

The Ross twins were at it again! "Dad!" James yelled. "Mark is making his loud bears roar!"

"James is throwing paper snow on me," added Mark.

Dad took away the paper hole punch and the paper. Mom took off Mark's soft, fuzzy bear slippers. "Why are you wearing these in bed? Quit bothering each other!"

"Go to sleep. You are bunk bed brothers." Dad said. He shut off the light.

Morning came. The twins were still annoyed with each other. Dad's warm pancakes couldn't even help. Mark put down his fork. "I want to live by myself."

"Me, too," James added.

"Good idea," Dad said. He held the pancake turner high. He made a face like a judge. "I rule that you must not play together."

The boys went back to their room and got dressed. Then James grabbed a suitcase. He put in a water bottle. He put in drawing paper. Mark got his backpack. He went to the kitchen. He put snacks in his backpack.

James and Mark took the quilts off their beds. Both boys grabbed their belongings. They went outside.

James took his quilt and tossed it over the bar on the swings. "This is my fort. Don't come in!" yelled James.

Mark took his quilt and threw it over the table. He shouted, "This is my tent. Stay away!"

James made believe he was a tracker. He gathered shiny rocks. But he couldn't decide where to hide them.

Mark pretended he was on a camp out. He piled sticks. He used them to make a bird nest. But he couldn't put the nest in the tree.

It was noontime. The boys just sat. James was outside his fort. He drank a little water, but he wanted food. Mark was outside his tent. He nibbled on some apple, but his mouth was dry.

"Want some water?" James asked.

"Want some apple?" Mark asked.

The brothers shared. Then they hid James's stones and found a place for Mark's nest.

Listen as your teacher reads. Look at the pictures as you listen.

What makes this story different from a text that gives information?

Bunk Bed Brothers

100   Unit 5 ■ Reading Literature: Craft and Structure

Unit 5 ■ Reading Literature: Craft and Structure   101

Preview the Focus Skills

Do a second reading of the read aloud as children look at the pictures. As you read, pause briefly where indicated below. Use the suggested think alouds to preview the unit's targeted reading skills and model how children might use the skills independently during shared reading.

- Pause after reading the description of Mark's slippers. Say: *When I read a story, I pay attention to words that describe sounds, smells, sights, feelings, and tastes. This author helps me hear a bear roar, see paper snow, and feel soft fuzzy slippers.*

- Pause after reading the scene in the kitchen. Say: *Sometimes it is not easy to figure out whether a story is real or made up. This story is about twins who are arguing. That could really happen. However, the pictures are drawings, not photos. The author used a lot of dialogue. That makes the people in this writing seem like characters to me, even though they are doing realistic things.*

- Read to the end of the story. Say: *I will understand this story better if I figure out who is telling it. This story has four characters, Mom, Dad, Mark, and James. None of the characters uses the word I when they speak. That means this story is told by an outside narrator, not by one of the characters.*

Digital Connection

Preview and watch a video from an online Web site and talk about conflict resolution. Discuss the conflicts the twins have. Ask children to use the information in the video to assess how the twins resolve their conflict.

Guided Instruction

OBJECTIVES
- **Identify sensory and feeling words.**
- **Answer questions about key details in a text read aloud.**

Genre: Narrative Poem

Explain to children that a narrative poem tells a story.

Set the Purpose

Help children understand the purpose for learning to identify sensory language by asking: *What are the five senses?* (seeing, hearing, smelling, tasting, touching) *What sense does the word salty go with?* (taste)

Model and Teach

Read the text aloud as children follow along in their books.

Teacher Talk: Find Evidence

To support children in identifying sensory language, say: *It is helpful to read a poem a few times. The first time I pay attention to the meaning. Now I will pay attention to the language. I will look for sensory words.*

Focus on the first stanza. Say: *I see sensory words. The mixer is* old *and* green. *The chair is* shiny *and* red. *These details help me know how the mixer and chair look. What sense do these words go with?* (seeing) *In stanza 4, what are two words that tell about the can?* (tall, cold) *What senses do these words go with?* (seeing and touching) Encourage children to respond in complete sentences, as appropriate.

Identifying Sensory Words

Words to Know

blaze
sting

Ice Cream Music
(Genre: Narrative Poem)

1 I help Gram. We put the old green mixer
On the kitchen floor,
In front of the shiny red chair.

2 Uncle Dan brings the heavy bag.
White and gray. Salty pieces.
From sand to rocky blocks.

3 I reach in for some to make pretty rings.
My salt rocks **sting** my cut.
I lick away the **blaze**.

4 Gramps lugs the ice on his shoulder.
Aunt Fay reaches for the tall, cold can.
Smoke comes out with the creamy, sweet mix.

Guided Instruction

Teacher Talk: Find Evidence
Tell children that authors use words to tell how things look, feel, smell, taste, or sound. Say: *I want to know how the chair looks.* Underline *shiny* and *red* in stanza 1. Say: *These words tell me how the chair looks.* Ask: *What words in stanza 4 tell about the can?* Have children circle the words.

102   Unit 5 ■ Reading Literature: Craft and Structure

Words to Know

blaze (*noun*): burning
sting (*verb*): sharp hurt

Working with Word Meaning Have children create picture dictionary entries for the words *blaze* and *sting*. Have them draw a picture to show each word. Then, have them label the picture with the word.

Craft and Structure

5   Gramps snaps the handle shut.
    Then he begins to crank.
    Clink clank, clink clank.
    That sound makes me happy.

6   Fill it up, he tells me.
    I bring cup after icy cup,
    Until the bottom is full.
    Gramps shouts, "Stop!" and puts on salt.

7   We add ice, salt, ice, salt.
    Gramps keeps on.
    Then Uncle Dan takes over.
    We are excited.

Teacher Talk: Find Evidence

Say: *Some words tell about feelings. In stanza 5, the sound of the ice cream crank makes the girl feel happy.* Circle *happy.* Say: Happy *is a word that tells about a feeling.* Have children underline the word in stanza 7 that tells how everyone feels about making the ice cream.

Guided Instruction

Unit 5 ▪ Reading Literature: Craft and Structure **103**

Guided Instruction

Teacher Talk: Find Evidence

Say: *After I read once for meaning, I am going to stop again at the end of page 103 to reread. I will pay attention to the language the author chose.*

Stanza 5 has words that tell how the crank sounds. Did anyone notice those words? (clink, clank)

In stanza 6, can anyone find a word that tells how something feels? (icy) *What does the word* shouts *tell you about how something sounds?* (It is loud.) *What about a word that tells how something tastes in stanza 6?* (salt)

At the very end of stanza 7, I see a word like happy. *It is a word that tells about a feeling. What word is it?* (excited)

Use Visuals

To help children understand sensory details from information presented in visuals, have them look at the pictures on pages 102–104. Ask children to tell which part of "Ice Cream Music" each visual explains. Then say: *Sometimes poets use words to show how people feel on the inside, their emotions. Happy and sad are feelings or emotions. Look at the pictures on pages 103 and 104. What do you think the people are feeling? What words in stanzas 5 and 7 tell this?*

Support English Language Learners

Preview challenging vocabulary. Pair English language learners with proficient partners. Have children circle the action words in the poem and discuss or act out their meanings. Some difficult verbs include:

lug pull or carry with a lot of effort (*p. 102*)

snap move quickly or sharply (*p. 103*)

takes over take responsibility (*p. 103*)

spin turn round and round rapidly (*p. 104*)

Guided Practice

Read and Practice

Remind children that sensory language helps the reader imagine and experience the text. Have children talk about what they see in the drawing. Then read the first line of stanza 8 and discuss it with children. Have heterogeneous partners take turns reading the rest of the text on page 104 as you circulate to provide support. After they read the text once for meaning, have them read the text again to look closely at the language. Ask them to underline any words that tell about how something looks, tastes, smells, feels, or sounds. Ask them to circle words that tell about feelings. (underline: clink, clank, soft, round, fast, slow; circle: joyful, jolly)

Teacher Talk: Find Evidence

Ask children to underline the words in stanza 8 that tell the sound of the crank and to circle the words in stanza 9 that tell how the people feel. Ask volunteers to read aloud the words they underlined and circled. Monitor children's understanding of sensory language and ask a volunteer to state in complete sentences why authors use sensory and feeling words. (Sensory and feeling words add details that explain what the author is trying to say.)

Peer Collaboration

Have partners brainstorm alternative sensory and feeling words to replace the words they marked in their books. Then, have them choose some words to present to the class. Have volunteers read stanzas with alternative sensory and feeling words.

Identifying Sensory Words

Words to Know

mine
spin
treat

8 Clink clank, clink clank, he turns the crank.
Gramps takes Gram's soft hand.
Aunt Fay takes **mine**.
We **spin**, too.

9 Round and round, joyful, jolly.
Fast and faster first,
Then slow and slower,
We dance. The ice cream is done.

Guided Practice

Teacher Talk: Find Evidence
Review that authors use words to show how people feel and how things look, feel, taste, smell, or sound. Then have children underline the stanza 8 words that tell the sound of the crank, and circle the stanza 9 words that describe how the dancers feel.

104   Unit 5 ■ Reading Literature: Craft and Structure

Words to Know

mine (*pronoun*): belonging to me
spin (*verb*): to turn round and round
treat (*noun*): something special and good to eat

Working with Word Meaning Provide groups with a spinner that indicates a number from 1 up to the number of children in the group. For example, a group of 4 would have a spinner with the numbers 1 through 4. Each child is assigned a number. When the spinner points to a child's number that child asks another child: *What is your favorite treat?* Then the child responds: *Mine is _____.* Let groups spin several times.

10 We lift the lid and give everyone spoons.
    We lick the (smooth, rich) **treat**,
    And laugh at the mess on our faces.

Comprehension Check
MORE ONLINE
sadlierconnect.com

1. Which word tells how salt feels
   on a cut?

   a. icy

   b. sting

   c. shiny

2. Read stanza 10 again. How do you know that
   everyone is happy?

   Sample answer: They are laughing at one another as they

   eat ice cream and get it on their faces.

_____

_____

Teacher Talk: Find Evidence
Ask children to think about how the ice cream feels and tastes. Have
them circle the words that tell about the ice cream in stanza 10.

Independent Practice

Foundational Skills Review: Fluency Practice

Remind children that good readers set a purpose for reading. Ask them to
think about the poem "Ice Cream Music." What purpose could they have
for reading this poem? (entertainment, enjoyment, fun) Model reading
the first stanza with purpose. Then, have children chorally read the stanza
with you. Have them work in small groups to continue practicing reading
stanzas. Additional fluency passages and activities can be found at
sadlierconnect.com.

Read and Apply

Have children read stanza 10 on page
105 independently as you circulate.
Provide extra support to struggling
readers by reading chorally with them.

Teacher Talk: Find Evidence

Ask volunteers to share their own words
about how ice cream feels and tastes.
Then ask: *Which words in stanza 10 tell
how ice cream feels and tastes? Which
of our own words were the same as
these words? Which were different?*

Comprehension Check

Answer Explanations:

1. Choice **B** is found in stanza 3, on
   page 102.

2. Children may cite the use of the
   words *treat* and *laugh* as evidence
   of happiness.

Critical Comprehension

Use the following activity and question to
help children think more deeply about the
selection. Children should support their
answers with evidence from the text.

• *Compare making ice cream to getting
  ice cream from a store. Make a
  T-chart and write or draw about the
  differences. Then draw a picture to
  show what is the same.* (eating)

Assess and Respond
If children have difficulty answering the questions in the Comprehension Check . . .
Then reteach sensory and feeling words by working together as a class to list words for each of the five senses and words that show emotions.

Guided Instruction

OBJECTIVES

- Contrast the features of fictional and informational text.
- Answer questions about key details in a text read aloud.

Genres: Informational Text / Fantasy

Remind children that informational text tells readers facts about a subject and uses photos to show real things. Tell children they will compare an informational text and a fantasy story about bears.

Set the Purpose

Help children understand the purpose for learning the differences between fiction and nonfiction by asking: *If you want to learn facts about animals, do you read informational texts or stories?*

Model and Teach

Read the text aloud as children follow along in their books.

Teacher Talk: Find Evidence

Before reading, help children identify features of nonfiction texts. Say: *I notice that this text has a photo with a label that says* black bear. *I think this text will tell me facts about bears.* After you read paragraphs 1–3, say: *Paragraphs 1, 2, and 3 have facts. Underline a fact in paragraph 3.* Encourage children to respond in complete sentences, as appropriate.

Identifying Fiction and Nonfiction

Words to Know

silver
weigh

Black Bear, Brown Bear

(Genre: Informational Text)

1 There are many kinds of bears. Two kinds are named for their color. One is black. The other is brown.

2 Most black bears are dark as night. But they are not black all over. They have brown noses. They have some white fur. It is on the front.

3 Brown bears can be dark or light. A grizzly bear is a brown bear. It has some **silver** hairs. They are called guard hairs.

4 Another kind of brown bear can get very big. It can stand taller than a man! It can **weigh** as much as a class of first graders!

black bear

Guided Instruction

Teacher Talk: Find Evidence

Explain that texts that give information are called nonfiction. Point out the facts "Two kinds are named for their color," "One is black" and "The other is brown." Say: *Find a sentence in paragraph 3 that tells a fact about brown bears.* Have children underline the sentence.

106   Unit 5 ■ Reading Literature: Craft and Structure

Words to Know

silver (*adjective*): shiny gray or white
weigh (*verb*): to be the size of

Working with Word Meaning As a class, brainstorm things that are the color silver (coins, jewelry, metal, hair, tinsel), and things that weigh a lot (trucks, buildings, Earth), and a little (mice, dust, raisins).

Lunch with the Bears
(Genre: Fantasy)

1 Mama Bear packed berries and bugs. "Come, cubs. We will have lunch at the park."

2 "Lunch at the park?" asked Ted.

3 "What is the park?" asked Bell.

4 "A place for people," said Mama.

5 The bears walked through the forest. They stopped at a tall fence. Mama spread a sheet. The bears sat and ate. They watched the people.

6 Big people would clap for little people. The little people were running around a large green space.

7 "Look," Ted said, pointing. A boy threw a ball. A girl swung a stick at it.

Teacher Talk: Find Evidence

Tell children that made-up stories are called fiction. Say: *I know the bears are not real because real bears do not pack lunches.* Have children circle two sentences in paragraph 5 that show these are not real bears. Point out that some made-up stories have things that could really happen.

Guided Instruction

Unit 5 ■ Reading Literature: Craft and Structure **107**

Guided Instruction

Teacher Talk: Find Evidence

Before beginning to read the selection, ask volunteers to talk about what they notice in the picture. (Sample answers: It is a drawing, not a photograph. One bear is carrying a purse. Another bear is wearing a baseball cap, and another is wearing a bow. The bears are eating from a picnic basket.) Say: *Do these bears seem real? Do you expect this to be a story or to give information? Let's read, and see what we notice about the text.*

Read through paragraph 5. Then stop and say: *Made-up stories are called fiction. There are a lot of clues that this is a fiction story. For example, these lines in paragraphs 1 through 4 have dialogue. Dialogue is often a clue that a story is fiction. Plus, bears cannot talk! So, that is a pretty good clue. I have never heard of a real bear packing a picnic lunch. Have you? In paragraph 5, circle two details that show that these are not real bears.* (Mama spread a sheet. The bears sat and ate.)

Review: Identifying Sensory Language

Remind children that they identified sensory language in "Ice Cream Music." Focus attention on paragraph 6. Ask: *Which details tell about how things sound or look?* (clap, large, green)

Differentiate Instruction

To help children understand the differences between fiction and nonfiction, ask them to look at the images on pages 106 and 107 and tell the differences between the bears. List these on the board in a chart under the headers: *Fiction* and *Nonfiction*. (The bear in the photograph has bigger ears. The bears in the drawing are wearing a hat, bow, or purse.) Then ask children to offer synonyms and characteristics of fiction and nonfiction. List these next to the headings. (Fiction: stories, not true, made up, not real, drawings; Nonfiction: facts, photographs, information)

Guided Practice

Read and Practice

Have heterogeneous partners take turns reading page 108 as you circulate to provide support. Before children begin reading, remind them that knowing if a text is fiction or nonfiction can help them set a purpose for reading.

Explain that sometimes fiction has some parts that could be real, but that does not mean they are facts. Instruct children to find examples of things that seem real as they read.

Teacher Talk: Find Evidence

Have partners reread page 108 and circle sentences that could really happen. Then have them underline things that cannot happen.

Volunteers can share their answers for class discussion. Children might have different perspectives on what is realistic. For example, if a child says that paragraph 8 could really happen, clarify whether it is realistic for bears or people to talk.

Team Jigsaw

Have children work in teams of four. Assign each group to tell about 1. nonfiction text, 2. nonfiction pictures, 3. fiction text, and 4. fiction pictures. Each child on a team will describe the text or pictures of fiction or nonfiction. Then, they will share their ideas with other team members and then answer any questions.

Identifying Fiction and Nonfiction

Words to Know

dash
strange

8 "Don't point," said Mama. "It's not nice."

9 The girl hit the ball. She watched a boy **dash** to catch it. The ball flew over the fence.

10 "HOME RUN!"

11 The ball landed on the bears' lunch. Berries and bugs flew everywhere. Bell and Mama tried to save the lunch.

12 Ted picked up the ball. He threw it back over the fence. But no one was there to catch it. All the people had run away, screaming, "Bears!"

Guided Practice

Teacher Talk: Find Evidence
Remind children that a fiction story is a made-up story, but some parts of the story could actually happen. Have children circle the sentences that describe things that could actually happen. Then have them underline things that cannot happen.

108 Unit 5 ■ Reading Literature: Craft and Structure

Words to Know

dash (*verb*): to run
strange (*adjective*): hard to understand

Working with Word Meaning Write the Words to Know on index cards, one word on each card. Put the two cards in a hat or bag. Allow volunteers to draw a card and then use the word in a sentence. Record the sentences on the board. Repeat the activity several times so that children can see different examples for both words.

Craft and Structure

13 | The bears just shook their heads and laughed. |

14 "People are **strange**," said Ted.

15 "But they are fun to watch," said Bell.

Comprehension Check

(MORE ONLINE) sadlierconnect.com

1. Which of the following tells you that "Black Bear, Brown Bear" is nonfiction?

   a. It shows a bear wearing clothes.

   (b.) It gives facts about bears.

   c. It shows the bear talking.

2. In fiction, some things cannot really happen. Look back at "Lunch with the Bears." List some things that could not happen.

   Sample answer: Bears don't pack a lunch. Bears don't

   spread a sheet down to eat. Bears don't throw baseballs.

   Bears don't talk like we talk.

Teacher Talk: Find Evidence

Remind children of the differences between nonfiction and fiction. Then have them draw a box around the sentence in paragraph 13. Have them explain what the bears are able to do here that they cannot do in "Black Bear, Brown Bear."

Independent Practice

Unit 5 ■ Reading Literature: Craft and Structure **109**

Support English Language Learners

Preteach academic vocabulary that will help English language learners discuss fiction and nonfiction. Use self-stick notes to create labels with these terms defined: photograph, label, fact, character, dialogue, drawing, fantasy.

Place the labels on pages 106–107 on exemplars and discuss the meanings of these words.

Independent Practice

Read and Apply

Have children read paragraphs 13 through 15 on page 109 independently as you circulate. Provide extra support to struggling readers by reading the paragraph chorally with them.

Teacher Talk: Find Evidence

Ask volunteers to list the differences between fiction and nonfiction. Then put a box around paragraph 13 and read it aloud. Ask volunteers to tell why the sentence is fiction.

Comprehension Check

Answer Explanations:

1. Answer choice **B** is the only choice that is true of "Black Bear, Brown Bear."

2. Children may also write that bears don't wear hats or carry purses.

Critical Comprehension

Use the following questions to help children think critically about the two selections. Children should support their answers with evidence from the text.

- *What are the likely authors' purposes in writing these two texts?*

- *What are some possible readers' purposes in reading these two texts?*

Assess and Respond

If children have difficulty answering the questions in the Comprehension Check . . .

Then ask: *Why might you read a nonfiction text about bears? Why might you read a fiction story about people getting scared by bears?*

Guided Instruction

OBJECTIVES

- Determine the narrator of a story.
- Answer questions about key details in a text read aloud.

Genre: Adventure Story

Explain to children that an adventure story is a special kind of fiction. Adventure stories usually have danger, excitement, and a hero who has a problem to solve.

Set the Purpose

Help children understand the purpose for learning to identify the narrator by asking: *Can a story change when a different person tells it?* Explain that the person who tells a story is called the narrator.

Model and Teach

Read the text aloud as children follow along in their books.

Teacher Talk: Find Evidence

Pause at the end of paragraph 1. Say: *I want to know who is telling this story. There is an important clue in the first sentence. The clue is the word I. When I read "Alex and I were fast asleep," I know that the word I stands for the narrator of the story. I know that the narrator is a character in the story. Looking at the drawing, I see two boys and a woman. My guess is that one of the boys is telling the story. The other boy is named Alex.* Stop reading after paragraph 3. Ask: *What is the narrator's name?* (Ray) Encourage children to respond in a complete sentence.

Identifying the Narrator

Words to Know

check
sudden

Max's Monster

(Genre: Adventure Story)

1   Alex and I were fast asleep. Then all of a **sudden**, I sat up. Alex sat up. Max was barking outside!

2   "Why is Max barking?" I asked. "I need to go **check** on him."

3   Alex got out of bed. "Ray, please let me come," he said to me.

4   Mom heard us talking. She came to our room. "What is going on?" she asked us.

5   "Max is barking," Alex told Mom. "He might be in danger. I'm going with Ray."

Guided Instruction

Teacher Talk: Find Evidence

Explain that the narrator is the person who tells the story. *The first sentence reads* Alex and I. I *is a clue word. It tells me that a story character is telling the story. From paragraph 3, Ray must be the narrator.* Have children circle Ray's name. Discuss why Ray is the narrator.

110   Unit 5 ■ Reading Literature: Craft and Structure

Words to Know

check (*verb*): to look at to see if everything is all right
sudden (*noun*): fast and surprising

Working with Word Meaning Write these sentence frames for children to complete: All of a sudden, _____. I will check _____.

Then pantomime skits to help children think of different ways to complete the sentences. For example, for "All of a sudden," jump up from your desk and run to the door. For "I will check" look out the window as if you're checking the weather. Continue pantomiming different scenes until children are comfortable using the words and can generate their own sentences.

6 "Not without me!" Mom said. "Plus, it's late and dark."

7 I went and got the flashlight. The three of us crept outside. "Max is over there," I said. I pointed the flashlight toward Max's bark.

8 Alex looked up at the moon. It looked like cheese. "I'm hungry, Ray," he said.

9 "Me, too," I said.

10 Mom took Alex's hand. "We'll make a snack later. We need to find Max."

Teacher Talk: Find Evidence

Tell children that if a story character is the narrator, the narrator uses *I* and *me*. Have children underline what Ray says in paragraph 7. Ask: *How do you know that these are the words of the narrator?*

Guided Instruction

Unit 5 ■ Reading Literature: Craft and Structure **111**

Teacher Talk: Find Evidence

Remind children that "I" is an important clue word telling readers that the narrator is also a character in the story. Then explain that there is a difference between the dialogue in quotation marks, and the other words in the text. Show children that characters use the words *I* and *me* in dialogue, but that is different from the narrator, who uses *I* and *me* outside of the dialogue.

After reading paragraph 10, say: *I see that in paragraph 6, Mom says* "Not without me." *Mom is a character, and the words she says are called dialogue. In paragraph 9, Alex says* "I'm hungry, Ray." *These words are in quotation marks. They are dialogue, too. However, I see that in paragraph 7, the word I is not in quotation marks. That tells me that the narrator is speaking. That tells me that Ray is speaking.*

I am going to reread page 111. When I reread paragraph 9, I circle the words I and me when they stand for the narrator, Ray.

Review: Identifying Fiction

Remind children that they identified important features of fiction when they read "Lunch with the Bears." Ask: *What clues have you seen on pages 110 and 111 that tell you this is fiction?* (The genre is *story*; the pictures are drawings; there are characters and dialogue.) *Does this story include things that could not happen?* (So far, most things seem like they could really happen.)

Support English Language Learners

This story has phrases that may be difficult for English language learners. Take time to define these phrases and provide practice using them in sentences.

fast asleep: sleeping and not easy to wake up

all of a sudden: at once; happening quickly

sat up: moved from lying to sitting

Read and Practice

Read paragraph 11 aloud and model for children how to identify the narrator. Say: *I read "Alex took my hand." Then Alex says, "Ray." Those two clues help me know that Ray is the narrator.* Have heterogeneous partners take turns reading page 112 as you circulate to provide support. Before children begin reading, remind them to keep looking for clues about the narrator. As they read, have children circle the word *I* whenever it refers to the narrator. Remind them to be careful when they see the word *I* in dialogue.

Teacher Talk: Find Evidence

Once partners have finished reading the text, ask them to share examples they found of the word *I* meaning the narrator, Ray. (paragraphs 12, 14, and 17) Discuss the word *my* in paragraph 11. Ask: *Whose hand does Alex take?* (Ray's, the narrator's) Make sure all children have correctly circled two occurrences of *I* in paragraph 17.

Turn and Talk

Have partners discuss the question "How would this story be different if Max were the narrator?" After partners discuss, have volunteers share their ideas. Mention that if the dog were the narrator, it might be a fantasy story rather than an adventure story. Talking animal stories are either fables or fantasies.

Identifying the Narrator

Words to Know

scary
shone

11 An owl hooted. Alex took my hand. "Maybe Max is hurt, Ray," he said.

12 "Hear him bark?" I asked. "He is fine."

13 "What if Max found a monster?" asked Alex.

14 "Monsters don't live around here." I didn't want Alex to worry.

15 Suddenly, Max jumped from the dark. His tail was wagging. Then he ran to a log.

16 Max began to dig. The dirt flew and flew. It got in Mom's hair! It got in Alex's shoes!

17 I called to Max. "What is it, Max?" I **shone** the flashlight on the log. A dark shape moved. We all looked at it.

Guided Practice

Teacher Talk: Find Evidence
Review that children can look for clues such as *I, me,* and *my* to figure out who the narrator of a story is. Have children underline the sentence in paragraph 17 that tells that the narrator is the boy holding the flashlight in the illustration.

112   Unit 5 ■ Reading Literature: Craft and Structure

Words to Know

scary (*adjective*): causing someone to be afraid
shone (*verb*): glowed with light; gave off light

Working with Word Meaning Have children work in small groups to brainstorm lists of things that can be *scary*, and things that *shine*. Volunteers from each group can share examples with the class. Challenge children to share their examples in complete sentences. Help children to change their sentences to the past tense to use the word *shone*.

18 "Some monster!" I said to Mom and Alex.

19 "May we take it home?" asked Alex.

20 Mom smiled. "We should leave it alone. At least a box turtle isn't a **scary** monster!"

Comprehension Check

MORE ONLINE sadlierconnect.com

1. Which word is a clue that a story character is telling the story?

   a. he

   b. she

   c. me

2. Look back at paragraphs 11 and 12. How do you know that Ray is telling the story here?

   Sample answer: The words "my" and "I" are used. The

   narrator's name is Ray. I see the sentence "'Hear him

   bark?' I asked." The words "I asked" tell me Ray is talking.

Teacher Talk: Find Evidence

Have children put a box around the word in paragraph 18 that is a clue that the narrator is one of the story characters.

Independent Practice

Independent Practice

Read and Apply

Have children read paragraphs 18, 19, and 20 on page 113 independently as you circulate. Provide extra support to struggling readers by reading chorally with them.

Teacher Talk: Find Evidence

Read each word in paragraph 18 aloud and ask children to identify the one that shows that the narrator is a character in the story. Ask a volunteer to state in complete sentences how we know who the narrator is.

Comprehension Check

Answer Explanations:

1. Answer choice **C** is correct because the word *me* shows that a story character is telling the story.

2. Children should explain that Ray uses *I* and *my* in the paragraphs.

Critical Comprehension

Use the following question to help children think more deeply about the selection. Children should be prepared to support their answers with evidence from the text.

• *Summarize the action. What happens first, next, and last?*

Assess and Respond
If children have difficulty answering the questions in the Comprehension Check . . .
Then review the characters in the story. Show children examples of narration and dialogue. Focus on the use of *I* in paragraphs 14 and 17 to reteach the skill.

Extend Thinking: Critically Analyze Literature

Provide children with several simple stories from which they will choose one to read, based on their interest. All of the choices should be fiction told in the first person, like "Max's Monster." Assign children the task of identifying the narrator of the story.

Tell children that they will tell the class about the narrator and will share evidence from the story that they used to figure out which character was the narrator.

At your discretion, assign struggling students stories that you have read together as a class. As children read, circulate and provide support to struggling readers.

Foundational Skills Read Together

OBJECTIVE
Read decodable text featuring one-syllable CVC, CCVC, CVCe, and CCVCe words.

Prepare to Read

Tell children that you will be reading a story about a cat. As you read, children should listen for single-syllable words.

Introduce Phonics Skills

After you have read the selection once, read it again, this time focusing on the target phonics skills.

- *I see many words with one syllable. The first word,* Brad, *has one syllable. I know it has one syllable because it has one vowel sound. I hear four sounds when I say this word: /b/ /r/ /ă/ /d/.*

- *The name* Kate *also has one vowel sound and one syllable. It has the same number of letters as* Brad, *but it has only three sounds. /k/ /ā/ /t/. The* e *is silent. Because the* e *is silent, the sound of the* a *is long.*

- Cat *has one vowel sound. I hear three sounds in* cat. */k/ /ă/ /t/*

- *Look at line 4. Let's read the word* place *together. /p/ /l/ /ā/ /s/.* Place *has one vowel sound.*

- *I noticed two words with unusual spellings,* was *and* friends. *I want to memorize these words.*

Focus on Fluency

Draw children's attention to the dialogue in "Scat, Cat!" Remind children that fluent readers use punctuation to read accurately. Help children see that the quotation marks indicate a speaker's words, which should be read differently. Have partners chorally read the selection. Encourage them to use punctuation to read accurately.

As you read along, listen for words with one vowel sound.

Scat, Cat!

1 Brad and Kate had a fine home. But a fuzzy gray cat was king around the house.

2 When Brad sat, the cat wanted to sit. "Scat, cat! Find your own place!"

3 When Brad ate, the cat wanted to eat. "Scat, cat! Find your own food!"

4 When Brad slept, the cat wanted to nap. "Scat, cat! Sleep on the rug!"

5 "You like the same things," Kate fussed. "You need to be friends!"

6 Brad made a face. "Scat, cat!" The cat did.

7 That night a snake slid in! "Eek!" cried Kate. She jumped on the bed.

8 Brad raced in. The cat raced in. Oh, what a chase! Then the cat pounced. That cat scared the snake away.

9 "Nice cat!" Brad said. "Want to sleep on my lap?"

Focus on Phonological Awareness

Phoneme Identity

Use CVC and CVCe words for phoneme identification practice. Follow the steps below for the word pairs *it/ice, ant/ate, oat/on, use/us, egg/eat.*

- Tell children to listen as you pronounce the word.
- Ask what sound they hear at the beginning of the word.
- Ask whether the vowel sound is short or long.
- Pronounce the word together.

Foundational Skills Reader 1

DIRECTIONS: Cut and fold the book.

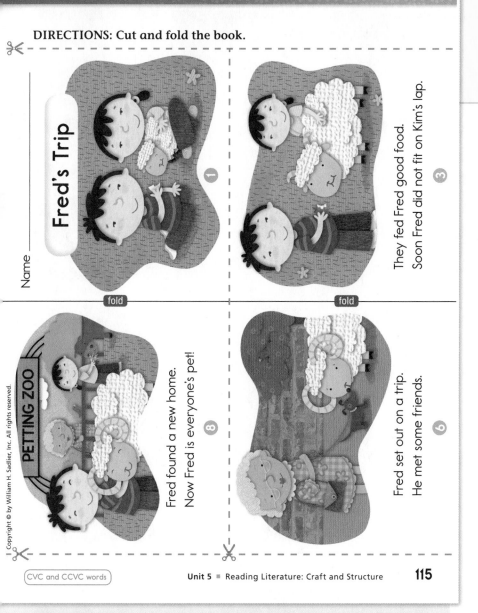

Name

Fred's Trip

①

fold

They fed Fred good food.
Soon Fred did not fit on Kim's lap.

③

fold

PETTING ZOO

Fred found a new home.
Now Fred is everyone's pet!

⑧

Fred set out on a trip.
He met some friends.

⑨

CVC and CCVC words

Unit 5 ■ Reading Literature: Craft and Structure **115**

Foundational Skills: Phonics Practice

Write the following words from the Read Together and Foundational Skills Reader 1 on the board or on a chart. Have children practice reading the words.

Read Together **CVC words:** had, but, cat, sat, sit, nap, rug, did, bed, lap; **CCVC words:** Scat, Brad, slid; **irregularly spelled words:** was, friends

Foundational Skills Reader 1 **CVC words:** Kim, Tam, got, him, fed, did, not, fit, lap, pen, ran, set, met, big, man, pet; **CCVC words:** Fred, trip, slim; **irregularly spelled words:** some

OBJECTIVES
* **Read decodable text featuring one-syllable CVC and CCVC words.**
* **Read along orally, using emotion and reflecting changes in characters.**

Prepare to Read
Tell children that they will be reading realistic fiction about a pet named Fred. Tell them they may share the book at home. Have them follow the directions to cut and fold the book.

Review Phonics Skills
Explain that this book features many words with one syllable and short vowel sounds. Remind them that they learned about these kinds of words when they read "Scat, Cat!" Review the targeted phonics skills.

* *Remember that a word with one vowel sound has one syllable. The names* Kim *and* Tam *are one-syllable words. Find more examples as you read. Some words have two consonants together.* Fred *and* trip *are both examples of words with two consonants together. Notice that both of these words have one vowel sound. Find more examples of words with two consonants together.*

* *The words* was *and* friends *have unusual spellings. What words in this book have unusual spellings?*

Introduce Reader 1
Divide the class into two groups. Assign each group to line 1 or 2. Have each group chorally read its corresponding line as you read each line aloud.

Read with a Partner

Form heterogeneous pairs of children so that your stronger readers can help those who struggle. Allow pairs to decide how they want to read the text together several times: chorally; alternating by sentences; or alternating by pages. Once the pairs are comfortable with one of their oral readings, have them record it for playing back later.

Focus on Fluency

Remind children that fluent readers read with emotion. Ask children to look at page 4 of the reader and identify how Fred might feel. (surprised) Have children echo read as you model reading page 4 in different ways, showing different emotions like excitement, fear, and surprise. Then ask children to choose which style of reading goes best with the picture. Model fluency by using the Fluency Practice activity below.

Reading at Home

Once children are comfortable reading the book, send it home for them to read to family members.

Assess and Respond
If children have trouble reading one-syllable CVC and CCVC words . . .
Then review the short vowel sounds and practice decoding the following words: bat, can, flag, pen, ten, step, win, pin, skip, log, pot, spot, bug, cup, drum.

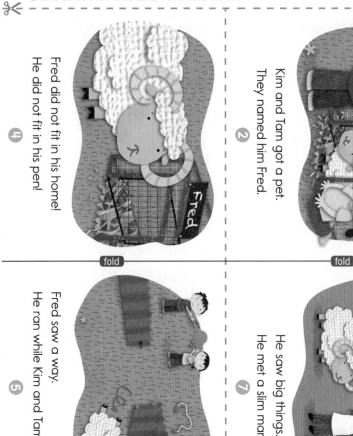

Foundational Skills Reader 1

DIRECTIONS: Cut and fold the book.

④ Fred did not fit in his home!
He did not fit in his pen!

② Kim and Tam got a pet.
They named him Fred.

fold fold

⑤ Fred saw a way.
He ran while Kim and Tam played.

⑦ He saw big things.
He met a slim man.

116 Unit 5 ▪ Reading Literature: Craft and Structure Fluency: Read with expression

Foundational Skills: Fluency Practice

Explain to children that it is important to pay attention to emotions when they read. Being aware of emotions will help with comprehension and fluency. Work with children to read page 8 with emotion. Ask: *What punctuation do you see on this page? What does that tell you about the emotion?* Model reading the page with emotion. Then chorally read the page. Additional fluency passages and activities can be found at **sadlierconnect.com**.

Foundational Skills Reader 2

DIRECTIONS: Cut and fold the book.

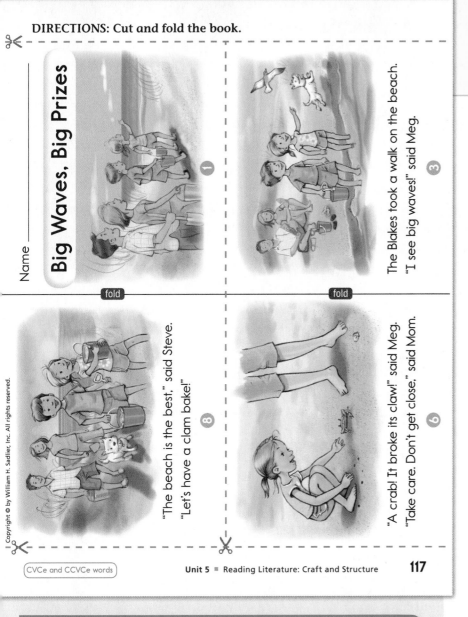

Name

Big Waves, Big Prizes

1

The Blakes took a walk on the beach.
"I see big waves!" said Meg.

3

"The beach is the best", said Steve.
"Let's have a clam bake!"

8

"A crab! It broke its claw!" said Meg.
"Take care. Don't get close," said Mom.

9

CVCe and CCVCe words

Unit 5 ■ Reading Literature: Craft and Structure   **117**

Prepare to Read

Tell children that they will be reading realistic fiction about a trip to the beach. Have them follow the directions to cut and fold the book.

Review Phonics Skills

Explain that this book features many words with one syllable and long vowel sounds. Remind them that they learned about these kinds of words when they read "Scat, Cat!" Review the targeted phonics skills.

Say: *Remember that a one-syllable word that ends in e usually has a long vowel sound. The word* wave *ends in e. The sound of a is long. We know that it is long because it says its name: /w/ /ā/ /v/. Find more examples of words with long vowel sounds as you read.*

Words that have two consonants together at the beginning of the word and end in e also usually have long vowel sounds. Prize *has two consonants together at the beginning. What are they? (p and r). We know the vowel i is long because it says its own name: /p/ /r/ /ī/ /z/. Look for more words that begin with two consonants and have long vowel sounds in this book.*

Introduce Reader 2

Divide the class into two groups. Assign each group to line 1 or 2. Have each group chorally reads its corresponding line on each page of the book as you read each line aloud.

Write the following words from the Read Together and Foundational Skills Reader 2 on the board or on a chart. Have children practice reading the words.

Read Together CVCe words: Kate, fine, home, like, same, made, nice;
CCVCe words: place, snake

Foundational Skills Reader 2 CVCe words: dune, race, came, take, nine, five, bake; **CCVCe** words: Steve, slope, close, broke

Read with a Partner

Form heterogeneous pairs of children so that your stronger readers can help those who struggle. Allow pairs to decide how they want to read the text together: chorally, alternating by sentences, or alternating by pages. Have pairs read the text several times. Once the pairs are comfortable with one of their oral readings, have them record it for playing back later.

Focus on Fluency

Remind children that fluent readers read with emotion and make changes to give voices to different characters when they read dialogue. Ask children to practice this skill by reading pages 2–3 aloud. Read pages 4–5 chorally if children need additional practice.

Reading at Home

Once children are comfortable reading the book, send it home for them to read to family members.

Assess and Respond
If children have trouble reading one-syllable CVCe and CCVCe words . . .
Then review the long vowel sounds, and practice decoding the following words: tape, plate, skate, game, grape, line, bike, drive, spine, joke, nose, spoke, huge, flute.

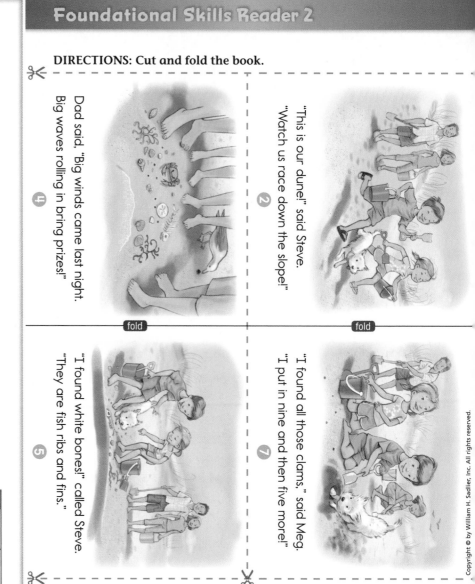

Foundational Skills Reader 2

DIRECTIONS: Cut and fold the book.

④ Dad said, "Big winds came last night. Big waves rolling in bring prizes!"

② "This is our dune!" said Steve. "Watch us race down the slope!"

⑤ "I found white bones!" called Steve. "They are fish ribs and fins."

⑦ "I found all those clams," said Meg. "I put in nine and then five more!"

118 Unit 5 ■ Reading Literature: Craft and Structure

Fluency: Read with expression

Foundational Skills: Fluency Practice

Ask pairs of children to identify and underline all the dialogue in the Reader 2. Then ask pairs to circle the end punctuation for each sentence of dialogue. Discuss each punctuation mark, the pictures, and how the dialogue fits into the story to decide how to read each quote. Model reading the quotes and ask children to repeat, imitating your emotions. Additional fluency passages and activities can be found at **sadlierconnect.com**.

OBJECTIVES

- **Identify sensory and feeling words.**
- **Contrast the features of fictional and informational text.**
- **Determine the narrator of a story.**

Blue Flube
(Genre: Fantasy)

1   Crista and I heard a sound. Bump! Pop! It came from under the porch. Who or what could it be? "Maybe it's mice!" said Crista, her eyes wide. She did not like mice one bit!

2   I got a light. "Let me shine this in here. Let's look."

3   There, in the darkest place, was a thing. It was bigger than a cat. It was blue. It had wide lips. It looked a bit like a bear. It had smoke coming out of its nose.

4   Crista began to shake. "Who or what are you?"

5   I asked, "Why are you here?"

Unit 5 ■ Reading Literature: Craft and Structure   **119**

Genre: Fantasy

Remind children that in fantasy stories, something happens that would not happen in normal life. Tell children to look for extraordinary things to happen in "Blue Flube."

Path Options

You may wish to have children read the text independently and apply the skills learned in this unit. Or you may wish to do a close reading with children; if so, use the supports provided on these pages. As a third option, set up a buddy system, with some heterogeneous and some homogeneous pairs, to fit the needs of your class. Regardless, children should read the text more than once to facilitate understanding and to be able to answer the Comprehension Check questions correctly.

Support English Language Learners

Prepare English language learners to succeed by talking about made-up words before they read "Blue Flube."

After reading paragraph 6, discuss how you can use context clues to discover what the author means by *Flube*. Use questions like the following to explore the text.

What do you notice about capital letters?

Did the author use an article such as a or the?

Do you think Blue Flube is a name or a thing?

Support First Reading

Circulate to check children's understanding. As needed, use the following comprehension and strategy check-ins to support basic understanding of the selection as children read.

Check-in Questions

- **page 119** *How does the author describe the "thing" that is under the porch?* (bigger than a cat, blue, wide lips, looked a bit like a bear, smoke coming out of its nose)

- **page 120** *Is Blue Flube friendly? How can you tell?* (Yes, he comes to make friends.)

- **page 121** *How does the story end?* (Sample answer: Blue Flube leaves, but he will visit again someday.

Review: Identifying Sensory Language

Reread paragraph 1 with children. Ask: *How do the children know that something is under the porch?* (They heard the sounds *Bump! Pop!*)

Review: Identifying Fiction and Nonfiction

Ask children to tell some important clues that this is fiction. (It has drawings, not photographs. It has characters. It has dialogue. It has no facts. It has events that are imaginary.)

Close Reading

6   "I am Blue Flube. I come from space. I am here to make friends," it said.

7   "Would you like to play a game with Jax and me?" asked Crista.

8   "Yes, I will hide," said Blue Flube. "You and Jax will hunt for me. That will be fun."

9   Just then we heard more sounds. Zip! Snap! A spaceship floated down.

10   "Oh, oh! Mom is here for me! She let me come here. She gave me time to make friends. But I must go home. I want to come back. We can play lots of games. So long, Jax and Crista," said Blue Flube.

120   Unit 5 ■ Reading Literature: Craft and Structure

Differentiate Instruction

If children are unable to read the text, read the text aloud once. Then, read the text sentence by sentence in a call and response fashion allowing time for children to repeat each sentence after you read it aloud. Then, let children read the text independently, asking for help as needed.

11 We waved when Blue Flube shot up into the sky.

12 "Blue Flube was nice, Jax. It made me smile," said Crista.

13 "We had fun. We made a space friend!" I said. "Next time, we will play tag."

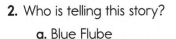

Comprehension Check

1. What words help you hear the sound of the spaceship landing?
   a. Play tag
   b. Zip! Snap!
   c. Oh, oh!

2. Who is telling this story?
   a. Blue Flube
   b. Jax
   c. Crista

121

Strategic Reading

Support all readers by reminding them of the importance of making predictions while reading. This strategy will help them have more fun reading, and it will help them understand what they are reading, too.

Model the strategy. Say: *Paragraph 1 has a lot of opportunities to make predictions. The sounds "Bump!" and "Pop!" come from under the porch. The author asks, "Who or what could it be?" I think maybe it is an animal, like a raccoon. What do you think? Crista thinks it is mice. Did you agree? I do not agree. I think "Bump!" and "Pop!" do not sound like mice. Crista might just be scared. I predict that Crista is wrong about the mice.*

Review: Identifying the Narrator

Reread the last paragraph with children. Ask: *Who is speaking in the last paragraph?* (Jax) *How can you tell that this person is the narrator of the story?* (He says "I.")

Multiple Readings for Critical Comprehension

Have children reread this selection, and pose questions that focus on critical comprehension. Remind children that they can mark the text.

- *How do Jax and Crista change during this story?* (At first they are afraid. At the end they are excited about having a new friend.)

- *What clues tell you that Blue Flube will return?* (Blue Flube says, "I want to come back." Jax says, "Next time, we will play tag.")

Comprehension Check

Score children's understanding of unit skills and texts using the Comprehension Check on this page and the next. Use children's total score to determine their readiness for the Unit 5 Review on page 125.

Multiple-Choice Questions: *1 point each*

1. Answer choice **B** is correct, because "Zip" and "Snap" are both words that stand for sounds. The sentence following these words also shows that these are spaceship sounds: "A spaceship floated down."

2. Children can deduce that Jax is the narrator by noticing that in paragraph 1, the word "I" is used. That means the narrator is a character in the story. We can tell the narrator is not Crista from paragraph 7. Readers find out the name of the narrator when Blue Flube says, "You and Jax will hunt for me." Thus, answer choice **B** is correct.

Short-Answer Questions:
3 points each

Item 3 Rubric

3	Children cite 3 or more sentences as text evidence that accurately supports the statement "Blue Flube is happy to be with the children."
2	Children correctly cite 1 or 2 sentences as text evidence.
1	Children provide an explanation, but do not cite text evidence.
0	No response, or the response is unrelated to the question.

Item 4 Rubric

3	Children cite two or more kinds of evidence that "Blue Flube" is fiction. They may cite evidence about the genre, characters, dialogue, types of events, or pictures.
2	Children cite one kind of evidence that "Blue Flube" is fiction but give more than one example.
1	Children provide one correct example.
0	No correct response is given.

Theme Wrap-Up

Lead children in a discussion of the theme "All in a Family," and how that theme was part of selections they read. Choose to discuss any of the texts: "Bunk Bed Brothers," "Ice Cream Music," "Lunch with the Bears," "Max's Monster," "Scat, Cat!," "Fred's Trip," "Big Waves, Big Prizes," or "Blue Flube." Talk about how families are different and how they are the same.

Close Reading

3. What sentences from the story let you know that Blue Flube is happy to be with the children?

Sample answer: She gave me time to make friends. I want

to come back. We can play lots of games.

_____

_____

_____

4. How do you know "Blue Flube" is fiction? Find and list story details that tell.

Sample answer: Blue Flube came from space. The

children talked to it. Blue Flube's mom came down

from space to get it. It went back up in a spaceship.

_____

_____

_____

Assess and Respond (pages 119–122)

If	Then
Children scored 0–3 points, they are **Developing** their understanding of unit skills …	Provide children with reading support and more intensive modeling of skills.
Children scored 4–6 points, they are **Improving** their understanding of unit skills …	Use children's scores to target areas that are weak and review those specific skills.
Children scored 7–8 points, they are **Proficient** in their understanding of unit skills …	Have these children move on. They are ready for the formal assessment.

Compare and Contrast Texts

Look at the pictures from three texts you have read. What kinds of words did the authors use to tell their stories? How did they give information? Be ready to talk about your ideas.

Black Bear, Brown Bear   **Max's Monster**

Blue Flube

Return to the Essential Question

How can readers recognize different kinds of texts?

Talk about the pictures and ideas in the texts. How do they help you to know what kinds of texts they are?

Unit 5 ■ Reading Literature: Craft and Structure   **123**

Discussion Skills

Help children understand what it means to listen with care. Explain that most people have a hard time listening when they are also trying to think about what they will say.

Place children in pairs to practice listening. Tell them that their goal is to tell the class their partner's thoughts about one of the selections, using the same words their partner used. They may need to ask their partner questions to complete the task. Encourage children to speak in complete sentences.

Compare and Contrast Texts

Read aloud the directions on page 123. Then provide some information about each of the featured texts, to help children as they recall the key ideas.

Say: *The selection "Black Bear, Brown Bear" is nonfiction. It is an informational text. How did the author give information?* (The author tells facts about bears.)

The selection "Max's Monster" is fiction. It is an adventure story. Do you remember who the characters are? Do you remember what they are doing? What kind of fiction story is this? (adventure)

We just read "Blue Flube." What kind of story is it? (fantasy) *What characters are in it?* (Crista, Jax, Blue Flube, Mom) *What events do you remember? What kinds of words does the author use?*

Give children time to organize their thoughts about the texts. Have them ask any questions they have about the texts before you begin. Then lead the Essential Question discussion.

Support Essential Question Discussion

Read the Essential Question aloud. Then prompt children to share their ideas about the selections. Remind children to listen to others with care, and build on others' talk by responding to the comments of others.

- *Which image from these selections is unlike the other two? How is it different? Why is it different?*

- *How do drawings show ideas in "Max's Monster" and "Blue Flube"?*

- *How are "Max's Monster" and "Blue Flube" alike and different?*

- *Which selection would you use to write a report, and why?*

OBJECTIVE
Identify verbs and their inflected forms.

Guided Instruction

Read aloud the Guided Instruction section on page 124. Say: *The word* looked *is a verb. It tells what Alex did. The word has two parts. It has a root word,* look. *It also has an ending,* ed. Ask: *Can you think of other verbs?* Discuss whether the words children think of are root words or whether they are root words with endings.

Guided Practice

Group children in pairs to complete items 1 through 4 of the Guided Practice. Circulate and provide support to children who are having difficulty. At your discretion, challenge proficient children to use the words they formed in a sentence.

Independent Practice

If children have difficulty circling the root word, review the endings *s, ed,* and *ing.* Then ask them to identify the ending first, and then circle the root word.

Apply to Reading

Have children return to "Blue Flube." Focus their attention on paragraph 11 on page 121. Challenge children to identify a verb that has a root word and an ending. (wave/waved) Talk about the dropped *e.*

Language

Verb Endings *s, ed, ing*

Guided Instruction **Verbs** are action words. Verbs tell what someone or something does. Verbs can end in the letter *s,* or the letters *ed* or *ing.*

Read this sentence from "Max's Monster":

> Alex **looked** up at the moon.

Looked is a verb. *Look* is the root word. The letters *ed* are the ending.

Guided Practice Add the ending to each root word to make a new verb.

1. tell + s = _____tells_____
2. play + ed = _____played_____
3. rest + ing = _____resting_____
4. jump + s = _____jumps_____

Independent Practice Read each verb. Circle the root word.

5. (fix)ing
6. (kick)ed
7. (melt)s
8. (land)ed
9. (ask)s
10. (bump)ing

Support English Language Learners

Preteach the skill to English language learners. Then they will be able to follow the class instruction.

Say: *Many words have a root word and an ending. The root word is the part that carries the meaning. It is the main part of the word.*

Explain: *An ending is the letters you add to the end of a root word. The ending changes the root word. You can use both the root and the ending to understand a word.* Write the word *looked.* Underline the word *look* and circle the ending *-ed.* Define the root word *look:* to move one's eyes to see. Then, explain that the ending *-ed* changes the word to the past tense.

Unit 5 Review

Read along with the following selection.

A Cooking Tip

Spice Cake Mix

1　I had to bake a cake, so I asked Dad for tips. He knows the best way to make a cake. He said to use a mix.

2　Dad drove me to the store. I picked a spice cake mix. I read the box. The steps told how to make the cake.

3　At last, the cake was done. It was warm, and it smelled sweet. I was proud of my cake. "Yum!" Dad said. "You did a great job, Sam!"

Fill in the circle of the correct answer.

1. Which word tells how the cake smelled?

○ sweet

○ warm

○ mix

Unit 5 ■ Reading Literature: Craft and Structure　**125**

Unit Summary

Children have had instruction and practice in identifying sensory language and words used to describe feelings. They have learned that fiction and nonfiction texts have different purposes and that they use different kinds of text and pictures to reach their purposes. Children have practiced identifying the narrator in fiction that has multiple characters and dialogue. They have practiced decoding single-syllable words, and identifying root words in inflected forms of verbs. They should be well prepared for the review section.

Introduce the Review

Explain to children that they will read a new story along with you that is related to the unit's theme and the texts they have already read. Then they will answer the questions on pages 125 and 126.

Answer Explanations

Scoring: Items 1, 2, 5, 6, 7, and 8 on pages 125–126 are worth 1 point each. Explanations for the correct answers are given below and on the next page. Also see the rubrics on the next page for guidance in scoring the short-answer questions on page 126.

1. Only the first answer choice, *sweet*, describes a smell. It appears in the text in paragraph 3.

2. In the last line of the story, Dad calls the narrator *Sam*. Therefore the final answer choice, *Sam*, is the correct one.

Self-Assessment: Progress Check

Have children revisit the Progress Check on page 97 and respond to the questions again. Ask them to compare their Before and After responses.

Create peer teaching opportunities for children who feel especially confident in a certain skill. Create a group for each skill, and instruct them to create a lesson for their peers.

Answer Explanations

Item 3 Rubric

2	The child specifically mentions facts.
1	The answer is general. It is correct but not specific.
0	No answer is given.

Item 4 Rubric

2	The child cites evidence from the text that shows that Sam was proud of his cake.
1	The child states that Sam was proud, but does not supply text evidence.
0	No response is given.

5. Children should circle the word *smelled*.

6. Children should underline the word *knows*.

7. Children should box the words *cake* and *bake*.

8. Children should underline the word *Yum*.

Unit 5 Review

2. Who is telling this story?

   ○ the cake   ○ Dad   ● Sam

3. Read these steps for checking if a cake is done.

   1. Put a toothpick in the cake.
   2. Take out the pick. The cake is done if the toothpick comes out dry.

   How do you know the text above is nonfiction?

   It gives me facts on how to tell if a cake is done.

4. How does Sam feel about his cake? What words in the story tell you?

   He feels proud. The story says, "I was proud of my cake."

5. Circle the verb in paragraph 3 with the *ed* ending.

6. Underline the verb in paragraph 1 with the *s* ending.

7. Put a box around the words in the first sentence in paragraph 1 with a long *a* vowel sound.

8. Read the sentence below. Underline the word with the short *u* vowel sound.

   I was proud of my cake. "Yum!"

Analyze Scores

8–10 pts Strong	Child has a good grasp of the skills and concepts taught in this unit. Point out any mistakes the child has made and explain the correct answers if necessary.
4–7 pts Progressing	Child is struggling with some skills or concepts. Identify the specific skills that are problematic to target a review of instruction.
0–3 pts Emerging	Child has difficulty understanding the skills and concepts taught in this unit. Child may need further instruction with a higher level of support and detailed explanation of the unit's skills and concepts.

Introducing UNIT 6

In this unit, you will write a made-up story, or narrative. You will make up the events and add some details. Good writers tell the story events in order. They give details and use words to show what happens first, next, and last. They write a good ending for their story. Many stories have been written about families. Your made-up story will be about a family, too.

Progress Check

The Progress Check is a self-assessment feature that children can use to gauge their own progress. Research shows that when children take accountability for their own learning, their motivation increases.

Before children begin work on Unit 6, have them check the boxes next to any item that they feel they can do well. Explain that it is fine if they don't check any of the boxes. Tell them that they will have an opportunity to learn about and practice all of these items while studying the unit. Let them know that near the end of the unit, they will have a chance to reconsider how well they can do each item on the list.

Before children begin their Unit 6 Review on page 140, have them revisit this page. You can use this information to work with children on any items they don't understand before they tackle the Review.

Progress Check Can I?

Before Unit 6		After Unit 6
☐	Write a made-up story about a family.	☐
☐	Write the events in order with details.	☐
☐	Use words such as *first* and *next* to show time order.	☐
☐	Write an ending for the story.	☐
☐	Use pronouns and adjectives.	☐

Unit 6 ■ Text Types and Purposes: Write Fictional Narratives

Student Page 127

HOME◆CONNECT...

The Home Connect feature is a way to keep parents or other adult family members apprised of what their children are learning. The key learning objectives are listed, and some ideas for related activities and discussions are included.

Explain to children that they can share the Home Connect page with their parents or other adult family members in their home.

Encourage children and their parents or other adult family members to share their experiences using the suggestions on the Home Connect page.

HOME◆CONNECT...

In this unit, your child will learn about writing a **fictional narrative**, or made-up story, about a theme he or she has studied in class.

As your child gets ready to write a fictional narrative, he or she will have to think of events and tell what happened in order, as well as add details. Talk with your child about his or her favorite stories and why they are favorites. Ask questions such as *What was the best part of the story? Why? What happened first in the story? What happened next? How did the story end?*

Invite your child to talk about the story he or she will write for this unit. Ask questions about the steps in writing the story, such as *What is your story about? Who are the characters? Where does the story take place? What happened first? What happened next? What happened last?* Then, once your child has written the story, encourage him or her to share it with you. Talk with your child about the way he or she felt when sharing the story with you.

On the Go: With your child, visit your local library and look at the books in the children's section. Read a few books together and talk about the events and the order in which they happen. Look for words such as *first, then, after that, at last,* and so on that help readers understand what happens first, next, and last in a story. Read a few of your child's favorite books together.

IN THIS UNIT, YOUR CHILD WILL...

- Create a fictional narrative in response to a theme.
- Write two or more story events in time order and use time-order words such as *first, next, last,* and *finally* to show the order of events.
- Use details to describe events.
- Write an ending for a story.
- Focus on a topic when writing and respond to questions and suggestions from peers.
- Use a variety of digital tools to produce and publish writing.
- Use pronouns such as *I, me, my, they, their, your, someone,* and *everything.*
- Use adjectives to describe nouns.

WAYS TO HELP YOUR CHILD

Remind your child that stories can be about people, animals, or things. Encourage your child to use his or her imagination and creativity. You may wish to help your child draw upon your own family adventures or experiences to make up a story about fictional characters. Then have your child share the story with another family member.

ONLINE
For more Home Connect activities, continue online at sadlierconnect.com

128   Unit 6 ■ Text Types and Purposes: Write Fictional Narratives

Student Page 128

UNIT PLANNER

Theme: All in a Family Curriculum Connection: Social Studies	Focus
WRITING MODEL pp. 130–131	*Fly, Birdy, Fly!*
WRITING ACTIVITY pp. 132–135	**ORGANIZATIONAL STRUCTURE:** Chart
LANGUAGE MINI-LESSONS pp. 136–137	• Pronouns • Adjectives
SPEAKING AND LISTENING pp. 138–139	• Share Your Writing • Be a Good Listener • Return to the Essential Question
UNIT 6 REVIEW p. 140	Language Skills Summary

Objective(s)

- Write a fictional narrative about a family, including a beginning, middle, and end; time-order words; details explaining the events; and a strong ending.

- Create a fictional narrative in response to a theme studied in class.

- Plan a fictional narrative about a family, arranging events in time order.

- Draw pictures, complete sentence starters, and compose fictional narrative text about a family.

- Use personal, possessive, and indefinite pronouns.

- Identify adjectives in sentences and use an adjective for self-description.

- Use determiners correctly.

- Orally present a fictional narrative, using sentences with detail and answering questions after the presentation.

- Participate respectfully in presentations as an active listener who asks questions and joins in the discussion.

Unit Assessment

- Unit 6 Review *p. 140*

Additional Assessment Options

- Performance Task 1 *pp. 141–144*
  ALSO ONLINE

- Performance Task 2 *pp. 259–262*
  ALSO ONLINE

Optional Purchase:

- iProgress Monitor **ONLINE**

- Progress Monitor Student Benchmark Assessment Booklet

ONLINE Digital Resources

- Home Connect Activities
- Additional Practice
- Teacher Resources
- iProgress Monitor (optional purchase)

Go to SadlierConnect.com to access your Digital Resources.

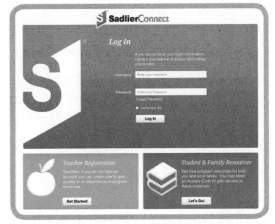

For more detailed instructions see page T3.

LEARNING PROGRESSIONS

In this unit, children will learn to write a fictional narrative in which they recount two or more events in time order. They will learn to include details about events, as well as temporal words that signal event order. Their narratives will include some sense of closure. In order to learn the skills necessary to craft a fictional narrative, children will further develop skills learned in kindergarten. They should be encouraged to retain these skills, as they will continue to build on them in second grade.

Sequencing Events

- By the end of kindergarten, children have experienced combining drawing, dictating, and writing to narrate a single event or several loosely linked events.

- Children learn to write narratives in which they sequence two or more events in time order in grade 1.

- Second-grade children are able to write about multiple events in a narrative, and are able to sequence them in the order in which they happened.

Describing Events

- A kindergartner can tell about events and may provide some details.

- By the end of grade 1, children are able to furnish some details about events.

- In their writing, second graders include more details about what happened as well as descriptions of what their characters think and feel about the events.

Using Time-Order Words

- Time-order words are not formally introduced in kindergarten. However, children are expected to tell events in order.

- In first grade, children learn to use some time-order words to show the sequential order of events.

- Children in grade 2 are able to draw from a larger bank of time-order words and use them to show how a well-elaborated event unfolds.

Providing a Sense of Closure

- Kindergarten children are not yet ready to provide a sense of closure to their stories.

- Grade 1 children begin to provide some sense of closure when recounting sequenced events.

- In second grade, children learn to provide a true sense of closure at the end of their narratives.

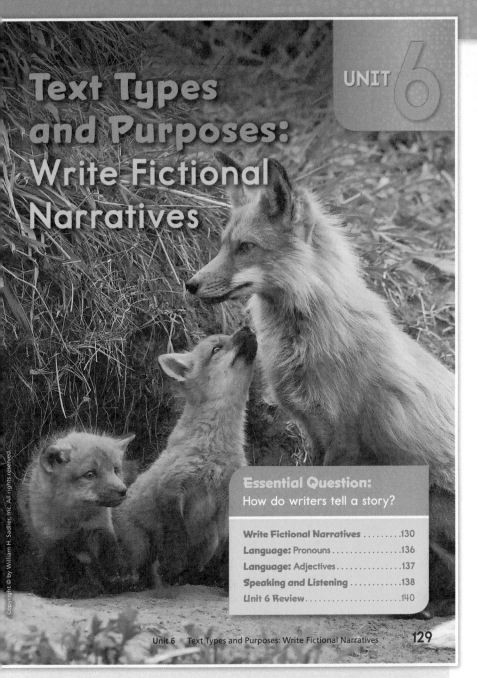

Text Types and Purposes: Write Fictional Narratives

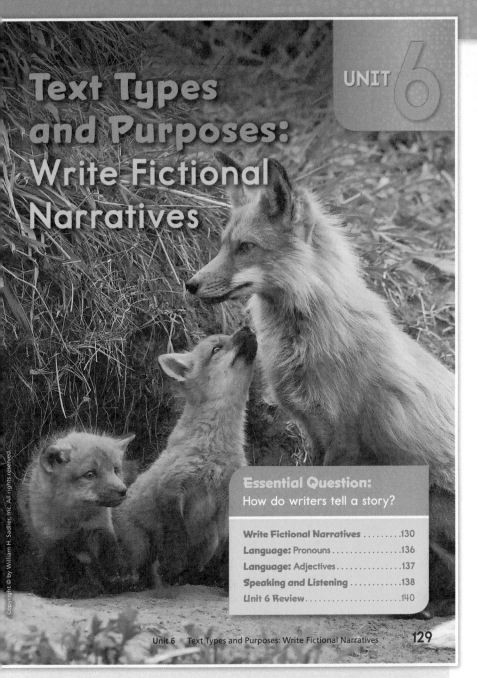

UNIT 6

Essential Question:
How do writers tell a story?

Unit 6　Text Types and Purposes: Write Fictional Narratives　**129**

Essential Question:
How do writers tell a story?

Children will learn to write a story about a family. They will be introduced to time-order words that help to describe a sequence, as well as learning to create a sense of closure.

Theme: All in a Family

Children will carry forward from Unit 5 the theme of families—both realistic and imaginary families—as they read a narrative model about a bird family.

Curriculum Connection: Social Studies

Children will apply their reflections on the different types of families when they write their own fictional narratives about a family.

Connect Reading to Writing

Remind children that they read many different narratives about families in Unit 5. They read "Bunk Bed Brothers," about brothers who resolved a conflict (Student Book, pages 100–101), "Ice Cream Music," about a family having fun making ice cream (Student Book, pages 102–105), "Lunch with the Bears," about a family of bears having a picnic (Student Book, pages 106–109), "Max's Monster," about a family that investigates a sound in the night (Student Book, pages 110–113), and even more. Now children will have an opportunity to describe and connect two or more events in a narrative about a family.

Writing Handbook

To assist children in writing a fictional narrative, use the *Writing Handbook* on pages 263–268 to guide children through the writing process. The *Writing Handbook* gives children detailed instruction on planning, drafting, revising, and editing their writing, as well as providing tips on producing and publishing.

Have children turn to page 263 and review all of the parts of the *Writing Handbook*. Then lead them through the suggestions on page 264 on selecting a topic and organizing their information. Once children get started on their narratives, return to the *Writing Handbook* for information on each part of the writing process.

OBJECTIVES

- **Write a fictional narrative about a family,** including a beginning, middle, and end; time-order words; details explaining the events; and a strong ending.
- **Create a fictional narrative in response to a theme** studied in class.

Introduce: Organizational Structure

Tell children that they will be writing a fictional narrative about a family. They will write two or more things that happened, in the order they happened. As you read the model, clarify each event and explain how the writer created a sense of closure at the end.

Analyze a Student Model

Title: Tell children that a title should grab a reader's attention. The title may also give a clue about what the story is about. Ask: *What kind of characters do you expect to read about?* (birds)

Beginning: After you read the first paragraph, say: *The beginning of this story helped me see that the* Birdy *from the title is a character's name.*

Event: Ask: *What is the first event that happens?* (Birdy is ready to fly.) *How does Birdy feel?* (afraid) Say: *That is a detail.* Work through the Teacher Talk on page 130 with children.

Write Fictional Narratives

Read a Student Model

Taylor wrote a story, or a narrative, about a baby bird. Think about what happened first, next, and last. Look for words that describe events, too.

Fly, Birdy, Fly!

Birdy was ready to fly. But he was not sure he could. He felt scared.

"Do not be scared," Mama said. "You can do it because you are brave!"

Teacher Talk: Find Details

Tell children that details in stories, or narratives, help readers understand events, or what happens in a story. Ask: *What is Birdy ready to do? How does Mama help Birdy?* Have children underline the details that tell the answers.

130   Unit 6 ■ Text Types and Purposes: Write Fictional Narratives

Genre: Fictional Narrative

Remind children that they wrote a personal narrative in Unit 2. Tell children that the difference between a personal narrative and a fictional narrative is that a fictional narrative is made-up. It may be a story that seems like real life. On the other hand, it might be fantasy. A fantasy story has parts that are very unlike real life; for example, a fantasy story might have animal characters that talk, as in the model they are reading.

Make sure children know that a fictional narrative has characters, a setting, and events. Define *events* as "things that happen." Tell children that good stories have a beginning, middle, and ending.

(First) Birdy hopped to the edge of the nest.

(Next) Birdy flapped his little wings. (Then) he flew away! "I did it!" he chirped.

Birdy came back to the nest. "I am a brave bird!" he said.

Teacher Talk: Find Time-Order Words and Find Ending
Tell children that a good story lets readers know the order of events. Point out that the words *first, next,* and *then* help tell about order. Have children circle those time-order words on the page. Then ask: *How does this story end?* Underline the part that is the ending.

Unit 6 ■ Text Types and Purposes: Write Fictional Narratives **131**

Support English Language Learners

This student model contains the modal helping verbs *can* and *could*.

Write these sentences from the student model on the board:

"You can do it because you are brave!"

He was not sure he could.

Define *can* as *be able to.* Remind children that the characters are talking about flying. Point out how the verbs *can* and *could* work with other verbs. In the first sentence, the verb *can* works together with *do.* In the second sentence, *could* stands for *could fly.*

Analyze a Student Model

Details: Explore details on this page with children. Ask: *How does Birdy move?* (He hops.) *How does he speak?* (He chirps.) *What do these details do?* (They show that Birdy is a bird.)

Time-Order Words: After you read page 131, help children understand how time-order words help readers sequence events. Ask: *What was the first thing Birdy did to fly?* (hopped to the edge of the nest) *What word helped you know that this was first?* (The author used the word *first.*) Continue this line of questioning for the words *next* and *then.* Then work through the first part of the Teacher Talk on page 131 with children.

Ending: Tell children that a good ending tells what happened *last.* Explain that readers want to know what happened at the end and how everything worked out. Say: *I remember that at the beginning of the story, Birdy was feeling afraid. When Birdy said, "I am a brave bird!" at the end of the story, I felt good. I noticed that Birdy made a big change in this story.* Work through the last part of the Teacher Talk together.

Visual Literacy

Use Pictures: Use the pictures on pages 130 and 131 to talk about setting. Say: *What do you see in the picture?* (birds) *Where are the birds?* (in a nest) *Where things happen in a story is called the setting. Tell me more about the nest.* (Sample answer: It is made of sticks.) *The sticks that make the nest are a detail about the setting. This detail tells me more about the setting. Details tell more about something.*

Model: Organizational Structure

Explain to children that strong stories, or fictional narratives, start with good planning and organization. When writers plan their narratives, they put events in order. They use time-order words to show what happened first, next, and last. They use details about the events, and they write a good ending.

Discuss the chart that Taylor used. Point out the information in the three boxes.

- The Beginning box tells about Birdy and Mama. Birdy is afraid to fly.

- The Middle box tells what happened next. Birdy did two things: he hopped to the edge of the nest and then he flew!

- The Ending box tells the last thing that happens in the story: Birdy flew back to the nest!

Point out to children that Birdy and Mama are the characters in the story and that it takes place in a nest in a tree.

Heterogeneous Pairs

Pair children appropriately so that one can help the other compare the annotated graphic organizer to the Writer's Model. Have children discuss the parts of the graphic organizer and find them in the Writer's Model.

Write Fictional Narratives

Taylor used this chart to plan her story. She wrote the events in the order in which they happened. She wrote details. She also wrote the ending.

Beginning
Birdy was scared to leave the nest.
Mama said Birdy can do it.

Middle
Birdy hopped to the edge of the nest. He flew.
He said, "I did it!"

Ending
Birdy flew back to the nest to be with Mama.

Review: Fiction and Nonfiction

Remind children of the difference between fiction and nonfiction. Explain that Taylor's story is a fictional narrative that uses photos Taylor took from a magazine article. Guide children to understand that Birdy and Mama are not real birds, because real birds do not talk. Ask children to find the sentences in Taylor's story that show Birdy and Mama are not real birds.

Plan Your Narrative

Use this chart to plan your story about a family. Write the events in order. Use time-order words. Use details to tell about the events. Remember to write an ending.

Beginning

Middle

Ending

OBJECTIVE
Plan a fictional narrative about a family, arranging events in time order.

Introduce the Writing Process

Explain that writing takes place over several steps and does not happen all at one time. The first step is planning. The graphic organizer that Taylor filled out helped her to plan her story. Tell children that they will fill out a graphic organizer before writing their narratives.

Plan a Narrative

Think About Organization

Remind children of how Taylor organized her narrative. She first talked about the characters and their problem. In the middle, she told about what happened next. She finished with an ending. Children should follow this organization for their stories.

Plan

Explain to children that they will complete the graphic organizer, using information for their narrative about a family, the theme they have been studying. Explain that this will help them plan their writing. Ask leading questions for each box. Encourage children to draw and write notes or complete sentences in the boxes. Ask: *What will happen first? Who is in your story?* Continue with the other boxes. Circulate to provide individual support as children use the boxes to plan their narrative.

Peer Collaboration

Have pairs use their graphic organizers to talk through their fictional narratives in preparation for writing. Expanding orally on their ideas should help them generate vocabulary and ideas that will support their writing. Encourage children to communicate their ideas clearly and for partners to comment and ask questions in return. Children should attempt to respond to their partners' questions in their discussions and to respond to their partners' suggestions when they begin their drafting in the next step of the process.

OBJECTIVE
Draw pictures, complete sentence starters, and compose fictional narrative text about a family.

Draft a Narrative

Tell children that they will now use the ideas from their chart to make a draft. When writers make a draft, they put their ideas in sentences. Emphasize that a draft is not a finished product and that they will have a chance to make changes and corrections later.

Show children the boxes provided for drawings. Offer them the alternative of cutting and pasting images into the boxes. Say: *Taylor used photographs in her story "Fly, Birdy, Fly!" You might want to do that if your story is like real life.*

Emphasize that good writers add details to make their ideas clearer and their stories more interesting. Show children the sentence starters. Say: *Once there was . . . This might be a good place to introduce the characters and the setting.* Then point out the time-order word *First*. Say: *The word* first *means that this is where I should write the first thing that happens in the story. On page 135, I will write what happens next, and what happens last, in order.*

Write Fictional Narratives

Create Your Narrative

In the boxes on pages 134–135, draw pictures to go with your story.

Then use your chart on page 133 to help you as you write. Start by completing the sentences below.

Once there was <u>Sample answer: a baby horse</u>

_____.

First, <u>Sample answer: the baby horse could barely stand</u>

<u>up beside its mother</u>.

Differentiate Instruction

Some children may benefit from composing their thoughts orally.

For example, one child could dictate his or her story to a peer who could fill in the sentence starters on a separate sheet, or on a photocopy of pages 134 and 135. Then these children will be able to copy the sentences into their workbooks to create the draft of their fictional narrative.

_____

_____

_____

Answers will vary. Children should write the events in order,

using time-order words, and give details about the events.

They should write an ending to their narratives.

Unit 6 ■ Text Types and Purposes: Write Fictional Narratives **135**

Revise and Edit: Peer Collaboration

Once children have finished their drafts, have them work in pairs to read their drafts to each other and suggest revisions. Remind them to pay special attention to what happens in the story and when each event happens. It is important for a story to have at least two things happen. Encourage listeners to ask for more details if part of what happens is unclear, or if they are just interested and want to know more.

Partners can then read each other's revisions and then make suggestions for ways to improve the draft.

Narrative Rubric

4	The story uses details to describe more than one event in time order, and ends with a sense of closure. Time-order words are used to signal event order.
3	The story has most of the elements listed under "4" above, but there are problems with sentence mechanics.
2	The story shows serious difficulties with either describing what happened, sequencing what happened, using time-order words, or providing closure.
1	The story shows little or no understanding of the elements of a narrative.

Assess and Respond

If children have difficulty creating a narrative from the planning chart . . .

Then provide a problem such as wanting to learn to ride a bike. Suggest a character, such as a favorite animal. Then pair struggling children with proficient writers to compose a narrative sequence about how the character overcomes the problem.

Digital Connection

Children who like to compose orally can use a recording application that is on some phones to record their story. Some children will be able to copy these sentences into their book. Others may be able to print their stories directly or e-mail their recording to a person who has a printer.

Encourage children to read along with their own recording. You may wish to let children swap stories and listen to their classmates' stories as well.

OBJECTIVE
Use personal, possessive, and indefinite pronouns.

Guided Instruction

Read through the Guided Instruction together. Point to the word *he* in the first example. Elicit that *he* is used because Joey is a boy.

Point to the word *backyard* in the last example. Say: *Who does this backyard belong to?* Elicit that this backyard belongs to Bill and Emma.

Provide and discuss examples for *her* (used to describe something owned by a girl), and *everything* (all the things). Continue your discussion until most children feel comfortable enough to work independently.

Guided and Independent Practice

Place children in pairs to complete items 1 through 6. Point out items 1 through 3 and tell partners to circle one pronoun in each sentence.

Point out items 4 through 6. Show children the word choices in parentheses, and tell them they will choose one word to write in the blank. Circulate as partners work through the Guided and Independent Practice, providing support as needed.

Assess and Respond
If children have difficulty with items 1 through 6 . . .
Then invite children who have successfully completed the assignment to explain how they arrived at their answers.

Pronouns

Guided Instruction **Pronouns** are words that take the place of nouns.

> **Joey** lives next door. **He** is my neighbor.

The word **he** takes the place of **Joey**.

- Words such as **I, he, she, we, me, my, their, his, her, our,** and **everything** are pronouns.

> **She** likes to play kickball.

> Bill and Emma play in **their** backyard.

Guided and Independent Practice Circle the pronouns in the sentences.

1. (I) would like to go home.

2. Kayla could not find (her) boots.

3. Mack found (everything) in the bag.

Choose the missing word. Write it on the line.

4. Mom and Dad put on ____their____ hats. (her/their)

5. Tom will go, but ____he____ will be late. (I/he)

6. Jill will ride ____her____ bike. (her/me)

Support English Language Learners

Preteach vocabulary that will help English language learners understand the instruction. Use definitions such as the following:

I the person who is speaking or writing

my having to do with me; belonging to me

noun a word that is the name of something

pronoun a word that is used instead of a noun

them a pronoun used in place of the names of people, places, or things

Adjectives

Guided Instruction Some words tell about nouns. They are called **adjectives.** Adjectives describe, or tell more about, nouns.

Jane has **long** hair.

The boy told a **funny** story.

The **big** mouse ate the cheese.

The **brown** dog barks a lot.

Guided and Independent Practice Circle the word that tells more about the underlined noun in each sentence.

1. I held the (soft) lamb.

2. The (large) rabbit hopped away.

3. A frog swims in the (muddy) pond.

4. The cat sleeps in a (green) basket.

5. My horse likes (sweet) apples.

6. Write an adjective that describes YOU!

   Sample answer: smart

Unit 6 ■ Text Types and Purposes: Write Fictional Narratives **137**

OBJECTIVES

- **Identify adjectives in sentences and use an adjective for self-description.**
- **Use determiners correctly.**

Guided Instruction

Read through the guided instruction together. Explain that the words in dark print are adjectives. Discuss what each adjective tells about the noun it describes.

Then introduce the words *a, an, the, this, that, these*, and *those*. Explain that these words also go with nouns. They come before a noun and let people know whether the noun is a specific one or could be any. Offer the examples of "a bird," "the bird," "this bird," and "that bird."

Guided and Independent Practice

Explain that children will circle the word that tells more about the underlined noun in each sentence.

Tell children that in order to identify the adjective in sentence 1, they can ask themselves "Which word tells me what kind of lamb it is?"

Point out the instructions for item 6. Make sure children know to write one word that describes themselves.

Have children rewrite sentences 3 and 4 to refer to a specific animal by using *this* or *that*.

Assess and Respond

If children have difficulty identifying and using adjectives . . .

Then offer a group of adjectives and a group of nouns. Ask children to choose one word from each group, read the phrase they have made, and identify which is the noun and which describes the noun.

Differentiate Instruction

Use realia to teach adjectives. Bring objects into the classroom for children to describe. List the adjectives children contribute as they describe the objects. For example, a cotton ball might be described as *light, white*, and *soft*. Encourage children to use all of their senses to describe how each thing feels, smells, looks, sounds, and (as appropriate) tastes.

OBJECTIVE

Orally present a fictional narrative, using sentences with details and answering questions after the presentation.

Share Your Writing

Tell children that they will present their stories by reading them aloud. Ask them to share their inspiration for their story by completing this sentence: "I chose to write about _____ because _____." Point out to children that this is a complete sentence.

Remind children that they used details to describe what happens in the story. Tell them that as they read aloud, they will have a chance to hear whether or not their details express their ideas and feelings clearly. Explain that reading aloud helps many writers improve their writing.

Get Ready

Place children in pairs to practice introducing themselves and reading their stories. Guide them to apply the speaking skills they have learned: use sentences with details, speak in complete sentences, and look at their listeners.

Present

Have children present in small groups. Monitor to be sure children are listening carefully and waiting their turn when they ask questions of the presenter.

Share Your Writing

You will present your story. Tell your ideas clearly and in complete sentences. Remember to use sentences with details. Look at your listeners when you speak.

I like the way you added details to the events!

138   Unit 6 ■ Text Types and Purposes: Write Fictional Narratives

---

Discussion Skills

Prompt children for further participation with questions such as "Can someone say what they liked about the story?"

Provide this sentence frame: I liked the story because _____.

When appropriate, encourage children by saying: *Say more about that.*

Be a Good Listener

Remember to follow the rules for speaking and listening. Listen carefully when a classmate reads a story. As you listen, think of questions you have about what you hear.

Why did you end the story that way?

After the story, ask any questions you might have. Then think about how the answers help you understand the story.

Return to the Essential Question

How do writers tell a story?

Think about these questions before the class discussion:

• What words did you use to tell what happened first, next, and last in your story?
• How can writers help readers understand events?

Unit 6 ■ Text Types and Purposes: Write Fictional Narratives **139**

OBJECTIVE
Participate respectfully in presentations as an active listener who asks questions and joins in the discussion.

Be a Good Listener

Remind children that good listeners are curious about what they hear, and they ask questions. Give children this sentence frame to help them ask for more details: *Can you tell me more about _____?.*

Return to the Essential Question

Give children time to think about the questions before the discussion. After discussing those questions, have children suggest other ways that writers tell a story.

Support English Language Learners

Encourage all group members to participate by using a talking stick. A talking stick can be any object that makes it clear whose turn it is to speak. When a person is holding the talking stick, their self-expression can be facilitated by prompting questions, by use of visuals, or by simplifying the language to facilitate understanding. Make sure that each child who listens to a story formulates a question about the story for the writer.

Introduce the Review

Explain to children that this review will give them a chance to use the language skills that they have studied and practiced in this unit. It will also give them a chance to share what they have learned about being a good speaker and listener.

Language Skills Summary

Prepare children to answer questions in which they identify and use pronouns and adjectives.

- Write this sentence on the board: My old cat sat on my lap. Say: *Raise your hand if you see a pronoun in this sentence. Raise your hand if you see an adjective.*(My, old)

- Say: *Use the pronoun in your own sentence. Use the adjective in your own sentence.*

Answer Explanations

1–2. Make sure children understand the direction line. Have them read it to you aloud and tell it to you in their own words.

3–4. Ask struggling children: *What does a pronoun stand for? What kind of word is an adjective? Use a complete sentence to tell me something that you like to do. Can you hear the pronoun? Describe yourself to me. Do you hear the adjectives?*

5. Correct answers include but are not limited to the following: They raise their hands. They wait their turn. They listen carefully. They pay attention.

Self-Assessment: Progress Check

Have students revisit the Progress Check on page 127 and compare their answers now with the answers they gave before completing Unit 6.

Unit 6 Review

Choose the correct answer. Fill in the circle.

1. Which word is a pronoun that takes the place of <u>Mike</u>?

   Is Mike home? Yes, he is playing.

   ● he   ○ is   ○ home

2. Which word tells about the underlined noun?

   The bush has thorny <u>stems</u>.

   ○ bush   ○ has   ● thorny

3. Write a sentence that uses a pronoun.

   Sample answer: I like to read.

4. Write a sentence that uses an adjective.

   Sample answer: I saw a gray cat.

Think about speaking and listening.

5. Write a sentence about what good listeners do.

   Sample answer: Good listeners think about questions

   they have. They ask the questions after the speaker finishes.

Test-Taking Tips

Explain to children that they will take similar tests all throughout their school years. For that reason, it is very useful to ask about any question types that they find confusing. Encourage children to formulate and ask questions about the test.

Underscore the importance of taking the time to read the directions carefully. Give children this example instruction line:

Choose the correct answer. Fill in the circle and underline it.

Discuss how this change in the direction line would change how they would answer the questions.

There are three parts to this performance task. Your teacher will give you a copy of the story "The Cracked Pot."

Part 1: Text Questions

☐ Listen to and read along with "The Cracked Pot."

☐ Then answer the questions on pages 142–143.

Part 2: Literary Analysis

☐ Listen to and read along with "The Cracked Pot" again.

☐ Then listen to and read along with the directions for Literary Analysis on page 144. Use the page your teacher gives you to write your answer.

Part 3: Narrative Writing

☐ Listen to and read along with "The Cracked Pot" again.

☐ Then listen to and read along with the directions for Narrative Writing on page 144. Use the page your teacher gives you to write your answer.

Performance Task 1   **141**

Part 1 Text Questions

Listen to and read the questions and answer choices. Fill in the circle next to the correct answer.

1. When does this story take place?

- ● long ago
- ○ now
- ○ in the future

2. How does the cracked pot feel at the end of the story?

- ○ sad
- ● happy
- ○ angry

3. Which word from the story helps you know the answer to question 2?

- ● smiled
- ○ cried
- ○ pretty

Performance Task Overview

Overview

The Performance Tasks are designed to determine a student's ability to understand a read-along text, locate evidence to support text analysis, and create extended responses that show comprehension of the text. Each Performance Task has one part devoted to text questions and two parts devoted to writing.

Performance Task 1

Go to **sadlierconnect.com** to download the following resources for Performance Task 1:

ONLINE   **Digital Resources**

- **Texts:** "The Cracked Pot" (traditional tale)
- **Prompts:** response sheet; model responses
- **Answer Keys and Rubrics**

Administration Procedure

Part 1 Introduce the Task Explain that children will read a story along with you. Then they will answer questions and write about what they read.

- **Selected response items** ask about the story; some items ask children to find evidence from the story that points to the correct answer.
- **Constructed response items** are writing prompts based on the story; they require children to use story details for support.

Reading Children follow as you read the story aloud.

Selected Response Children complete the multiple choice items.

Part 2 Reading Children follow along as you read.

Constructed Response (Literary Analysis) Distribute the prompt. Read the prompt, and make sure children understand the directions. Then have children respond.

Part 3 Constructed Response (Narrative Writing) Repeat the steps followed for the Literary Analysis Constructed Response.

Text Questions

ONLINE Download "The Cracked Pot" and the Answer Key.

Core Task: Children read along with a traditional tale and respond to six selected response items. In answering the items, children must analyze the story and identify the evidence that supports their answers.

Depth of Knowledge Levels:

Item 1:	Item 2:	Item 3:	Item 4:	Item 5:	Item 6:
Level 1	Level 1	Level 1	Level 2	Level 2	Level 3

Literary Analysis

ONLINE Download "The Cracked Pot" and the Answer Key and Rubric.

Core Task: Children read along with a traditional tale and respond to a literary analysis prompt. Children's responses must: 1) retell the story, including important details, events in order, and the story's lesson; 2) use linking words and provide a conclusion; 3) construct sentences properly; 4) demonstrate a general command of conventions, including spelling, punctuation, and capitalization.

Depth of Knowledge Level: Level 3

Narrative Writing

ONLINE Download "The Cracked Pot" and the Answer Key and Rubric.

Core Task: Children read along with a traditional tale and respond to a prompt that requires them to write a new story ending. Children's responses must: 1) create a well-elaborated event that fits in with the original story, using appropriate details to describe actions, thoughts, feelings; 2) use time-order words, provide a sense of closure; 3) construct sentences properly; 4) demonstrate a general command of conventions, including spelling, punctuation, and capitalization.

Depth of Knowledge Level: Level 3

Scoring

Selected response items: 1 point per item (up to 6 points)

Constructed response items: up to 3 points per item (possible total of 12 points)

Note: When analyzing constructed responses, have student volunteers share their responses. Discuss key elements of the scoring rubric and ask children to make one significant change to improve their responses.

---

4. What does the word **leak** mean in this sentence from "The Cracked Pot"?

They grow because of the **leak** in your pot.

- ○ flowers
- ○ woman
- ● crack

5. Which word best describes the old woman?

- ○ bossy
- ○ silly
- ● kind

6. Which sentence from the story helps you know the answer to question 5?

- ○ "Long ago an old woman went to the river every day."
- ○ "Water dropped out of this pot."
- ● "The old woman had made the cracked pot grow flowers."

Part 2   Literary Analysis

Listen to and read the directions. Use the paper your teacher gives you to respond.

Write about why the cracked pot feels so sad. Retell the story "The Cracked Pot" for someone else to read. Use your own words to tell details from the text. End by writing the lesson the story teaches.

Part 3   Narrative Writing

Listen to and read the directions. Use the paper your teacher gives you to respond.

The story tells what the old woman does for the cracked pot. Look at the pictures. Write a paragraph to add to the story's ending. Write what happens next. Tell what the old woman does next. Be sure the details fit in with the rest of the story.

Introducing UNIT 7

This unit is about neighborhoods. The texts in it are all about places and helpers in our neighborhoods.

You will learn to ask and answer questions to help you understand words. You will learn ways to find facts and information. And you will learn how to use both pictures and words to get information.

 Before Unit 7

Progress Check Can I?

After Unit 7

- ☐ Ask and answer questions to find the meaning of words in a text. ☐
- ☐ Use parts of a text to find information. ☐
- ☐ Tell whether pictures or words give information in a text. ☐
- ☐ Use what I learn to read new words. ☐
- ☐ Use word parts to figure out the meaning of new words. ☐

Unit 7 ■ Reading Informational Text: Craft and Structure

Student Page 145

Progress Check

The Progress Check is a self-assessment feature that children can use to gauge their own progress. Research shows that when children take accountability for their own learning, their motivation increases.

Before children begin work on Unit 7, have them check the boxes next to any item that they feel they can do well. Explain that it is fine if they don't check any of the boxes. Tell them that they will have an opportunity to learn about and practice all of these items while studying the unit. Let them know that near the end of the unit they will have a chance to reconsider how well they can do each item on the list.

Before children begin their Unit 7 Review on page 173, have them revisit this page. You can use this information to work with children on any items they don't understand before they tackle the Review.

HOME CONNECT...

The Home Connect feature is a way to keep parents or other adult family members apprised of what their children are learning. The key learning objectives are listed, and some ideas for related activities and discussions are included.

Explain to children that they can share the Home Connect page with their parents or other adult family members in their home. Let children know how much time the class will be spending on this unit so they can plan their time accordingly at home.

Encourage children and their parents or other adult family members to share their experiences using the suggestions on the Home Connect page. You may wish to make a place to post some of this work.

HOME CONNECT...

IN THIS UNIT, YOUR CHILD WILL...

- Ask and answer questions to understand word meanings.
- Use text features such as headings and captions to locate information.
- Gather information from words and pictures in a text.
- Read words spelled with long *a* or long *i*.
- Read words spelled with *ar*, *er*, *ir*, *or*, or *ur*.
- Read and understand the meaning of words with the prefix *re* or the suffix *ful*.
- Compare and contrast three different texts on the same topic.

 Nonfictional narrative texts, such as magazine articles, may contain words that readers don't know and understand. As you read a nonfictional narrative with your child, **ask and answer questions** to help him or her **understand the meanings** of new words. For example, you might ask, *Have you seen or heard this word before? Are there other words in the sentence that can help you figure it out? Is there a base word that you know?*

Authors often include **text features,** such as headings and captions, to help readers understand what they read. Look at a print or online magazine article that has headings and captions. Read one of the headings together, and guess what the section will be about. Then read on to see if you are correct. Read the captions and talk about what you learn from them.

Find a nonfictional narrative text that includes both **words and pictures.** Together, talk about what you learn from the words. Then, talk about what else you learn from the pictures.

WAYS TO HELP YOUR CHILD

Look for frequent opportunities to read informational texts to or with your child. For example, look at newspaper and magazine articles together. Point out recipes or assembly instructions that you read and follow. Draw your child's attention to any pictures and invite him or her to tell what kind of information the pictures add to the topic.

On the Go: Walk around your neighborhood with your child. Take turns pointing out places you see, such as a school, a library, a park, stores, a police station, or a fire station. Also point out neighborhood helpers, such as a police officer or a trash collector. Talk about how their jobs are helpful to people in the neighborhood.

ONLINE
For more Home Connect activities, continue online at sadlierconnect.com

146 Unit 7 ■ Reading Informational Text: Craft and Structure

Student Page 146

UNIT PLANNER

Theme: In My Neighborhood	Focus
READ ALOUD *pp. 148–149*	*Walking with Grandpa* **GENRE:** Nonfictional Narrative
UNDERSTANDING WORD MEANINGS *pp. 150–153*	*We Need a Dog Park* **GENRE:** Opinion Piece **LEXILE®:** *450L* **WORDS TO KNOW:** build, exercise, mayor, rake, rule
USING TEXT FEATURES *pp. 154–157*	*Neighborhood Helpers* **GENRE:** Informational Text **LEXILE®:** *380L* **WORDS TO KNOW:** bottle, carrier, librarian, trash, vegetable
DISTINGUISHING WORDS AND PICTURES *pp. 158–161*	*Fire Drills* **GENRE:** Procedural Text **LEXILE®:** *330L* **WORDS TO KNOW:** alarm, certain, drill, practice
FOUNDATIONAL SKILLS READ TOGETHER *p. 162*	*Farm Neighborhoods* **GENRE:** Informational Text
FOUNDATIONAL SKILLS READER 1 *pp. 163–164*	*Who Am I?* **GENRE:** Informational Text
FOUNDATIONAL SKILLS READER 2 *pp. 165–166*	*Firefighters at Work* **GENRE:** Informational Text
CLOSE READING *pp. 167–170*	*Who Works at Night?* **GENRE:** Informational Text **LEXILE®:** *400L*
CONNECT ACROSS TEXTS *p. 171*	Compare and Contrast Texts
LANGUAGE *p. 172*	Prefix *re* and Suffix *ful*
UNIT 7 REVIEW *pp. 173–174*	**WHO WORKS IN SCHOOL?** **GENRE:** Informational Text **LEXILE®:** *350L*

Objective(s)

- Ask and answer questions to figure out the meaning of words.
- Use text features to find information.
- Distinguish between information given in pictures and information given by words.

Ask and answer questions to figure out the meaning of words.

Use text features to find information.

Distinguish between information given in pictures and information given by words.

Read decodable text featuring long *a* words, long *i* words, and *r*-controlled vowels.

Read decodable text featuring long *a* words and long *i* words

Read decodable text featuring *r*-controlled vowels, long *a* words, and long *i* words.

Same objectives as pages 150–153; pages 154–157; and pages 158–161

Use -*ful* and *re*- as clues to word meaning.

Unit Assessment

- Unit 7 Review, *pp. 173–174*
- Unit 7 Performance Task (ONLINE)

Additional Assessment Options

- Performance Task 1 *pp. 141–144*
  (ALSO ONLINE)
- Performance Task 2 *pp. 259–262*
  (ALSO ONLINE)

Optional Purchase:

- iProgress Monitor (ONLINE)
- Progress Monitor Student Benchmark Assessment Booklet

(ONLINE) Digital Resources

- Home Connect Activities
- Unit Performance Task
- Additional Practice
- Full-Length Reading Selections
- Foundational Skills Practice
- Teacher Resources
- iProgress Monitor (optional purchase

Go to SadlierConnect.com to access your Digital Resources.

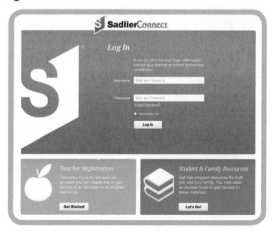

For more detailed instructions see page T3.

LEARNING PROGRESSIONS

In this unit, children will learn to ask and answer questions to understand the meaning of words and phrases. They will also learn to use various text features and distinguish between information in words and images. In order to learn the skills in this unit, children will further develop skills learned in kindergarten. They should be encouraged to retain these skills, as they will continue to build on them in second grade.

Understanding Word Meanings

- When prompted, children can ask and answer questions about unknown words in a text.

- By the end of first grade, children are able to ask and answer questions to clarify the meaning of words and phrases in a text.

- As second grade draws to a close, children can determine the meanings of words and phrases in grade-level content-area texts.

Using Text Features

- Proficient kindergartners are able to identify the front cover, back cover, and title page of a book.

- First-graders are then expected to know and use text features to locate key facts or other information in a text.

- In second grade, children are able to know and use an increasing number of text features to locate key facts or other information in a text with proficiency.

Distinguishing Words and Pictures

- By the end of kindergarten, children can name the author and illustrator of a text and describe the role of each.

- In first grade, children are able to tell the difference between information provided by the illustrations and information provided by the words.

- Second-grade children can identify the main purpose of a text, including what the author wants to answer, explain, or describe.

Reading Informational Text: Craft and Structure

Essential Question:
How do the parts of an informational text work together?

Essential Question:
How do the parts of an informational text work together?

In this unit, children will learn to describe how the parts of an informational text work together. Specifically, children will be able to analyze the role of words, illustrations, and text features.

Theme: In My Neighborhood

In this unit, children will read selections about community helpers and neighborhood features. They will develop a greater understanding of the important roles that people play in a neighborhood and how people in a community are connected.

Curriculum Connection: Social Studies

As children enjoy the selections in this unit, they will learn and explore the roles of various community helpers.

Vocabulary Overview

alarm 159, bottle 156, build 152, carrier 155, certain 160, drill 158, exercise 150, librarian 155, mayor 150, practice 158, rake 152, rule 151, trash 156, vegetable 156

OBJECTIVES

- **Ask and answer questions to figure out the meaning of words.**
- **Use text features to find information.**
- **Distinguish between information given in pictures and information given by words.**

Using the Read Aloud

Tell children that you will read a text aloud (see right) as they look at the pictures in their books. Read the text, pausing at the numbers to pose questions.

Picture

What is happening here? (Firefighters are washing their truck.)

Read caption 1 together.

Picture

What information does the caption give you about the photograph? (It shows what eggplants look like.)

Read caption 2 together.

Picture

What are these people doing? (watching their dogs in a dog park)

Read caption 3 together.

Picture

How does the caption help you understand the picture? (It tells me the building is a public library.)

Read caption 4 together.

Turn and Talk

Have pairs discuss the following questions: *Which of these places in the community would you like to visit? Why?*

Walking with Grandpa

Will loves walking around town with Grandpa. That's because Grandpa seems to know everyone! One day, they walked to the store. They passed a fire station along the way. Grandpa said "hi" to the firefighters who were washing the fire truck. Grandpa talked with his friends. A firefighter let Will try on a helmet and some boots. They were huge! **1**

Will and Grandpa walked on. They stopped at the community garden. Grandpa knew everyone in the garden that day. His friends gave them some vegetables. A man gave them some beans. A lady gave them an eggplant. **2**

Will and Grandpa walked on. They stopped at the park. They saw some men playing checkers there. Grandpa knew them. Sometimes he plays checkers with them. Will saw some friends playing baseball. They asked Will to play, but Will said no. He wanted to keep walking with Grandpa.

Next to the park was a dog park. Will and Grandpa stopped to watch the dogs. Most of them were chasing balls. Grandpa knew some people in the dog park. They talked to one friend who had a puppy. The puppy ran after all the balls. She never got one, but she never gave up! **3**

The park was on a busy street. The policeman at the corner was a friend of Grandpa's. He stopped the cars so Will and Grandpa could cross the street.

Will and Grandpa passed the library where Will's mother worked. He wanted to stop and get some books. Grandpa said they should stop on the way home. Then they would not have to carry the books as far. **4**

Will and Grandpa finally arrived at the store. They bought food and put it into bags. The bags were a little heavy. Grandpa thought that they should take a taxi home. Will said he would carry the bags. He wanted to walk home with Grandpa!

Read Aloud

Listen as your teacher reads. Ask questions about words that are new. Try to answer your questions.

Look at the pictures as you listen. What information do you learn from them?

Walking with Grandpa

1 Grandpa and Will stopped by the fire station.

2 A lady gave them an eggplant at the garden.

Preview the Focus Skills

Do a second reading of the read aloud as children look at the pictures. As you read, pause briefly where indicated below. Use the suggested think-alouds to preview the unit's targeted reading skills and model how children might use the skills independently during shared reading.

- Pause after reading paragraph 3. Say: *Sometimes when I'm reading, I find a word I don't know. One way to figure out a word I don't know is to ask questions about it. If I don't know the word* checkers, *I can ask, "What do the men do with the checkers?" I can read again and see that the men are playing checkers, so I know that checkers is a game.*

- Pause after reading paragraph 4. Say: *One way readers get information is from captions. Those are the words or sentences below a picture. I'm going to read the caption below picture 3. This caption helps me understand that this is the dog park, where dogs can walk, run, or play.*

- Pause after reading paragraph 6. Say: *I notice that both the words and photograph 4 are about the library. When I first saw the photograph, I wondered if Grandpa and Will visited the library. The words help me understand that they didn't stay at the library.*

Digital Connection

Have children work in groups to search the Internet for Web sites of different community organizations, such as the library, fire department station, or community center. Allow them to share the Web sites they found and what information is provided on the sites as they build background knowledge for this unit.

Craft and Structure

3 Grandpa and Will stopped at the dog park.

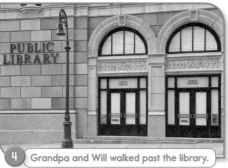

PUBLIC LIBRARY

4 Grandpa and Will walked past the library.

Guided Instruction

OBJECTIVES

- Ask and answer questions to figure out the meaning of words.
- Answer questions about key details in a text read aloud.

Genre: Opinion Piece

Tell children that authors sometimes write texts to share their opinions, or beliefs, with others. Usually, the authors of opinion pieces want to convince readers that their opinions are right.

Set the Purpose

Help children understand the purpose for asking and answering questions to determine word meaning by asking: *What can you do when you find a word you do not know?*

Model and Teach

Read the text aloud as children follow along in their books.

Teacher Talk: Find Evidence

Say: *When I find a word I do not know, I first sound it out.* Model sounding out *explore. I also need to understand what it means. So, I ask myself questions such as "Does the author give me the meaning?" or "Is there an example?" Then I read around the word to look for clues. I notice the word "or." This is a clue telling me the author gives the meaning of the word. Can you find the meaning?* Encourage children to give the meaning in a complete sentence.

Understanding Word Meanings

Words to Know

exercise
mayor
rule

We Need a Dog Park

(Genre: Opinion Piece)

1 Dear **Mayor** Hardy,

I have a puppy. Her name is Spot. She has white spots on her dark fur. Spot needs a lot of **exercise**! She is very playful. Spot likes to explore, or look around, new places.

2 My family lives in an apartment. We do not have a yard. Spot cannot run outside. She cannot explore outside.

3 Our city is not a good place for dogs. We have a park in our city. It is a nice place for people. But dogs cannot enter, or (go into), the park.

4 Our city needs a park for dogs. People could throw balls to their dogs there. The dogs could play with other dogs. Spot would love that. She carries her ball everywhere!

> This sign shows that dogs cannot come into this park.

Guided Instruction

Teacher Talk: Find Evidence

Model how to figure out the meaning of *explore* in paragraph 1. *I ask myself, "Are there words in the sentence that give the meaning of* explore*?" I see that the words* look around *tell the meaning.* Have children find and circle the words that give the meaning of *enter* in paragraph 3.

Words to Know

exercise (*noun*): regular activity to keep healthy
mayor (*noun*): leader of a town or city
rule (*noun*): what is allowed or not allowed; law

Working with Word Meaning Explain to children that a mayor is the leader of a town or city. Play a game of Simon Says, but change it to Mayor Says. The mayor asks children to do exercises. After the game, ask: *What did the* **mayor** *do? What* **rule** *did the mayor give? Did you like to* **exercise**?

Craft and Structure

The dogs are safely playing inside a fence at a city dog park.

5 Other cities have dog parks. I have read about them. They have high fences. They have lots of grass. Some parks have short trails. People walk their dogs on these dirt paths. The parks have pails of water for dogs to drink. They have hoses to refill the pails.

6 Dog parks have a **rule** that says only friendly dogs can come into the park. Also, dog owners have to remain. They have to stay with their dogs. People cannot bring food into the park. Dogs might grab it. They might fight over the food. These rules keep dogs and people safe.

Teacher Talk: Find Evidence

Model how to figure out the meaning of *cities* in paragraph 5. *I ask myself, "What base word is in the word* cities*?" The base word is* city. *Knowing the meaning of* city *helps me understand* cities. Have children circle *friendly* in paragraph 6 and use *friend* to give its meaning.

Guided Instruction

Unit 7 ■ Reading Informational Text: Craft and Structure **151**

Support English Language Learners

Build an understanding of a dog park before reading. Show children pictures of dog parks. Point out the fence surrounding it and special features such as toys and water. Explain that dog parks are special areas where dogs can play and exercise safely. Ask children to use the photograph to tell what a dog might do at a dog park.

Guided Instruction

Teacher Talk: Find Evidence

Say: *When I read opinion pieces, I know that they often have special vocabulary. Writers often give clues to the meanings of these words. They give a definition or give examples. For instance, the author gives several examples of exercise in paragraph 4. Dogs catch balls and play with other dogs.*

Continue reading the text. Stop after paragraph 5. Say: *As I read the word* cities, *I notice the ending -es. I know that many plural words have this ending.* Write *families* and *puppies* on the board. *The base words are* family *and* puppy. *I know that* families *is more than one family, and* puppies *is more than one puppy. Because* city *ends in a y, the y is changed to i when es is added. Cities is more than one* _____. *Looking for base words and word endings can help me understand word meanings. Turn and tell your partner a question you can ask about base words or endings to figure out the meaning of a word.* (Do I see a base word that I know?)

After going through the Find Evidence instruction, help children sum up strategies for finding the meaning of a word. Ask them to tell questions they can ask and answer to find the meanings of unfamiliar words.

Use Visuals

To help children figure out the meanings of unfamiliar words, have them look at the visuals on pages 150–151. Ask how the photograph on page 151 helps them understand what a dog park is. Ask children to use a sentence to explain the meaning of the word, using the visual.

Guided Practice

Read and Practice

Remind children that they can ask and answer questions about the text to understand the meaning of a word. For example, they can ask: "Does the author give me clues?" "Does the author tell the meaning near the word?" and "Do I know the base word and ending?" Have heterogeneous partners take turns reading the rest of the text as you circulate to provide support. While they read the text, remind them to pay attention to clues to the meaning of unknown words.

Teacher Talk: Find Evidence

Reread paragraph 8 aloud. Then have children give some questions they could ask to help them define the word *leaves*. If they need help, remind them about asking about context clues (words near the word) or base words (the main part of the word). As children ask each question, help them work together as a class to underline the word or word parts that answer the question. If children need more support, point out the word *rake*. Ask children to explain how the word *rake* helps them understand the word *leaves*.

Turn and Talk

Have children find the word *collect* in paragraph 7. Have children work in pairs to ask questions that will help them find the meaning of the word. Then ask the pairs to find clues in the sentence to the word's meaning. Finally, ask each pair member to use a complete sentence to create a definition for the word *collect* and share with their partner. Ask several pairs to share with the class.

Understanding Word Meanings

Words to Know
build
rake

7   Do you think our city could **build** a dog park? My friends and I could help. We could collect, or take in, money for the park. We could walk dogs for people. Many people in the city would pay us to do that.

8   My family will help, too. My dad can build a high fence. My brothers will **rake** the leaves. I think our neighbors will be helpful, too.

9   Dog parks are good for the neighborhood. They are places where people can meet their neighbors.

Some dogs just like to lie on the grass and rest in the park.

Guided Practice

Teacher Talk: Find Evidence
Review that asking and answering questions about context clues and base words can help readers figure out the meanings of new words. Have partners figure out the meaning of *neighborhood* in paragraph 9. Ask them to underline the base word that gives a clue to its meaning.

152   Unit 7 ■ Reading Informational Text: Craft and Structure

---

Words to Know

build (*verb*): to make something out of wood or other materials
rake (*verb*): to scrape or sweep up

Working with Word Meaning Have children do motions to show how to *build* a snowman. Then ask them to make motions to show how to *rake* leaves. Ask: *Which would you rather do: build a snowman or rake leaves? Why?*

Craft and Structure

10   Please respond, or (write back), to me. Please,
Mr. Mayor, Spot and I are hopeful about getting a dog
park. Maybe we could name it "The Bark Park"!

Yours truly,
Gail

Comprehension Check   (MORE ONLINE) sadlierconnect.com

1. Which base word can help you figure out the
meaning of *carries* in paragraph 4?

    a. car

    (b.) carry

    c. cherry

2. Ask and answer a question that can help you figure
out the meaning of *remain* in paragraph 6. Use your
understanding of *remain* to explain the rule.

    Sample answer: The dog owners have to stay with their

    dogs. They can't leave them there.

Teacher Talk: Find Evidence
Have children ask and answer a question that could help them figure
out the meaning of *respond* in paragraph 10. Ask them to circle the
words in the text that give a clue to its meaning.

Independent Practice

Unit 7 ■ Reading Informational Text: Craft and Structure   **153**

Foundational Skills Review: Fluency Practice

Remind children that it is important to read with expression. Say: *Reading
with expression means that you read with feeling. You pay attention
to the punctuation to tell you if something is read as a question or
with excitement.* Model reading paragraph 10 for children. Point out
the exclamation mark that shows the author wants to add emphasis
to this sentence. Then go back to the beginning of the paragraph and
have children chorally read the paragraph. Have them work in groups of
three to continue practicing with another paragraph. Additional fluency
passages and activities can be found at **sadlierconnect.com**.

Read and Apply

Have children read paragraph 10
independently as you circulate. Provide
extra support to struggling readers by
choral reading with them.

Teacher Talk: Find Evidence

Have children share questions they could
ask to help them understand the word
respond. If necessary, remind children they
can ask questions about context clues or
word parts. As children ask questions,
review the text to circle the answers. As a
class, use these words to understand the
meaning of the word *respond*.

Comprehension Check

Answer Explanations:

1. Choice **B** is the base word.

2. Children should note that the sentence
after the word *remain* explains that
owners must stay with their dogs.

Critical Comprehension

Use the following activity and question
to help children think more deeply
about the selection. Children should be
prepared to support their answers with
evidence from the text.

• *Why does Gail ask the mayor to
respond to her?* (She wants to know if
she has persuaded the mayor.)

Assess and Respond
If children have difficulty answering the questions in the Comprehension Check . . .
Then work with them to create an anchor chart listing questions they can ask when reading to help them determine the meaning of an unknown word.

Guided Instruction

OBJECTIVES
- Use text features to find information.
- Answer questions about key details in a text read aloud.

Genre: Informational Texts

Remind children that informational text presents facts. People usually read informational text to learn information.

Set the Purpose

Help children understand the purpose for learning the reading skill by asking: *What special text or images do you notice on this page? How do these special features help you find things?*

Model and Teach

Read the text aloud as children follow along in their books.

Teacher Talk: Find Evidence

Pause at the end of paragraph 3. Say: *As I read, I see words that are in dark orange print. These words are called headings. Headings are at the beginning of a section. Headings make it easy for readers to find information. Where will I find information on helpers who keep people healthy? Where will I find information about people who fight fires?* Encourage children to reply in complete sentences.

Using Text Features

Words to Know

carrier
librarian

Neighborhood Helpers
(Genre: Informational Text)

1   There are many neighborhood helpers. Which helper keeps you safe? Maybe you thought of a police officer. Police officers do help people. There are other neighborhood helpers. These are some of them.

Doctors and Nurses

2   Doctors and nurses are helpers. They keep people healthy. They make us feel better. Doctors and nurses may work all night. Has a doctor or a nurse ever helped you?

Firefighters

3   Firefighters are helpers. They put out fires. They save people. Firefighters teach people to "Stop, Drop, and Roll." That is helpful to remember if your clothes are burning.

This fire started in dried grass.

Guided Instruction

Teacher Talk: Find Evidence
Explain that authors include section headings to let readers know what they will read about and where to find information. Point out the headings. Ask: *Which heading helps you find information about doctors and nurses?* Have children circle the heading.

154   Unit 7 ■ Reading Informational Text: Craft and Structure

---

Words to Know

carrier (*noun*): person who takes things from place to place
librarian (*noun*): person who works in a library

Working with Word Meaning Help children understand the words by asking them to draw pictures of a mail *carrier* and a *librarian*. Then ask children: *What would you like a mail carrier to bring to your house? What kinds of things does a librarian carry?*

Craft and Structure

Librarian

4   A **librarian** is a helper. Librarians help people find books in a library every day. Did a librarian help you find a book when you visited the library? Will you visit the library again soon?

Bus Drivers

5   Bus drivers are helpers. Bus drivers stop to pick up people in the neighborhood. They take them where they need to go. Did a bus driver drive you to school?

Mail Carriers

6   A mail **carrier** is a helper. Mail carriers bring us letters. Some of them walk. They carry large bags of mail. Others drive cars or trucks. Has a mail carrier ever brought you a card or a letter?

Mail carriers also bring magazines to people.

Teacher Talk: Find Evidence
Explain that a caption is a sentence that tells more about a picture. Point out the photograph on this page and ask children to describe it. Then have children circle the caption. Ask: *What else do you learn about the mail carrier from the caption?*

Guided Instruction

Guided Instruction

Teacher Talk: Find Evidence

Pause before reading the text on page 155. Point out the photograph of the mail carrier. Say: *I know that in informational texts, I can learn information from the illustrations too. As I look at the photograph, I see a mail carrier. Since this text is about community helpers. I know that a mail carrier is a community helper.*

Sometimes authors want to give you specific facts or information about the picture. They write words near the picture that explain the picture. These words are called a caption. I know it is important to read the captions in a text. Can you circle the caption on the page? When I read this caption I learn new information about mail carriers. In the text, it said mail carriers bring letters. The caption adds information. What information does it add? (Mail carriers bring magazines to people.)

Tell children that you are going to continue using the text features such as headings and captions to help you find out important information in the text.

Review: Understanding Word Meanings

Remind children that informational texts can have some unfamiliar words. To help figure out word meanings, readers can ask themselves questions. Ask: *What questions can we ask to help us understand the word* brought? (Are there words like it nearby? Do I know any word parts of the word?) *I see the word* bring *in a sentence before* brought. *These words look a lot alike. I know* bring *means to take, so* brought *may mean something like that.*

Differentiate Instruction

To help children understand different text features, have a text feature scavenger hunt. Give children several informational texts. Ask children questions similar to those below and allow them to work with a partner to find text features that would answer the questions. Then allow them to share their examples.

What text feature helps us figure out what words mean? (glossary and bold-faced print)

What text feature explains a picture? (caption)

What text feature tells what a section is about? (heading)

Guided Practice

Read and Practice

Have heterogeneous partners take turns reading page 156 as you circulate to provide support. Before children begin reading, remind them to pay attention to text features such as headings and captions. These text features will help them identify and learn important information.

Teacher Talk: Find Evidence

Remind children that a caption is the words that tell more about a picture. Ask children to find and read aloud the caption. Monitor children's understanding of text features and ask volunteers to state in complete sentences how captions, pictures, and headings help them understand a text better. If necessary, provide the following sentence frames: Captions help us understand a text better by _____. Pictures help us understand a text better by _____. Headings help us understand a text better by _____.

Team Jigsaw

Divide the class into groups of five. Assign group members one paragraph from paragraphs 4, 5, 6, 7, or 8. Ask members to decide on the most interesting fact from the assigned paragraph and write a sentence about the community helper. Put the sentences together and have each group share what they have learned about community helpers.

Using Text Features

Words to Know
bottle
trash
vegetable

Trash Collectors

7   **Trash** collectors are helpers. We all throw away trash. What if no one took it away? Our neighborhoods would be dirty! A trash collector may pick up a **bottle** in your neighborhood. The glass can be reused. Are you glad that there are trash collectors?

Farmers

8   Farmers are helpers. What is your favorite **vegetable**? Some farmers grow vegetables such as corn. Others grow grain. Farmers sell the food they grow.

This farmer sells vegetables at a market.

Guided Practice

Teacher Talk: Find Evidence
Review that captions tell more about photographs or other pictures. Tell children to find and underline the caption for the photo on this page. Have children talk about what information they learn from the caption.

Words to Know

bottle (*noun*): glass container
trash (*noun*): things people no longer need or want; garbage
vegetable (*noun*): plant grown as food

Working with Word Meaning Give each child three index cards. Ask them to write each Word to Know on one side of an index card and draw a picture showing the meaning of the word on the other side. Then ask children to form pairs and lay out their index cards picture side up. Have children take turns naming the word that each picture shows. Then have them take turns saying a sentence using each word. Finally, have volunteers share their sentences with the class.

Craft and Structure

Teachers

9   Teachers are helpers, too. They teach children to read. They teach them to write. What did you learn from your teacher today?

Comprehension Check

MORE ONLINE sadlierconnect.com

1. What heading helps you find facts about helpers who bring letters?

   a. Trash Collectors

   b. Mail Carriers

   c. Bus Drivers

2. What does the photograph on page 154 show? What else do you learn in the caption?

   Sample answer: The photo shows a fire burning. The

   caption tells where the fire started.

Teacher Talk: Find Evidence
Have children circle the heading on this page. Tell them to underline the sentences that explain why teachers are neighborhood helpers.

Independent Practice

Unit 7 ■ Reading Informational Text: Craft and Structure   **157**

Independent Practice

Read and Apply

Have children read the paragraph on page 157 independently as you circulate. Provide extra support to struggling readers by choral reading the paragraph with them.

Teacher Talk: Find Evidence

Together, circle the heading and underline the sentences about teachers. Ask children to tell how the heading helps them understand the text.

Comprehension Check

Answer Explanations:

1. Only choice **B** describes people who might carry letters.

2. Children should tell what they learned from both the photograph and the caption.

Critical Comprehension

Use the following question to help children think critically about the selection. Children should be prepared to support their answers with evidence from the text.

• *Think about the people in the headings. Why are they called neighborhood helpers?* (They do jobs that help people near them.)

Assess and Respond
If children have difficulty answering the questions in the Comprehension Check . . .
Then ask pairs to work together to use different colored highlighters or light markers to highlight each text feature.

Peer Collaboration

Have children work with a partner to create picture cards using magazine pictures showing different neighborhood or community helpers including those in the text and other helpers such as police officers, crossing guards, teachers, and paramedics. Help children to name each worker. Then ask children to give a sentence about what each person does.

Guided Instruction

OBJECTIVES

- Distinguish between information given in pictures and information given by words.
- Answer questions about key details in a text read aloud.

Genre: Procedural Text

Explain that a procedural text tells how to do something or make something. Instructions, directions, and recipes are all types of procedural texts.

Set the Purpose

Help children understand that words and pictures both provide information: Say: *Imagine you were trying a recipe. What could you learn from the words? How could the pictures help you?*

Model and Teach

Read the text aloud as children follow along in their books.

Teacher Talk: Find Evidence

Say: *The title of an informational text often tells me the topic. I know from the title that this text is going to explain something about fire drills. As I read, I want to pay attention to the words that tell me what to do and study the pictures to learn more about how to do a fire drill.* Then read paragraph 3 and have children underline the sentence that tells how many fire drills. Ask: *How do the picture and the words work together?* Ask children to explain in a complete sentence.

Distinguishing Words and Pictures

Words to Know

alarm
drill
practice

Fire Drills
(Genre: Procedural Text)

1 Think about things you **practice**. Do you practice playing the piano? Maybe you practice playing soccer. People practice things so they can do them well.

2 In school, you practice reading. You practice adding numbers. A fire **drill** is practice, too. You practice what to do if there is a fire.

Schools have a plan for fire drills.

Guided Instruction

Teacher Talk: Find Evidence
Explain that children can get information from both words and pictures in informational text. Point out that the text in paragraph 3 tells about fire drills. Ask: *How many fire drills do schools have each year?* Have children find that fact on page 159 and underline it.

158   Unit 7 ■ Reading Informational Text: Craft and Structure

---

Words to Know

alarm (*noun*): very loud noise to get attention
drill (*noun*): going through steps to prepare for a real situation
practice (*verb*): to do something to get better, often over and over

Working with Word Meaning Have children practice a fire *drill*. Afterwards ask: *What happens when you hear the* alarm*? What do you do in a fire drill? Why should we* practice*?*

Craft and Structure

3 There are not many fires in schools. But you need to know what to do if there is one. Most schools have 8 to 12 fire drills every year. That may seem like a lot. But fire drills are helpful. They help you remember what to do.

4 There are steps to follow in a fire drill. Your teacher will tell you what do. Listen carefully. Do what your teacher says.

5 **Step 1** When you hear the fire **alarm** ring, stop what you are doing.

6 **Step 2** Line up in your classroom. Line up quickly, but do not run. Do not push. Be careful not to trip and get hurt.

7 **Step 3** Do not talk. Wait for your teacher to tell you to start walking.

Fire alarms make a very loud noise.

Teacher Talk: Find Evidence

Point out that pictures can show what people, animals, places, and things look like. Have children circle the fire alarm. Say: *Describe what the fire alarm looks like.* Then have them find and underline the words in the caption that tell more about fire alarms.

Guided Instruction

Unit 7 ■ Reading Informational Text: Craft and Structure **159**

Guided Instruction

Teacher Talk: Find Evidence

Ask children to point to the place on the page that shows what a fire alarm looks like. Circle the photograph together. Ask: *What information does this photograph give?*

Pause after paragraph 3. Say: *As I read the words, I am listening for facts about fire drills. Paragraph three tells me about practicing for fire drills. The words tell me why it is important.*

Pause after reading paragraph 7. Remind children that the pictures give important information. Say: *In the picture on page 158, I see children standing in a line in the hall. This shows me what it looks like to do a fire drill. Pictures add details to a text.*

Next, I will read the caption. These are the words in the box next to the picture. From the caption, I learn that schools plan fire drills.

The pictures and the text both taught me information about fire drills, but I learned different things from each place. I know that good readers pay attention to both the words and the pictures when they read. What do you think the teacher is doing in the picture? How does this help you understand more about fire drills?

Review: Using Text Features

Remind children that many informational texts have special features like headings and captions. Ask volunteers to identify the special features on this page. Ask: *How do these features help you understand the text better? Which feature helps you find special words? Which feature explains the picture?*

Support English Language Learners

Build background knowledge about fire drills with the children. Read the steps in the text on pages 159–160. Then have the children participate in a fire drill. Take photographs of each step. Ask the children to compare the photographs to the steps. Discuss how the photographs help create a visual image of the words. Point out things that are in the photographs but are not in the words. Then point out details that are in the text, but not shown in the photograph.

Guided Practice

Read and Practice

Remind children that images support and often add to the information provided in the text. Have them study the photograph on the page and read the caption. Then read the first two sentences of paragraph 8. Have heterogeneous partners take turns reading the rest of the text as you circulate to provide support. While they read the text, have them consider what information is presented using words and what information is presented through the pictures.

Teacher Talk: Find Evidence

Ask children to look at the picture and reread Step 5 (paragraph 9). Ask: *What part of Step 5 does the picture show?* Together, underline the sentence. Then ask children to describe in their own words the key idea shown by the photograph and the text. (In a fire drill you should go to a safe meeting place.) Ask volunteers to explain in complete sentences how words and pictures work together.

Reciprocal Teaching

Place children in groups of four. Assign each member a role: summarizer, questioner, clarifier, and predictor. Have children discuss the text and the pictures with each child contributing according to his or her assigned role.

Digital Connection

Allow children to use a word-processing program to write steps to follow during a fire drill at their home. They may add photographs or other illustrations to enhance the text. Encourage children to post their fire drill plans at home.

Distinguishing Words and Pictures

Words to Know

certain

8 **Step 4** Get in line when you leave your classroom. Do not take anything with you. Stay right behind the person in front of you. Do not turn around. Do not walk away from your class.

9 **Step 5** Go with your teacher. <u>She will walk with you to a meeting place outside.</u> Your teacher will count the children in line. She might recount the children. She needs to be **certain** that the whole class is there.

10 **Step 6** Remain, or stay, in line. Fire drills are not a time to play.

11 **Step 7** Your teacher will know when it is safe to go inside. Walk quietly in line.

These children are going to a safe meeting place with their teacher.

Guided Practice

Teacher Talk: Find Evidence
Review that readers can get information from both words and pictures in a text. Have children find information in paragraph 9 that matches the information that they get from the picture. Have them underline the sentence.

160 Unit 7 ■ Reading Informational Text: Craft and Structure

Words to Know

certain (*adj*): sure

Working with Word Meaning To review the Words to Know from this unit, have children play a game of Charades. Divide the class into two teams. Call a volunteer from each team and whisper one of the words in each volunteer's ear. Then say, "Go!" Each volunteer must act out the same word for their team. The first team to guess correctly earns a point for their team. Words to Know from this unit: exercise, mayor, rule, build, rake, carrier, librarian, bottle, trash, vegetable, alarm, drill, practice, certain.

Craft and Structure

12   Maybe firefighters will come to your school. They might tell you more about fire safety. They might tell you more about fire drills. Listen to what they tell you. Pay attention when you have a fire drill. Fire drills save lives!

Comprehension Check   MORE ONLINE sadlierconnect.com

1. Look at the picture on page 159. What do you learn from the caption?

   a. Fire alarms can be red.

   b. Fire alarms are very loud.

   c. Fire alarms can be on the wall.

2. Look at the picture on page 158. What does it show that you also read in the text?

   Sample answer: It shows children in line for a fire drill. They

   wait for their teacher to tell them to start walking. Their

   teacher makes sure they listen.

Teacher Talk: Find Evidence
Have children find information in paragraph 12 that tells which neighborhood helpers teach children about fire safety. Ask them to underline the sentence that tells that information. Then have them circle what else children learn from firefighters.

Independent Practice

Unit 7 ■ Reading Informational Text: Craft and Structure   **161**

Independent Practice

Read and Apply

Have children read the final paragraph on page 161 independently as you circulate. Provide extra support to struggling readers by choral reading the paragraph with them.

Teacher Talk: Find Evidence

Ask children to underline the sentence about who teaches fire safety. Discuss what else we learn from firefighters. Say: *Describe a picture that would go with this paragraph.*

Comprehension Check

Answer Explanations:

1. Only answer **B** contains information from the caption.

2. Children should indicate information that is in both the words and the picture.

Critical Comprehension

Use the following questions to help children think critically about the selection. Children should be prepared to support their answers with evidence from the text.

• *What are some other community helpers? How do they help people?* (Doctors and nurses keep people healthy.)

Assess and Respond

If children have difficulty answering the questions in the Comprehension Check . . .

Then work with them to create a web showing the main ideas and key details. Include details from the photographs. Discuss where you found each detail as you add it.

Extend Thinking: Form Opinions

Have volunteers name the neighborhood helpers they have learned about so far. Ask each child to choose a neighborhood helper they think is important. Then have each child draw pictures of that neighborhood helper that show a reason why the helper is important. Remind children that their reasons should be strong enough to convince others to agree with them. Ask children to share the neighborhood helper they selected and use a complete sentence to explain the reason their picture shows.

Copyright © by William H. Sadlier, Inc. All rights reserved.

OBJECTIVE
Read decodable text featuring long *a* words, long *i* words, and *r*-controlled vowels.

Prepare to Read
Tell children that you will be reading an informational text about the people who live in farm neighborhoods. As you read, children should look for words that have the long vowel sounds of *a* and *i* as well as words that have an *r* after a vowel.

Introduce Phonics Skills
After you have read the selection once, read it again, this time focusing on the target phonics skills.

- *Listen to the word* pie. *The letters* ie *stand for the long* i *vowel sound. Can you find more words with a long* i? *(*might, like*) Can you find words with the long* a *sound? (*make, raise*)*

- *Direct children to* farm. *Look at the letters as I say each sound: /f/ /ahr/ /m/. Which letters made the /ahr/ sounds? When r follows a vowel, it changes the sound of the vowel.*

- *A syllable is a word or word part with one vowel sound. Some words have one syllable. Some words have more than one syllable. Listen to the word* turkey. *Clap with me on each syllable. How many claps? (*two*) The word has two syllables. Can you find more two-syllable words? (*people, others, outside, farmers, horses*)*

Focus on Fluency
Remind children that it is important to read at an appropriate rate. A good rate is close to the one we use when we talk. Model reading paragraph 1 at different rates. Ask children to identify the best rate and tell why it is.

Foundational Skills Read Together

As you read along with the text, listen for long *a* words, long *i* words, and words spelled with *ar, ir, er, or,* or *ur.*

Farm Neighborhoods

1   Some people live in the city. Others live outside the city. They might live on a farm.

2   Some farmers raise cows. Some raise turkeys. Others have horses. The animals live in a barn. Some farmers grow corn. People and horses eat corn.

3   Vets might live near farms. They are animal doctors. Vets care for animals that are hurt. Some take care of big animals like cows. Others help care for small animals like hens.

4   Clerks sell things in stores. Some stores are near farms. Farmers need to buy things. A farmer might buy a shirt. She might buy plums to make pie. She might buy a tray to serve the pie.

> This vet takes care of large animals.

Focus on Phonological Awareness

Blending phonemes
Read the phonemes for each word below. Ask children to orally blend the words.

/f/ /ā/ /s/ (face)

/b/ /ē/ /k/ (beak)

/ch/ /ĕ/ /k/ (check)

/m/ /ū/ /l/ (mule)

Foundational Skills Reader 1

DIRECTIONS: Cut and fold the book.

Name _____

Who Am I?

1

I can bake a very big cake.
I can make a pie, too. Who am I?

3

I work with hammers.
I work with nails. Who am I?

8

I wear a white coat.
I make people feel better. Who am I?

6

(long a and long i)   Unit 7 ■ Reading Informational Text: Craft and Structure   **163**

OBJECTIVES

- **Read decodable text featuring long *a* words and long *i* words.**
- **Read along orally, using context to confirm or self-correct.**

Prepare to Read

Tell children that they will be reading an informational text about people and their jobs, or work they do. They can take the book home to share when they are done reading. Have them follow the directions to cut and fold the book.

Review Phonics Skills

Explain that this book features many words with long vowel sounds and two-syllable words that they learned about in the Read Together. Review the vowel spellings *a_e*, *ay*, *ai*, *i_e*, *ie*, and *igh*.

- *Remember that vowels can stand for a long or short sound. There are many spellings for long vowel sounds. Words can end in e or have a vowel team like* ai *or* ie.

- *Remember that words can have more than one syllable. We can clap to see how many syllables a word has. Breaking a long word into syllables helps us read it more easily.*

Introduce Reader 1

Divide the class into two groups. Assign each group to line 1 or 2. Have each group chorally read its corresponding line on each page as you read each line aloud.

Foundational Skills: Phonics Practice

Write the following words from Read Together and Foundational Skills Reader 1 on the board or on a chart. Have children practice reading the words.

Read Together long-vowel words: might, raise, take, like, pie, tray;
2-syllable words: people, city, others, outside, farmer, turkeys, horses, doctors

Foundational Skills Reader 1: long-vowel words: bake, cake, make, pie, nails, white, tie, smile, hay, night, bright, light, waves, save;
2-syllable words: very, hammers, people, better, horses, always, carry

Read with a Partner

Form heterogeneous pairs of children so that your stronger readers can help those who struggle. Allow each pair to decide how it wants to read the text together several times: chorally, alternating by sentences, or alternating by pages. Once the pairs are comfortable with one of their oral readings, have them record it for playing back later.

Focus on Fluency

Remind children that fluent readers reread to self-correct or confirm their understanding. Model fluency of the entire reader by using the Fluency Practice activity below.

Reading at Home

Once children are comfortable reading the book, send it home for children to read to family members.

Assess and Respond
If children have difficulty reading words with long vowels . . .
Then make a chart with all the different ways to spell long *a* and long *i*. List a sample word from the reader in each row, and then ask pairs of children to find more examples from the reader.

Foundational Skills Reader 1

DIRECTIONS: Cut and fold the book.

④ I grow hay for my horses to eat. I grow food for you. Who am I?

② I wear a wig and a funny tie. I make people smile. Who am I?

⑤ I swim in the waves. I save lives. Who am I?

③ I always work at night. I carry a bright light. Who am I?

fold   fold

Fluency: Use context to confirm or self-correct

164   Unit 7 ▪ Reading Informational Text: Craft and Structure

Foundational Skills: Fluency Practice

Explain to children that when reading, it is important to pay attention to the words and meaning. If they are unsure of the meaning or they have misread a word, then they should go back and reread. Model reading a page of "Who Am I?" Mispronounce one of the words, and then go back to reread and self-correct. Additional fluency passages and activities can be found at **sadlierconnect.com**.

Foundational Skills Reader 2

DIRECTIONS: Cut and fold the book.

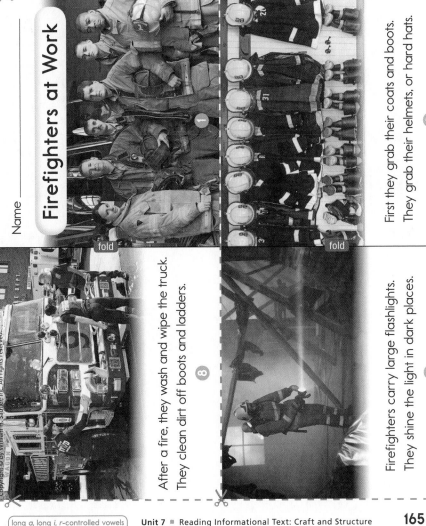

Name

Firefighters at Work

fold

First they grab their coats and boots.
They grab their helmets, or hard hats.

fold

After a fire, they wash and wipe the truck.
They clean dirt off boots and ladders.

Firefighters carry large flashlights.
They shine the light in dark places.

long a, long i, r-controlled vowels

Unit 7 ■ Reading Informational Text: Craft and Structure **165**

Foundational Skills: Phonics Practice

Write the following words from Foundational Skills Reader 2 on the board or on a chart. Have children practice reading the words.

word with r-controlled vowels: first, hard, after, dirt, dark, or, for, horn, cars, are, enter, hurt

long a words: places, way, aid, brave

long i words: shine, light, wipe

OBJECTIVES

- **Read decodable text featuring r-controlled vowels, long a words, and long i words.**
- **Read along orally, using context to confirm or self-correct.**

Prepare to Read

Tell children that the next informational text they will be reading tells them about firefighters. Once they have read the book, they can take it home to share. Have them follow the directions to cut and fold the book.

Review Phonics Skills

Review r-controlled vowels (ar, or, ir, er, and ur):

- *Remember that when* r *comes after a vowel, it changes the sound of the vowel. Say these words with me: car, store, bird, her, fur.*
- *What words do you see in this reader that have a vowel followed by an* r? (first, hard, after, dirt, dark, for, fire, cars, are, enter)
- *This book also has long* a *words and long* i *words. What long* a *spellings do you see? What long* i *spellings do you see?*

Introduce Reader 2

Have the class echo read the book with you. You read a sentence, and then they echo the sentence. When reading, be sure to model rereading to self-correct by pausing after a sentence and saying: *That didn't make sense. Let me reread that sentence.*

Read with a Partner

Form heterogeneous pairs of children so that your stronger readers can help those who struggle. Allow each pair to decide how it wants to read the text together several times: chorally, alternating by sentences, or alternating by pages. Once the pairs are comfortable with one of their oral readings, have them record it for playing back later.

Focus on Fluency

Remind children that fluent readers reread to self-correct. Ask them to explain why rereading is important. (This helps readers understand and make sense of what they are reading.) Focus children's attention on page 166. Ask them to follow along with their eyes and raise their hands when you misread a word and should reread. Model returning to the beginning of the sentence to reread it.

Reading at Home

Once children are comfortable reading the book, send it home for children to read to family members.

Assess and Respond
If children have difficulty decoding words with *r*-controlled vowels . . .
Then write pairs of words with the same vowel—one with an *r*-controlled vowel and one without (e.g., *car* and *cat*). Write a pair for each vowel. Read each word slowly and have children repeat the words after you.

Foundational Skills Reader 2

DIRECTIONS: Cut and fold the book.

The fire alarm rings at the firehouse. Firefighters get ready for the fire.

The fire truck has a loud horn! Cars move out of the way.

Firefighters help people who are hurt. They give them help called first aid.

They are brave. They enter the house that is on fire.

Fluency: Use context to confirm or self-correct

Foundational Skills: Fluency Practice

Remind children that when reading it is important to pay attention to the words and meaning. If they are unsure of the meaning or they have misread a word, then they should go back and reread. Model reading a page of "Firefighters at Work" by replacing the word "helmet" for "helpers." At the end of the sentence say, "That doesn't sound right." Then model rereading to self-correct. Additional fluency passages and activities can be found at **sadlierconnect.com**.

Close Reading

Who Works at Night?

(Genre: Informational Text)

1 Many people work at night. They work while you are sleeping. Who works at night?

Bakers

2 Many bakers work at night. They bake bread. The bread is ready in the morning. It is fresh, or just baked. It is not dried out.

Truck Drivers

3 People drive trucks at night. Some drive bread to stores. Some drive mail. They drive a long way in the dark. It is hard to see at night. Drivers must be very careful.

Truck drivers may drive all through the night.

167

OBJECTIVES

- **Ask and answer questions to figure out the meaning of words.**
- **Use text features to find information.**
- **Distinguish between information given in pictures and information given by words.**

Genre: Informational Text

Remind children that informational text presents facts. People usually read informational text to learn something about a topic. Instruct children to pay attention to the headings to help them identify the key facts and details to remember.

Path Options

You may wish to have children read the text independently and apply the skills learned in this unit. Or you may wish to do a close reading with children. If so, use the supports provided on these pages. As a third option, set up a buddy system with some heterogeneous and some homogenous pairs to fit the needs of your class. Regardless, children should read the text more than once to facilitate understanding and to be able to answer the Comprehension Check questions correctly.

Support English Language Learners

If you do decide to have children read the text on their own, be aware that English language learners may struggle to read it independently. You may wish to build background knowledge by showing the children photographs of each profession and discuss what each person does at work, embedding key concepts.

Support First Reading

Circulate to check children's understanding. As needed, use the following comprehension and strategy check-ins to support basic understanding of the selection as children read.

Check-in Questions

- **page 167** *Which section does the picture on page 167 describe?* (truck drivers)

- **page 167** *What do you learn about truck drivers from the picture and caption on page 167?* (Truck drivers work at night sometimes.)

- **page 168** *What base word helps you figure out the word* easier *in paragraph 6?* (easy)

Review: Understanding Word Meanings

Remind children that asking and answering questions helps them to find the meaning of words in a text. Have them turn to talk with a partner and ask and answer questions about a tricky word, such as "Are there any clues near the word?" "Does the author give an example?" "Do I recognize a base word?"

Review: Using Text Features

Explain that strategic readers pay attention to text features such as headings and captions. Ask them to reread paragraph 5. Ask: *How does the heading help you understand what this section is about?* (It lets me know that this section will describe what clerks do.) *What information does the first caption give about clerks?* (It tells me that they put out cans and jars at night.)

Close Reading

Nurses

4   Many nurses work at night. People can get sick at night. People can get hurt at night. Their families need help. Nurses are helpful. They take care of all these people.

Clerks

5   Some clerks work at night in stores. They fill up empty shelves. They put out more jars of food. They put out more cans. They put out more bags and boxes of food, too.

Clerks fill empty shelves with cans and jars at night.

Cleaners

6   Some people clean streets at night. Roads have fewer cars on the road then. This makes the job easier. Some people clean buildings at night. They clean dirt from floors. They wash germs from sinks. Cleaning is easier when a building has just a few people.

Street cleaners drive large machines at night.

168   Unit 7 ■ Reading Informational Text: Craft and Structure

---

Differentiate Instruction

For children who struggle to identify and use text features, provide two different highlighters to pairs of children. Have partners highlight the headings in one color and the captions in another. Then have the children use these to predict what each section will be about.

Close Reading

Firefighters

7   Do fires start only in the day? No! A fire can start at any time. A forest fire can burn through the day and night. Some fires restart after firefighters put them out. That is why firefighters work at night.

A building can burn at night.

Comprehension Check

1. Which heading helps you find facts about helpers who care for sick people?

   a. Cleaners

   (b.) Nurses

   c. Clerks

2. Which base word helps you figure out the meaning of the word *families* in paragraph 4?

   (a.) family

   b. fame

   c. farm

Strategic Reading

Support all readers by reminding them of the importance of figuring out unknown words. Explain that as they read they may ask themselves questions to find context clues and base words to help them figure out the word meaning. They should not just skip over a tricky word. If they need more help, they can consult a dictionary or glossary to find the meaning.

Review: Distinguishing Words and Pictures

Remind children that when you read a text it is important to pay attention to the words and the pictures. Ask children to explain what information they learn from the photograph on page 169. (I learn that buildings can burn at night.)

Multiple Readings for Critical Comprehension

Have children reread this selection, and pose questions that focus on critical comprehension.

- *Why are some jobs such as cleaning and clerks performed at night?* (Streets and stores are less busy.)

- *What might be a challenge of working at night?* (The workers might be sleepy. They need special equipment, like lights for firefighters.)

Comprehension Check

Score children's understanding of unit skills and texts using the Comprehension Check on this page and the next. Use the children's total score to determine their readiness for the Unit 7 Review on page 173.

Multiple-Choice Questions: *1 point each*

1. Answer choice **B** is correct because nurses are community helpers that care for sick people.

2. Answer choice **A** is correct. The base word *family* is found in the word, *families*. The *y* at the end is changed to an *i* and the ending *-es* is added.

Short-Answer Questions:
2 points each

Item 3 Rubric

2	Children relate that street cleaners drive large machines and work at night.
1	Children tell one fact but not both.
0	Children cannot tell a fact from the caption.

Item 4 Rubric

2	Children tell at least one fact from the text and at least one fact from the picture.
1	Children tell either a fact from the text or a fact from the picture but not both.
0	Children are unable to tell a fact about fires at night.

Theme Wrap-Up

Lead children in a discussion on what they have learned from the theme: "In My Neighborhood." Ask them to share what they learned about people and places found in neighborhoods.

Close Reading

3. What do you learn about street cleaners from the caption on page 168?

Sample answer: I learn that street cleaners drive large machines to clean streets at night.

4. What do you learn about fires from paragraph 7 on page 169? What do you learn from the picture?

Sample answer: In the paragraph, I learn that forest fires burn day and night. In the picture and caption, I learn that buildings burn at night, too.

170   Unit 7 ▪ Reading Informational Text: Craft and Structure

---

Assess and Respond (pages 31–34)

If	Then
Children scored 0–2 points, they are **Developing** their understanding of unit skills …	Provide children with reading support and more intensive modeling of skills.
Children scored 3–4 points, they are **Improving** their understanding of unit skills …	Use children's scores to target areas that are weak and review those specific skills.
Children scored 5–6 points, they are **Proficient** in their understanding of unit skills …	Have these children move on. They are ready for the formal assessment.

Connect Across Texts

Compare and Contrast Texts

Think about the words and pictures in these texts. Be ready to talk about them.

Neighborhood Helpers

Fire Drills

Who Works at Night?

Return to the Essential Question

How do the parts of an informational text work together?

Talk about the words and pictures in these texts. What did you learn about neighborhoods from the words? What did you learn from the pictures?

Compare and Contrast Texts

Read aloud the directions on page 171. Then provide some information about each of the featured texts, to help children as they recall the key details.

The selection "Neighborhood Helpers" is about different community helpers. Do you remember some people who help in your community? (firefighters, librarians, doctors, bus drivers, mail carriers, trash collectors, farmers, and teachers)

The selection "Fire Drills" is a procedural text. It explains what to do in a fire drill. Do you remember the first step? (When you hear the fire alarm, stop what you are doing.)

The selection "Who Works at Night?" is an informational text that describes different jobs people do at night. What are some night jobs? (firefighter, truck driver, baker, nurse, clerk, and cleaner)

Give children time to organize their thoughts about the texts. Remind them to ask questions about any confusion they have about the texts before you begin. Then lead the Essential Question discussion.

Support Essential Question Discussion

Read the Essential Question aloud. Then prompt children to share their ideas about their selections. Remind children to raise their hands and wait for you to call on them.

- *How does seeing pictures of neighborhoods help you understand them?*
- *How do captions work together with the pictures?*

Discussion Skills

As children work on the Essential Question prompts, encourage them to ask questions to understand the reasoning behind their answers. They might give examples or explain what text features or evidence in the text supports their answer. Encourage the children to ask questions such as the following:

Why do you think that?

How did you arrive at that answer?

Say more about that!

OBJECTIVE
Use *-ful* and *re-* as clues to word meaning.

Guided Instruction

Read aloud the Guided Instruction section on page 172. Be sure children understand that prefixes and suffixes are word parts added to a base word that change its meaning. Ask: *What does the prefix re-mean?* (again) *What does the suffix -ful mean?* (full of)

Guided Practice

Explain that children are to write the new word and its meaning. Direct children to refer to the chart if they need help figuring out the meaning.

Independent Practice

If children struggle to find the correct word, have them read the sentences aloud, trying each word.

Apply to Reading

Have children return to "Who Works at Night?" on page 168. Point to the word *helpful* in paragraph 4. Ask children to identify the suffix or prefix and the base word. Then ask them to turn to a partner and discuss what a person who is *helpful* might do. Remind children that the suffix *-ful* means "full of." (A helpful person is full of help for other people.)

In this and all discussions, encourage children to use words such as *because* and *so* to explain relationships between or among ideas.

Language

Prefix *re* and Suffix *ful*

Guided Instruction A **prefix** is a word part. It is added to the beginning of a word. A **suffix** is a word part added to the end of a word. Read this sentence from "Fire Drills":

She might recount the children.

Recount means "count again." It has the prefix **re.** The prefix **re** means "again." The suffix **ful** means "full of."

Word Part	Word	New Word	Meaning
re	play	replay	play again
ful	joy	joyful	full of joy

Guided Practice Join the prefix or suffix to the word. Write the new word and the meaning.

	New Word	Meaning
1. re + heat =	reheat	heat again
2. pain + ful =	painful	full of pain

Independent Practice Complete each sentence with the correct word above.

3. Falling off your bike can be _____painful_____.

4. I will _____reheat_____ my soup.

Support English Language Learners

Guide children in understanding the meanings of words with the prefix *re-* and the suffix *-ful.* Write words such as *reheat, refill, cheerful,* and *colorful* on index cards. Provide picture cards to illustrate each word. Let the children work with partners to read the words and match it to the action. Then have children explain the meaning of each word part, using the pictures to illustrate.

Unit 7 Review

Read along with the following selection.

Who Works in School?

Glass   Paper

Glass bottles can also be reused.

Teachers

1   Some teachers help you write. Others help you create, or make, (colorful) art. Others teach you to play games.

Nurses

2   Nurses help when you get hurt in school. Nurses can clean cuts. They can help if you have a |pain|.

Cleaners

3   Some people keep your school clean. Some might work at night. They sweep dirt from the floor. They collect paper. You can reuse the paper. That means you can use it again.

Fill in the circle next to the correct choice.

1. Which heading would you use to find information about the people who help you when you get hurt?

○ Teachers   ● Nurses   ○ Cleaners

Unit 7 ■ Reading Informational Text: Craft and Structure   **173**

Self-Assessment: Progress Check

Have children revisit the Progress Check on page 145 and respond to the questions again. Ask them to compare Before and After responses.

Review children's responses to get an idea of their confidence with the unit skills. Based on these responses and on children's success with the Comprehension Check in Close Reading, you may want to conduct additional review and practice of one or more of the unit skills.

Unit Summary

Children have had instruction and practice in reading different types of informational texts that provide facts and opinions about neighborhoods. Children have learned to ask and answer questions to help them determine the meaning of an unknown word in a text. Children have used text features such as headings and captions to help them locate information. They have distinguished between facts learned from the words and facts learned from the illustrations in a text. They have progressed toward completing an independent close reading of text, practiced applying the concepts across texts, and used context clues and word parts to refine their understanding of words.

They have read long *a* and long *i* words and words with and *r*-controlled vowels. They should be well prepared for the review section.

Introduce the Review

Explain to children that they will read a new passage along with you that is related to the unit's theme and the selections they have already read. Then they will answer the questions on page 173 and 174.

Answer Explanations

Scoring: Items 1, 2, 3, 4, 5, and 6 on pages 173 and 174 are worth 1 point each. Explanations for the correct answers are given below and on the next page. Also see the rubrics on the next page for guidance in scoring the short-answer questions on page 174.

1. The heading *Nurses* would contain information about people who help when you are hurt.

2. The word *create* does not have a base word or affix, so the first answer is the best response.

Answer Explanations

3. Both *car* and *art* have *ar*.

4. The word *reuse* means "to use again."

5. The word *colorful* has the suffix *-ful*.

6. *Pain* has the long *a* sound.

Item 7 Rubric

2	Child identifies two things learned from the heading.
1	Child identifies one thing learned from the heading.
0	Child cannot identify anything learned under the heading.

Item 8 Rubric

2	Child identifies the picture and explains the information in the paragraph.
1	Child identifies the picture or explains the information in the paragraph, but not both.
0	Child cannot identify the picture or explain the information in the paragraph.

Unit 7 Review

2. Which question would help you understand the meaning of *create* in paragraph one on page 173?

- ● Are there words in the sentence that give the meaning of *create*?
- ○ Is there a base word in *create* that I know?

3. Underline the word in paragraph 1 that has sounds like those in *car*.

4. What is the meaning of *reuse* in paragraph 3?

Sample answer: Use again.

5. Circle a word in paragraph 1 that has the suffix *ful*.

6. Put a box around the word in paragraph 2 that has the vowel sound in *make*.

7. What do you learn under the heading "Teachers"?

Sample answer: Teachers help me write. They help me

make art and play games.

8. What do you learn from the picture and paragraph 3 on page 173?

Sample answer: Glass bottles and paper can be reused.

Analyze Scores

8–10 pts Strong	Child has a good grasp of the skills and concepts taught in this unit. Point out any mistakes the child has made and explain the correct answers if necessary.
4–7 pts Progressing	Child is struggling with some skills or concepts. Identify the specific skills that are problematic to target a review of instruction.
0–3 pts Emerging	Child has difficulty understanding the skills and concepts taught in this unit. Child may need further instruction with a higher level of support and detailed explanation of the unit's skills and concepts.

Introducing UNIT 8

In this unit, you will choose a favorite place in your neighborhood. Then you will write an opinion piece about it. An opinion piece gives a writer's opinion and reasons that back up that opinion. It ends by telling the opinion again. Begin your opinion piece by telling what your favorite place is. Give reasons to support your opinion. In your ending, share your opinion again.

Progress Check *Can I?*

Before Unit 8 → / After Unit 8 →

- [ ] Write an opinion about a topic. [ ]
- [ ] Give a reason to support my opinion. [ ]
- [ ] Write an ending for my opinion piece. [ ]
- [ ] Use words that help to tell when or where. [ ]
- [ ] Use words that connect ideas. [ ]

Unit 8 ▪ Text Types and Purposes: Write Opinion Pieces

Progress Check

The Progress Check is a self-assessment feature that children can use to gauge their own progress. Research shows that when children take accountability for their own learning, their motivation increases.

Before children begin work on Unit 8, have them check the boxes next to any item that they feel they can do well. Explain that it is fine if they don't check any of the boxes. Tell them that they will have an opportunity to learn about and practice all of these items while studying the unit. Let them know that near the end of the unit they will have a chance to reconsider how well they can do each item on the list.

Before children begin their Unit 8 Review on page 188, have them revisit this page. You can use this information to work with children on any items they don't understand before they tackle the Review.

HOME ◆ CONNECT...

The Home Connect feature is a way to keep parents or other adult family members apprised of what their children are learning. The key learning objectives are listed, and some ideas for related activities and discussions are included.

Explain to children that they can share the Home Connect page with their parents or other adult family members in their home.

Encourage children and their parents or other family members to share their experiences using the suggestions on the Home Connect page.

HOME ◆ CONNECT...

In this unit, your child will learn to write an **opinion piece** about his or her neighborhood. Your child will be asked to choose a neighborhood place to write about. When you are out in your neighborhood, talk about your child's favorite places, such as the library, a local museum, the park, or the playground. Talk with your child about why each place is important.

An opinion piece tells how a writer feels about a topic. When writing an opinion piece, writers give reasons to support their ideas and encourage others to agree with them. Talk to your child about the difference between a fact about his or her neighborhood and an opinion about the place. Ask questions such as *What is your opinion about this place in our neighborhood? Why do you think that?* Share your opinion about a neighborhood place with your child and give reasons to support your opinion.

Conversation Starter: Use facts and opinions to talk about favorite fruits with your child. Model stating a fact about your favorite fruit, such as *A blueberry is round. It grows on a bush.* Then model giving an opinion, such as *Blueberries are delicious. They are the best fruit.* Ask your child to give a fact and an opinion about his or her favorite fruit. Then, repeat the activity for favorite vegetables.

IN THIS UNIT, YOUR CHILD WILL...

- Form an opinion about a favorite neighborhood place.
- Write an opinion piece that includes reasons to support the opinion.
- Write a conclusion.
- Learn specific language skills and use them in writing an opinion piece:
  - Use prepositions such as *after, over,* and *during* to add details.
  - Use conjunctions such as *and, but,* and *or* to add and connect ideas.

WAYS TO HELP YOUR CHILD

Provide opportunities for your child to express opinions about a variety of topics. For example, when you discuss your child's day, ask for his or her opinion about activities, books, videos, games, and so on. Encourage your child to give reasons for his or her opinions.

ONLINE
For more Home Connect activities, continue online at sadlierconnect.com

176 Unit 8 ▪ Text Types and Purposes: Write Opinion Pieces

UNIT PLANNER

Theme: In My Neighborhood Curriculum Connection: Social Studies	Focus
WRITING MODEL pp. 178–179	*The Park*
WRITING ACTIVITY pp. 180–183	**ORGANIZATIONAL STRUCTURE:** Web
LANGUAGE MINI-LESSONS pp. 184–185	• Prepositions • Conjunctions
SPEAKING AND LISTENING pp. 186–187	• Share Your Writing • Be a Good Listener • Return to the Essential Question
UNIT 8 REVIEW p. 188	Language Skills Summary

Objective(s)

Write an opinion piece about a favorite neighborhood place, stating an opinion at the beginning, supporting the opinion with reasons, and ending with a concluding statement.

- Plan an opinion piece about a favorite neighborhood place, providing an opinion supported by reasons.

- Draw pictures, complete sentence starters, and compose an opinion piece about a favorite neighborhood place.

- Use prepositions to add details to writing.

- Use conjunctions to connect ideas.

- Orally present an opinion piece, answering questions after the presentation.

- Participate respectfully in presentations as an active listener who asks questions and responds to the comments of others.

Unit Assessment

- Unit 8 Review *p. 188*

Additional Assessment Options

- Performance Task 1 *pp. 141–144*
  ALSO ONLINE

- Performance Task 2 *pp. 259–262*
  ALSO ONLINE

Optional Purchase:

- iProgress Monitor **ONLINE**

- Progress Monitor Student Benchmark Assessment Booklet

ONLINE Digital Resources

- Home Connect Activities
- Additional Practice
- Teacher Resources
- iProgress Monitor (optional purchase)

Go to SadlierConnect.com to access your Digital Resources.

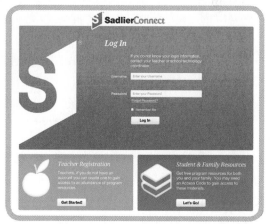

For more detailed instructions see page T3.

177B

LEARNING PROGRESSIONS

In this unit, children will learn to write an opinion text about a favorite place in their neighborhoods. The text will include illustrations and sentences. In order to learn the skills necessary to craft an opinion text, children will further develop skills learned in kindergarten. They should be encouraged to retain these skills, as they will continue to build on them in second grade.

Introducing the Topic

- Proficient kindergarteners are able to state an opinion or preference about a book or other topic.

- First-graders understand their topic and state an opinion on the topic.

- In second grade, children will show proficiency in understanding their topic and clearly stating an opinion.

Providing Reasons

- Kindergarteners are not expected to supply reasons to support their opinions.

- Proficient first-graders should be able to supply reasons to support their opinions.

- The expectation continues for second graders as they supply several reasons to support their opinions and use linking words to connect the opinion and their reasons.

Providing Closure

- Kindergarteners are not expected to provide closure when writing opinion texts.

- By the end of first grade, children are expected to provide some sense of closure at the end of an opinion text.

- Then as second graders, children should understand that the ending of an opinion text should have a concluding statement or section.

Text Types and Purposes: Write Opinion Pieces

UNIT 8

Essential Question:
How do writers present an opinion?

Essential Question:
How do writers present an opinion?

Children will learn to write an opinion piece that states a clear opinion, and support that opinion with reasons.

Theme: In My Neighborhood

Children will continue to think about the theme introduced in Unit 7, In My Neighborhood, as they read an opinion piece model about why the park is a child's favorite place in her neighborhood.

Curriculum Connection: Social Studies

In crafting an opinion piece about a place in their neighborhood, children will use what they know about places in their neighborhood to choose a location.

Connect Reading to Writing

Remind children that in Unit 7, they read an opinion piece about a girl requesting that a dog park be built in her neighborhood. Now, children will have a chance to write an opinion piece about something in their neighborhood.

Writing Handbook

To assist children in writing an opinion piece, use the *Writing Handbook* on pages 263–268 to guide children through the writing process. The *Writing Handbook* gives children detailed instruction on planning, drafting, revising, and editing their writing, as well as providing tips on producing and publishing.

Have children turn to page 263 and review all of the parts of the *Writing Handbook*. Then lead them through the suggestions on page 264 on selecting a topic and organizing their information. Once children get started on their opinion text, return to the *Writing Handbook* for information on each part of the writing process.

OBJECTIVE

Write an opinion piece about a favorite neighborhood place, stating an opinion at the beginning, supporting the opinion with reasons, and ending with a concluding statement.

Introduce: Organizational Structure

As you read the model together, point out how the author states her opinion at the beginning, next supports her opinion with reasons (one reason per paragraph), and then concludes by restating her opinion.

Analyze a Student Model

Topic and Opinion: Explain that the title of a text often gives clues about its topic. Read the title and the first sentence with children. Ask: *What is Carla's topic?* (the park) Explain that in an opinion piece, it is important to clearly state your opinion. Point out that it may not be the first sentence, but it will be near the beginning. Ask: *What is Carla's opinion about the park?* (She thinks it is the best place in the neighborhood.)

Reasons: Teach children that in an opinion piece, the writer tries to get readers to agree with the opinion. One way to achieve this agreement is to give reasons that support the opinion. Read the first paragraph aloud. Ask: *Which sentences give Carla's reasons for thinking that the park is the best place in her neighborhood?* (sentences 3 and 4) Have a volunteer read the sentences aloud.

Read a Student Model

Carla wrote an opinion piece about a neighborhood place. Notice how Carla states her opinion. See the reasons she gives for that opinion. Notice how Carla begins and ends her opinion piece.

The Park

Do you like to play at the park? It is the best place. You can meet people there and make new friends, too. You can spend time with your family.

I go to the park with my family.

Teacher Talk: Find Topic, Opinion, and Reasons

Explain that the topic is what the opinion piece is about. Have children box the topic. Ask: *What is Carla's opinion about the park?* Have children circle her opinion. Explain that Carla gives reasons to support her opinion. Have children underline the first reason.

178 Unit 8 ■ Text Types and Purposes: Write Opinion Pieces

Genre: Opinion Text

Emphasize that an opinion piece communicates something that the writer truly cares about. Most often, the writer of an opinion piece wants the reader to be convinced that the opinion is correct or the best. Many writers of opinion pieces state the opinion clearly at the beginning and supply *convincing* reasons that are connected to the opinion. Since the writer wants the reader to share the opinion, the writer usually mentions it again at the end.

We run and play at the park.

The park has a playground. It has a running track and fields, too. We run and play at the park to stay healthy.

I can be with my family or friends. The park is my favorite place.

Teacher Talk: Find a Conclusion

Explain that an author restates his or her opinion in the conclusion. Have children circle the ending sentence. Ask: *What words in the conclusion mean the same as "the best place" in the beginning?* Have children underline the words.

Unit 8 ■ Text Types and Purposes: Write Opinion Pieces **179**

Analyze a Student Model

Reasons: Point out that a good opinion piece gives more than one reason for the opinion. Point out that on page 179, Carla describes the park. She also gives another reason for her opinion. Ask: *What reason does Carla give?* ("We run and play at the park to stay healthy.") Have children reread the first paragraph on page 179.

Conclusion: Point out that the piece ends with a concluding statement. Remind children that the concluding statement reminds the reader of the opinion. However, it does not use the same words as the beginning. Ask: *How are the second and last sentences the same?* (They both say that Carla likes the park.) *How are they different?* (The concluding sentence tells that the park is her favorite place, while the beginning says it is the best place.)

Visual Literacy

Pictures: Ask children what the photos show and how they help the writer support her opinion. Point out that photos not only make the piece more interesting but also help show the reasons. Ask: *Which reasons do these photos show?* (The first shows the reason "You can spend time with your family." The second photo shows the reason "We run and play at the park to stay healthy.")

Support English Language Learners

You can support English language learners by giving them sentence frames to organize their writing. Provide the sentence frames below and encourage children to use these to state their opinion and supporting reasons.

I like _____.

I think _____ is _____ (great / fun / etc.).

My favorite place is _____.

You can _____ there.

You can also _____ there.

Model: Organizational Structure

Explain that strong opinion pieces start with good planning. In planning, the writer decides on an opinion and good reasons for the opinion. The writer puts the opinion and the reasons in an order that will help readers understand the writer's ideas.

Discuss the organizer that Carla completed when planning her opinion piece.

- Point out the opinion in the top oval. Say: *Notice that she wrote her opinion in a complete sentence. The opinion is clearly stated.*

- Point out the two circles below the opinion. Say: *A good opinion text gives at least two reasons for the opinion. Notice that Carla has written two reasons: one in each circle. Using the web helped her to write an opinion piece that is easy for readers to follow and helps the reader to understand why Carla thinks the park is so special.*

Peer Collaboration

Have children work in pairs or groups of three to compare Carla's organizer to her writing. They should find where Carla stated her opinion in the beginning and in the ending. Then they should locate Carla's reasons in the text. This will help them see how an opinion piece is structured with an introduction, body that gives and explains reasons, and a conclusion. It also reinforces the value of using an organizer to gather and arrange their ideas.

Write Opinion Pieces

Carla used this web to plan her opinion piece. She wrote her opinion in the top circle. Then she wrote two reasons to support her opinion in the other circles.

Opinion
The park is the best place in my neighborhood.

Reason
You can meet people and make new friends.

Reason
You can play there and stay healthy.

180 Unit 8 ■ Text Types and Purposes: Write Opinion Pieces

Review: Distinguish between Pictures and Text

Children learned how to distinguish between information provided in pictures and information provided by words in Unit 7. Remind children that both the pictures and the words in a text give important information. Guide children in understanding that Carla gives her reasons in words, but she also includes photographs to help show her reasons.

Plan Your Draft

Use a web like Carla's to plan your opinion piece.
Write your opinion about a place in your neighborhood.
Then write two reasons to support your opinion.

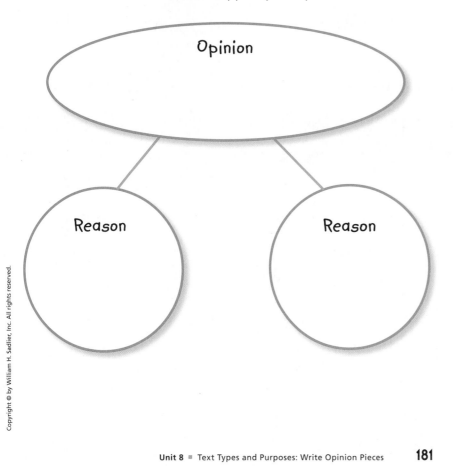

Unit 8 ■ Text Types and Purposes: Write Opinion Pieces **181**

OBJECTIVE
Plan an opinion piece about a favorite neighborhood place, providing an opinion supported by reasons.

Introduce the Writing Process

Explain that writing is a process with several steps. *The first step is planning. The web that Carla filled out helped her to plan her writing.* Tell children that they will fill out a web to plan their opinion pieces.

Plan an Opinion Piece

Think About Organization

Remind children of how Carla organized her opinion piece. Her opinion appears in the beginning. Then she gives reasons to support her opinion. Finally, she ends the piece with a concluding sentence that reminds readers of what her opinion is. Children should follow this organization for their texts.

Plan

Explain to children that they will complete the web to help them plan their writing. Ask leading questions for each circle in the web. Encourage children to draw and write notes or complete sentences in the circles. Point to the top oval. Ask: *What neighborhood place is your topic? What is your opinion about this topic?* Remind children that they need to clearly state their opinions about their chosen places. Point to the remaining circles. Ask: *What makes this place so special?* Circulate to provide individual support as children complete the organizer.

Peer Collaboration

Have pairs use their webs to talk through their opinion piece in preparation for writing. Verbalizing their ideas should help them generate language they can use in their writing.

Provide prompts such as the following to guide their discussion:

Is the opinion clear?

Is there another reason that will make readers share the opinion?

What words can be added to make readers agree with the opinion?

OBJECTIVE

Draw pictures, complete sentence starters, and compose an opinion piece about a favorite neighborhood place.

Draft an Opinion Piece

Point out the different areas provided for children to create their opinion piece: an area for illustrations, a sentence starter, and then write-on lines. Have children refer to their planning web. Guide children in completing the sentence starter. Say: *Remember that the beginning of your opinion piece should have your opinion. How can you finish this sentence starter to tell which place in your neighborhood is your favorite?* Then ask: *Why is this place your favorite?* Direct the children to find the web sections that contain their reasons. Guide children to write about their reasons. Say: *After you have given and explained your reasons, you should write an ending that reminds the reader of your opinion. How can you write your opinion in a different way?*

As children write their drafts, circulate to observe their development of spelling skills. Observe to see if they are learning to spell irregular words and words with common spelling patterns such as CVC and CVCe. In addition, monitor children's ability to draw upon their knowledge of letter sounds to spell untaught words. Provide additional instruction and practice as necessary.

Write Opinion Pieces

Write Your Opinion Piece

In the boxes on pages 182–183, draw pictures of a place in your neighborhood. Write your opinion about the place. Give two reasons that tell why you have that opinion.

Then use your chart on page 181 to help you as you write. Start by completing the sentence below.

In my neighborhood, the <u>Sample answer: school</u>

<u>playground is a place to have fun</u>

_____.

Differentiate Instruction

Some children may need support in articulating their reasons. For children who struggle, you may ask them probing questions such as the following about their favorite place.

Why do you like this place?

What do you do when you visit?

For emergent readers, you may want to provide sentence prompts such as:

I like _____.

You can _____ there.

_____

Answers will vary. Opinion pieces should clearly

introduce the topic, state an opinion about a favorite

neighborhood place, include two reasons to support

that opinion, and include a conclusion that

restates the opinion

_____

_____

_____

Unit 8 ■ Text Types and Purposes: Write Opinion Pieces **183**

Revise and Edit: Peer Collaboration

Once children have finished their draft, have partners read their draft to each other and suggest revisions. Explain that they should ask each other questions to make sure everything is clear. Partners might suggest words to describe the place, reasons that can be added, or sentences to delete that are not about the topic.

Partners can then read each other's revisions and make further suggestions for ways to improve the draft if needed.

Opinion Piece Rubric

4	The piece includes an opinion that is clearly stated at the beginning and end, and reasons that support the topic are presented in well-developed paragraphs.
3	The piece has the elements listed under "4" above, though they are executed less successfully.
2	The piece is missing one or more of the required elements.
1	The piece is unfinished or shows a minimal understanding of required elements.

Assess and Respond

If children have difficulty writing a conclusion . . .

Then pair them with a partner. Ask the children to brainstorm three different ways to restate the opinion using different words and then choose the one they like the best to use.

Digital Connection

Demonstrate for children how to conduct an Internet search to find the Web site for their neighborhood place. They may visit the parks and recreation site or city government site to find specific information about their location. As children draft their opinion piece and move into publishing, they can use these sources in their reasons to list features of a neighborhood place. Then, when publishing, they can use photographs from the sources to provide a picture of their location.

OBJECTIVE
Use prepositions to add details to writing.

Guided Instruction

Explain that each word in a sentence does a job. Read aloud the introduction and the first example sentence. Then point out the prepositional phrase, "at the park" and the preposition, *at*. Explain that "at the park" adds a detail because it tells where the speaker runs and plays. Read the sentence again, changing the prepositional phrase to "until lunch." Point out that "until lunch" tells when the speaker runs and plays.

Guided and Independent Practice

Point out that for items 1 through 3, children will add a word from the word box to tell when or where. For children who need more support, have them read the sentence with each word choice.

For items 4 through 6, children should complete the sentences by adding words after the word in dark type. To support children with item 6, brainstorm a list of options that could correctly complete the sentence.

Prepositions

Guided Instruction Some words help you add details to your writing. They help answer the questions **When?** and **Where?**

*We run and play **at** the park.*

*Kim is **inside** the library.*

Guided and Independent Practice Complete each sentence with a word from the box.

| after during over |

1. I can climb _____over_____ the stone wall.

2. Our class plays kickball _____during_____ recess.

3. We can see stars _____after_____ it is dark.

Use the word in dark print to add a detail to the sentence.

4. We walked **across** _Sample answer: the street_ .

5. I go outside **after** _Sample answer: lunch_ .

6. On _Sample answer: Tuesday_ , we work in our garden.

Support English Language Learners

English language learners may need extra support with prepositions because many languages do not use prepositions in the same way that English does. To provide practice, use a stuffed animal. Place it in various locations such as on a desk, under a table, in the closet, and on the rug. Model for children how to describe where the stuffed animal is located and ask the children to echo back the description. After children are familiar with the syntax, allow them to place the animal and describe its location using a prepositional phrase.

Conjunctions

Guided Instruction You can use the words *and, but,* and *or* to connect ideas.

I help Mom, **and** *she gives me a dollar.*

I want a toy, **but** *I need more money.*

I can save the money, **or** *I can spend it.*

Guided and Independent Practice Underline the two ideas. Circle the connecting word.

1. Jon plays soccer,(and)his sister plays softball.

2. I like to go to story hour,(but)I can't go today.

3. We can go to the dog park now,(or)we can go later.

Use the word in dark print to add a connecting idea.

4. Come to the lake with us, **and** Sample answer: bring your bathing suit .

5. I wanted to play kickball, **but** Sample answer: it was raining .

6. We can walk to the library, **or** Sample answer: we can ride our bikes .

Unit 8 ■ Text Types and Purposes: Write Opinion Pieces **185**

OBJECTIVE
Use conjunctions to connect ideas.

Guided Instruction
Read aloud the introduction. Then read each example sentence aloud and point out the conjunction. Point out each independent clause to show how the conjunction joins the two shorter sentences, each of which is a complete idea.

Guided and Independent Practice
Point out that for items 1 through 3, children will do two things: underline each idea and circle the connecting word. For items 4 through 6, children will complete the sentence by adding a complete idea after the conjunction.

Assess and Respond

If children have difficulty using conjunctions . . .

Then write the first half of compound sentences on the board. Ask volunteers to suggest conjunctions and second parts of the sentences. Record as many suggestions for each sentence as time allows.

Differentiate Instruction

Provide additional practice with using conjunctions to join two shorter sentences. Write the conjunctions: *and, but,* and *or* on a sentence strip and cut out each conjunction. Write two independent clauses on sentence strips. Read the two sentences aloud. Then allow the children to work with a partner to try each conjunction and select the one that best joins the two ideas. Repeat with other pairs of independent clauses until children feel confident.

OBJECTIVE
Orally present an opinion piece, answering questions after the presentation.

Share Your Writing

Tell children they will present their opinion pieces by reading them aloud.

Remind children that as they share, they should speak clearly and use complete sentences. They should be ready to answer questions about their topic. They can prepare by thinking about questions they might ask about their topic.

Explain that answering questions is part of a presentation. Tell children not to worry about knowing the answer to every question—it is fine to say "I don't know the answer to that question." Tell children to answer each question in a complete sentence.

Get Ready

Have children practice by presenting to a partner. Guide them to apply the speaking skills they have learned: speak clearly, use complete sentences, look at your listeners, and be ready to answer questions.

Present

Have children give their presentations in small groups. Monitor to be sure children are applying the listening skills they have learned: wait their turn, listen carefully, ask questions, build on what others say, and tell if they agree or disagree.

Share Your Writing

You will present your opinion piece. Speak clearly and in complete sentences. Look at your listeners. Be ready to answer questions about your writing.

Our school needs a new playground!

186   Unit 8 ■ Text Types and Purposes: Write Opinion Pieces

Discussion Skills

As you monitor the small group presentations, encourage the groups to engage in multiple exchanges after each speaker presents. Give children the following question and sentence starter to support their discussions.

Would you tell me more about why you like _____?

I like that place, too, because _____.

Be a Good Listener

Remember to listen carefully when a classmate presents an opinion piece. As you listen, think about whether you agree with the opinion.

> I think we need a new playground, too. Ours is too small.

After each opinion piece, your class will discuss ideas. Think about what others say. Add your ideas and opinions to theirs.

Return to the Essential Question

How do writers present an opinion?

Think about these questions before the class discussion:

• What is an opinion?
• Why is it important to give reasons to support your opinion?

OBJECTIVE
Participate respectfully in presentations as an active listener who asks questions and responds to the comments of others.

Be a Good Listener

Remind children that good listeners look at and listen to the speaker. Later, during the discussion, they listen to what others have to say, too. When they agree with another person, they should say things like "I agree with that idea because _____." When they disagree, they should present their point of view respectfully.

Return to the Essential Question

Give children time to think about the questions before discussion. After discussing the questions, have children suggest strategies that can help writers present their opinions to others.

Support English Language Learners

English language learners who are at the beginning stage of language development may be supported with the use of prompts or sentence frames such as the ones below.

I like _____ too!

Can you tell me more about _____?

I would like to go to _____!

Introduce the Review

Explain to children that this review will give them a chance to use the language skills that they have studied and practiced in this unit. It will also give them a chance to share what they have learned about being a good speaker or listener.

Language Skills Summary

Let children know that they are going to use what they learned about prepositions and conjunctions. Briefly review the main concepts they learned. Ask:

- *What are some examples of prepositions?* (at, near, under, before, after) *What questions can prepositions answer?* (when, where)

- *What do we call words that connect two ideas in a sentence?* (conjunctions) *What are some conjunctions?* (and, but, or)

Answer Explanations

1–2. Tell children that the word they select must make sense in the sentence. Prepositions help to tell when or where and conjunctions connect two ideas.

3–5. Highlight the boldfaced words *after, or,* and *over*. Tell children that the sentences that they create must make sense.

Self-Assessment: Progress Check

Have children revisit the Progress Check on page 175 and compare their answers now with the answers they gave before completing Unit 8.

Unit 8 Review

Choose the correct answer. Fill in the circle.

1. We walk _____ the hill to get to town.

   ● over   ○ during   ○ after

2. I want a banana, _____ we don't have any.

   ○ or   ○ and   ● but

Use the word in dark print to add a detail or a connecting idea.

3. We play soccer **after** _____ Sample answer: school _____

_____

4. We can make pancakes, **or** _____ Sample answer: _____

we can make eggs

5. The cat climbed **over** _____ Sample answer: the fence _____

_____

Think about speaking and listening.

6. Write a sentence about what a good speaker or listener does.

Sample answer: A good listener adds to another person's

ideas when it is time to discuss

Test-Taking Tip

Remind children that it is important to check their work. Once they have chosen an answer, they should read the sentence again with their answer choice in the blank to make sure that the answer sounds right.

Introducing UNIT 9

In this unit, you will read stories from different places. You will learn how to connect pictures and details to understand characters, settings, and events. You will find ways that stories are alike and different. You will also find ways that you are like story characters—and how you are different from them.

Progress Check

The Progress Check is a self-assessment feature that children can use to gauge their own progress. Research shows that when children take accountability for their own learning, their motivation increases.

Before children begin work on Unit 9, have them check the boxes next to any item that they feel they can do well. Explain that it is fine if they don't check any of the boxes. Tell them that they will have an opportunity to learn about and practice all of these items while studying the unit. Let them know that near the end of the unit, they will have a chance to reconsider how well they can do each item on the list.

Before children begin their Unit 9 Review on page 213, have them revisit this page. Use this information to work with children on any items they don't understand before they tackle the Review.

Progress Check Can I?

Before Unit 9 / After Unit 9

- ☐ Use pictures and story details to describe characters, setting, or events. ☐
- ☐ Tell how characters are alike and different. ☐
- ☐ Use what I learn to read new words. ☐
- ☐ Tell how similar words are different in meaning. ☐

Unit 9 ■ Reading Literature: Integration of Knowledge and Ideas

Student Page 189

HOME ✦ CONNECT...

The Home Connect feature is a way to keep parents or other adult family members apprised of what their children are learning. The key learning objectives are listed, and some ideas for related activities and discussions are included.

Explain to children that they can share the Home Connect page with their parents or other adult family members in their home. Let children know how much time the class will be spending on this unit so they can plan their time accordingly at home.

Encourage children and their parents to share their experiences using the suggestions on the Home Connect page. You may wish to make a place to post some of this work.

HOME ✦ CONNECT...

In this unit, your child will **use illustrations and story details** to describe characters, setting, and events. Pictures often show details that are not in the text. They also may support the text. Have your child choose a favorite picture book. Together, look at one page and read the text. Then have your child look for and describe additional details in the illustration.

Your child will also learn to **compare and contrast** the experiences and adventures of characters from different stories. As you read a story together, ask if the main character reminds your child of another story character. Discuss how the character goes about solving the problem in the story. Talk about ways that other characters may have solved a similar problem.

In addition, your child will **make other types of connections,** including connections to other cultures. Select a simple story about a character from another culture. Discuss similarities and differences between your child's experiences and the world of the story—its characters, where it takes place, and what happens.

Activity: Find a picture book that your child hasn't read. Have your child take a "picture walk" through the book, looking at the pictures and using them to tell what the story will be about. After you read the story, talk about how the pictures can help your child understand the text of the story.

IN THIS UNIT, YOUR CHILD WILL...

- ■ Use illustrations and details in a story to describe its characters, setting, or events.
- ■ Compare and contrast characters' experiences and adventures.
- ■ Make connections to cultures in stories.
- ■ Read words with long vowels *o, u,* and *e.*
- ■ Identify how similar words are different in meaning.
- ■ Compare and contrast texts on the same topic.

WAYS TO HELP YOUR CHILD

When you read aloud to your child, model how to read with expression. For example, read a character's words the way you imagine that character would sound, and change your voice when reading the words of different characters. Have your child take a turn. Invite your child to read with expression as you have done.

ONLINE
For more Home Connect activities, continue online at sadlierconnect.com

190 Unit 9 ■ Reading Literature: Integration of Knowledge and Ideas

Student Page 190

UNIT PLANNER

Theme: In a Land Far Away	Focus
READ ALOUD pp. 192–193	*Why the Desert Has So Many Stars* **GENRE:** Traditional Tale
UNDERSTANDING STORY ELEMENTS pp. 194–197	*Snake and Frog* **GENRE:** Folktale **LEXILE®:** *200L* **WORDS TO KNOW:** message, nature, serious, warn
COMPARING AND CONTRASTING CHARACTERS pp. 198–201	*Spider's Greed* **GENRE:** Folktale **LEXILE®:** *370L* **WORDS TO KNOW:** delicious, ignore, skitter, stomach, stuck, tasty
FOUNDATIONAL SKILLS READ TOGETHER p. 202	*The Missing Bag* **GENRE:** Realistic Fiction
FOUNDATIONAL SKILLS READER 1 pp. 203–204	*Robin's Trip to China* **GENRE:** Realistic Fiction
FOUNDATIONAL SKILLS READER 2 pp. 205–206	*Mule and the Deep Well* **GENRE:** Fable
CLOSE READING p. 207–210	*The Two Frogs* **GENRE:** Fable **LEXILE®:** *250L*
CONNECT ACROSS TEXTS p. 211	Compare and Contrast Texts
LANGUAGE p. 212	Shades of Meaning
UNIT 9 REVIEW pp. 213–214	*Farmer Bill's Carrot* **GENRE:** Traditional Tale **LEXILE®:** *350L*

Objective(S)

- Use story illustrations and text to describe characters, settings, or events.
- Make connections within a text by comparing characters.

Use story illustrations and text to describe characters, settings, or events.

Make connections across texts by comparing characters.

Read decodable text featuring long *o* words, long *u* words, long *e* words, and irregularly spelled words.

Read decodable text featuring long *o* words and irregularly spelled words.

Read decodable text featuring long *u* words and long *e* words.

Same objectives as pages 194–197; pages 198–201

Distinguish among words with similar meanings.

Unit Assessment

- Unit 9 Review, *pp. 213–214*
- Unit 9 Performance Task (ONLINE)

Additional Assessment Options

- Performance Task 1 *pp. 141–144*
  (ALSO ONLINE)
- Performance Task 2 *pp. 259–262*
  (ALSO ONLINE)

Optional Purchase:

- iProgress Monitor (ONLINE)
- Progress Monitor Student Benchmark Assessment Booklet

(ONLINE) Digital Resources

- Home Connect Activities
- Unit Performance Task
- Additional Practice
- Full-Length Reading Selections
- Foundational Skills Practice
- Teacher Resources
- iProgress Monitor (optional purchase)

Go to SadlierConnect.com to access your Digital Resources.

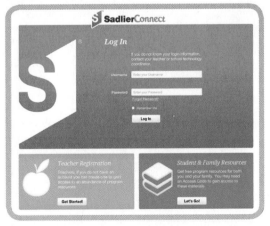

For more detailed instructions see page T3.

LEARNING PROGRESSIONS

In this unit, children will learn how to use illustrations and details in a story to describe its characters, setting, or events and how to compare and contrast these elements. In order to learn the skills in this unit, children will further develop skills learned in kindergarten. They should be encouraged to retain these skills, as they will continue to build on them in second grade.

Understanding Story Elements

- By the end of kindergarten, children can describe the relationship between the illustrations and the story in which they appear.

- In first grade, children are able to use illustrations and details in a story to describe characters, settings, or major events in a story.

- In second grade, children should demonstrate increased proficiency in using the illustrations and words in print or digital text to demonstrate understanding of its characters, setting, or plot.

Comparing and Contrasting

- Proficient kindergartners, with prompting and support, compare and contrast the adventures and experiences of characters in familiar stories.

- First-graders are able to independently compare and contrast the adventures and experiences of characters in stories.

- In second grade, children compare and contrast two or more versions of the same story by different authors or from different cultures.

Making Connections

- When prompted, children at the end of kindergarten can make connections between themselves, a text, and the world around them.

- By the end of first grade, children are able to make connections between themselves, a text, and the world around them.

- As second grade draws to a close, children should show proficiency at making connections between the text, and the world.

Reading Literature: Integration of Knowledge and Ideas

Essential Question:
Why are characters, settings, and events important?

Essential Question:
Why are characters, settings, and events important?

Unit 9 Reading Literature: Integration of Knowledge and Ideas **191**

In this unit, children will learn how to identify and interpret key ideas and details when reading literature by using illustrations and text. Specifically, children will be able to describe details about characters, settings, and main events and then use these details to compare different characters.

Theme: In a Land Far Away

Children will explore the theme, using various genres of literature from realistic fiction to fantasy and fables. The stories take place in a wide variety of settings from a desert to a rainforest, allowing children to explore how a setting influences the story.

Curriculum Connection: Language Arts

As children enjoy the selections in this unit, they will explore different places and times. As children read, they will make connections through various text sets and compare characters, settings, and events.

Vocabulary Overview

delicious 199, ignore 198, message 194, nature 196, serious 196, skitter 199, stomach 200, stuck 200, tasty 200, warn 194

OBJECTIVES

- **Use story illustrations and text to describe characters, setting, or events.**
- **Make connections within a text by comparing characters.**

Using the Read Aloud

Tell children that you will read a text aloud (see right) as they look at the pictures in their books. Read the text, pausing at the numbers to pose questions.

Picture 1

How does the illustration help you understand why the animals want to make the desert pretty? (The illustration shows a dry desert with little growing.)

Picture 2

How does this illustration help you understand the story events? (You see lazy Coyote sleeping in the cave. The other creatures are working while Coyote sleeps.)

Picture 3

What do you see in the illustration? (Coyote trying to eat the yellow bits) *Why do you think Coyote tries to eat the yellow bits?* (He thinks they are food.)

Picture 4

How does the illustration help you understand what the yellow bits are? (The characters are looking at stars in the sky.)

Turn and Talk

Have pairs discuss: *Why might the animals want to change the desert?*

Why the Desert Has So Many Stars

Long ago in the desert, the animals looked around and decided their home was not very pretty. The sky was dark. The animals wanted a brighter sky. They wanted everything to be more beautiful. **1**

The jackrabbits dug paths for cool streams and rivers for swimming or jumping across.

Owls planted a few trees along the rivers so that everyone could have shade. The snakes found big rocks and put them everywhere.

The deer colored the mountains by planting wildflowers. Then they hid in the mountains. Mountain lions grew cactus plants in funny and unusual shapes. Everyone laughed, as they played hide-and-go-seek.

Hairy spiders called tarantulas were busy gathering shiny yellow bits and putting them in a bag.

Everyone was busy working and having fun except Coyote. He couldn't be bothered. He just slept in a cave all day. **2**

At the end of the day, everyone was tired. Most everything in the desert was fixed up except the sky.

No one knew what to do with the spiders' shiny yellow bits. The spiders laid down the bag, and a few yellow bits had scattered out on the ground.

Coyote woke up at midnight. He looked around at the mountains, streams, cactus, trees, and wildflowers. Then he saw the shiny yellow bits on the ground near the bag. **3**

"What are these?" he wondered. He tried to eat them, but they were too hot.

"Useless!" Coyote yelled. Then he threw the yellow bits up into the air. **4**

The lazy coyote looked up to see that the yellow bits had turned into stars.

And to this day, if you go outside at night in the desert, a sky full of yellow stars will greet you!

Read Aloud

Listen as your teacher reads. Pay attention to story details.

Look at the pictures as you listen. How do the pictures and the details help you understand the story?

Why the Desert Has So Many Stars

Integration of Knowledge and Ideas

Preview the Focus Skills

Do a second reading of the Read Aloud as children look at the pictures. As you read, pause briefly where indicated below. Use the suggested think-alouds to preview the unit's targeted reading skills and model how children might use the skills independently during shared reading.

- Pause after reading the first section. Say: *As I was reading, I thought about the setting. I looked at the pictures and thought about the words to help me imagine where the animals lived. Using the pictures along with the words helps me to understand where the animals live.*

- Pause after reading the second section. Say: *When reading, I make connections between the characters and other stories I have read. I ask myself, "What other story characters have had something similar happen?" or "What characters felt that way?" Coyote sleeping in a cave while everyone else works reminds me of another folktale about a coyote under a table.*

- Pause after reading the final sections. Say: *As I was reading the last part of the story, I continued to make connections. When the author described the sky full of stars, I thought about a time that I was in the country and the stars seemed so bright. Good readers make connections like these between the text and the world around them.*

Digital Connection

Supervise children as they search for images of the desert. Then have them print their images to make a collage. In small groups, have them discuss why the setting is important to "Why the Desert Has So Many Stars."

Guided Instruction

OBJECTIVES
- **Use story illustrations and text to describe characters, setting, or events.**
- **Answer questions about key details in a text read aloud.**

Genre: Folktale

Explain that folktales are stories told and shared by people. Folktales often explain something in nature.

Set the Purpose

Help children understand the purpose for understanding story elements by asking: *How can you use pictures to help you understand characters, the setting, and story events?*

Model and Teach

Read the text aloud as children follow along in their books.

Teacher Talk: Find Evidence

Point out to children that they can use story details and pictures to learn about characters and setting. Say: *When I read page 194, I learn that there are two characters, Frog and Snake. I see the picture of the snake in the tree; I see the river and plants. Let's think about how the text and the picture help me to understand where Snake and Frog live. I'm going to look for the sentences on the page.* Monitor children's understanding and have a volunteer use complete sentences to state where each character lives.

Understanding Story Elements

Words to Know
message
warn

Snake and Frog
(Genre: Folktale)

1   Frog wanted to play outside. So did Snake. Their mothers agreed, but they told them that there could be trouble.

2   "Ribbit, ribbit!" Frog's mother said. "I **warn** you. Stay away from snapping turtles. Watch out for animals with beaks."

3   "Ssss," Mama Snake said. "Watch out for eagles. Watch out for animals with big claws."

4   Frog and Snake got the **message**. Be careful! Frog hopped from her swamp to the river. Snake began to slither from his tree to the river. There, they saw each other.

Guided Instruction

Teacher Talk: Find Evidence
Explain that we can use story details and pictures to learn about characters and setting. Guide children to circle the characters in the pictures on page 194 and at the bottom of page 195. Ask: *Where do Frog and Snake live?* Have children underline the details in the text.

194   Unit 9 ■ Reading Literature: Integration of Knowledge and Ideas

Words to Know

message (*noun*): something someone wants to tell someone else
warn (*verb*): to tell someone about danger

Working with Word Meaning Ask children if someone has ever given them a message. Ask: *What was the message? When could a message warn you about something? What might the message say?*

5 "Do you want to play?" asked Frog.

6 "Are you an eagle?" Snake asked. "Do you have big claws?"

7 "Are you a turtle?" Frog asked. "Do you have a big beak?"

8 "I'm not a turtle," said Snake. "I'm a snake. Snakes don't have beaks."

9 "So let's play!" Frog said.

10 First, they floated in the cool river. Then they sat on a log. They soaked up the hot sun. They talked and talked.

11 "Let's be friends," Snake said.

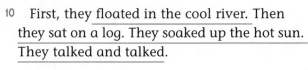

Teacher Talk: Find Evidence

Explain that we can use pictures and story details to find out more about events, the things that happen. Talk about what is happening in the picture at the top of the page. Ask: *What do Frog and Snake do together?* Have children underline words in paragraph 10 that tell.

Guided Instruction

Unit 9 ■ Reading Literature: Integration of Knowledge and Ideas **195**

Guided Instruction

Teacher Talk: Find Evidence

Point out to children that they can use pictures and story details to find out more about story events. Say: *I know that the events, or what happens in the story, are important details. So far, I know that Frog and Snake want to play outside, and that they meet. I also see that the picture at the top of the page shows Frog and Snake meeting and it looks like they're talking. When I read paragraphs 5–9, I learn that Snake and Frog have agreed to play. Let's reread the rest of the page to find the details that tell us what Frog and Snake are going to do together.*

After going through the Find Evidence instruction, help children name the characters, setting, and key events. Ask them to tell how they used the details from the text and the illustrations to describe the key story elements.

Use Visuals

To help children recall key details from information presented in visuals, have them look at the visuals on pages 194–195. Ask them to tell what they can learn about the characters, setting, and key events by studying each. Ask children to use a sentence to tell the important details in each visual.

Support English Language Learners

Build an understanding of a swamp setting. Show children several pictures of swamps. Point out the water surrounding the area and different animals found in a swamp, including frogs, snakes, turtles, and birds. Discuss what dangers there might be for a snake and a frog.

Guided Practice

Read and Practice

Read paragraphs 13 and 14 aloud. Have heterogeneous partners take turns rereading the paragraphs as you circulate to provide support.

Teacher Talk: Find Evidence

Have children look at the pictures and tell what they see. Remind children that pictures can add information to help them understand the characters and the events. Say: *I see Mother Frog and Mother Snake looking at and talking to their children. The mothers look unhappy, or angry. I will reread the page to find details that show the mothers are angry. That will help me to find the words the mothers use to tell Frog and Snake what to do. Then we can circle the part of the picture that shows the mothers are angry.*

Reciprocal Teaching

Have children meet in groups of four. Distribute one notecard to each member of the group identifying each person's unique role: summarizer, questioner, clarifier, and predictor. Allow time for children to use their role to have a group discussion about the events thus far.

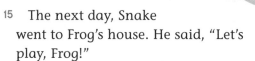

Understanding Story Elements

Words to Know

nature
serious

12 "Okay," Frog said.

13 Frog went home and told her mother about Snake. She became angry. "Don't *ever* do that again! Snakes EAT frogs! It's a law of **nature**. He can never be your friend!"

14 Snake went home and told his mother about Frog. She was furious. "Are you **serious**? Snakes eat frogs. They do not play with them. It's just a law of nature. Tomorrow you will show you are a snake. You will eat that frog!"

15 The next day, Snake went to Frog's house. He said, "Let's play, Frog!"

16 "GO AWAY!" said Frog. "I know what you want. You want to eat me."

Guided Practice

Teacher Talk: Find Evidence
Review that pictures and story details tell us about characters, setting, and events. Guide children to underline the words each mother uses to tell Frog and Snake what to do. Have them circle the part of each picture that shows how the mother looks when she speaks.

196   Unit 9 ■ Reading Literature: Integration of Knowledge and Ideas

Words to Know

nature (*noun*): the way animals and plants live and behave
serious (*adjective*): not teasing

Working with Word Meaning Have children demonstrate their understanding of the words by asking the following questions: *What types of things are in nature? When should you be serious?*

Integration of Knowledge and Ideas

17   So Snake went away. He missed his friend, but he knew one rule. Frogs and snakes don't play. It's just the law of nature.

Comprehension Check

MORE ONLINE
sadlierconnect.com

1. Look at the picture at the bottom of pages 194 and 195. What do Frog and Snake live near?

   a. a mountain

   b. a puddle

   c. a river

2. What happens in this story? Use the story details and pictures to help you remember the events.

   Sample answer: Frog and Snake go to the river. They meet

   and play. Their mamas find out and get mad. Frog and Snake

   learn that snakes eat frogs. Snake ends up playing alone.

Teacher Talk: Find Evidence
Have children underline the sentence that tells what Snake and Frog learn in this story.

Independent Practice

Unit 9 ■ Reading Literature: Integration of Knowledge and Ideas   **197**

Independent Practice

Read and Apply

Have children read paragraph 17 independently as you circulate. Provide extra support to struggling readers by choral reading the paragraph with them.

Teacher Talk: Find Evidence

Explain that this folktale tells something about nature and how some animals act toward each other. Have children underline the sentence that tells what we learn about snakes and frogs.

Comprehension Check

Answer Explanations:

1. The picture shows water. It is too big for a puddle, so choice **C** is the best answer.

2. Accept answers that clearly demonstrate a summary with key events.

Critical Comprehension

Use the following question to help children think critically about the selection. Children should be prepared to support their answers with evidence from the text.

How would the story have ended if both characters were frogs? (The animals would remain friends, since they were not natural enemies.)

Assess and Respond
If children have difficulty answering the questions in the Comprehension Check . . .
Then work with them to create a story map showing the characters, setting, and key events. Point out how the illustrations and text help them to find key details.

Foundational Skills Review: Fluency Practice

Remind children that it is important to read a story with accuracy, paying careful attention to the words to make sure they read them correctly. Point out that if children do not understand a word or it does not make sense with what they have read so far, they should go back and read the sentence again. Model reading paragraph 17, replacing *nature* with *natural*. After the miscue, pause and say, *That doesn't sound right*. Model rereading the sentence and self-correcting the error. Have children work in groups of three to continue practicing with another paragraph, self-correcting as needed. Additional fluency passages and activities can be found at **sadlierconnect.com**.

Guided Instruction

OBJECTIVES
- **Make connections across texts by comparing characters.**
- **Answer questions about key details in a text read aloud.**

Genre: Folktale
Remind children that folktales are stories told and shared by people. This folktale is written as a play.

Set the Purpose
Help children use the pictures to explore the purpose for learning the reading skill. Ask: *Are these characters like those in "Snake and Frog"? Are they different?*

Model and Teach
Read the text aloud as children follow along in their books.

Teacher Talk: Find Evidence
Explain that when we read, we can think about ways that story characters are alike and different. Say: *I read that Jade will gather fruit. Jade and Spider meet. Spider says something to Jade. Let's underline what Jade does that shows her feelings. Later, Spider's actions show how he feels about Jade. Let's look for the words in paragraph 5 that give his actions.* Monitor children's interactions and have them use complete sentences in their discussions.

Comparing and Contrasting Characters

Words to Know
delicious
ignore
skitter

Spider's Greed
(Genre: Folktale)

1 **Narrator:** Spider rests on a tree branch. It is the coolest spot in the forest. Spider is feeling hungry. He jumps up when he sees Jade. She comes to the forest to gather fruit for her mother.

2 **Spider:** Hello, Jade. You look very nice today.

3 **Narrator:** Jade decides to **ignore** Spider. She goes off to gather fruit.

4 **Spider:** Wait, my pretty girl! I want to come with you. I would like to be your friend.

5 **Narrator:** Jade agrees that Spider can help. So Spider follows her to a plum tree. He pushes Jade aside and climbs the tree. He eats every last plum.

Guided Instruction

Teacher Talk: Find Evidence
Point out that in "Snake and Frog," the characters have fun together, but Spider and Jade do not. Ask: *What does Jade do when Spider speaks to her? What does Spider do?* Have children underline the sentences in paragraphs 3 and 5 that tell this.

198   Unit 9 ■ Reading Literature: Integration of Knowledge and Ideas

---

Words to Know

delicious (*adjective*): yummy; very good to eat
ignore (*verb*): to pay no attention to
skitter (*verb*): to run in little steps

Working with Word Meaning Have children show their understanding of the words by having them act out each word. Use the following prompts:

Pretend you are eating something *delicious*.

Show what it looks like to *ignore* friends when they talk.

Show what it looks like to *skitter* across the floor like a spider.

Integration of Knowledge and Ideas

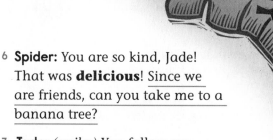

6 **Spider:** You are so kind, Jade! That was **delicious**! Since we are friends, can you take me to a banana tree?

7 **Jade:** (*smiles*) Yes, follow me.

8 **Narrator:** Jade leads Spider deeper into the forest. She shows him the banana tree. Again, Spider shoves Jade aside. He gobbles up all the bananas before she can pick one. That gives Jade an idea.

9 **Jade:** Spider, we are true friends. I would like to take you to get some honey.

10 **Narrator:** Spider is greedy, so he agrees. He follows Jade farther into the forest. She points to a hole in a very tall tree. Spider pushes Jade aside. He begins to **skitter** up the tree and enters the hole. He eats honey until he is full.

11 **Jade:** How is the honey, my friend?

Teacher Talk: Find Evidence

Explain that readers can compare the characters and their experiences. Ask: *Why does Spider want to be Jade's friend? What does he want?* Have children underline the sentence in paragraph 6 that tells. Ask: *Why are Snake and Frog friends? What do they want?*

Guided Instruction

Unit 9 ■ Reading Literature: Integration of Knowledge and Ideas **199**

Guided Instruction

Teacher Talk: Find Evidence

Point out to children that they can compare the characters and their experiences in the story. Say: *I know that Spider acts like he wants to be Jade's friend. In paragraph 6, Spider tells Jade she is kind and tells her the plums were delicious. Let's reread paragraph 6 and look for the sentence that tells what Spider wants.*

Pause after rereading paragraph 6. Say: *Now I'm going to think back to the story about Frog and Snake and why they wanted to be friends. I remember that Frog wanted to play outside, and so did Snake. Since they both wanted to play outside, that seems like a good reason to be friends.*

Tell children that you are going to continue looking at what the characters say and do in this story to see if there are any other comparisons to Frog and Snake.

Review: Understanding Story Elements

Remind children that illustrations can help them describe and understand characters, setting, and events. Have them study the pictures on the pages. Ask: *How do the illustrations help you to better understand the play?* (Sample answer: I know what the forest looks like, and I see that Jade is a girl. I also understand how Spider can get the plums from the tree.)

Differentiate Instruction

Use a Venn diagram to help children make connections between the two texts in this unit. Lead children in using the diagram to compare and contrast key elements such as characters, setting, events, and lessons. After children have completed the diagram, ask questions such as the following to help children connect to the texts, to themselves, and to the world:

How are the characters in "Snake and Frog" and "Spider's Greed" alike?

Have you read other stories with a problem like one in these stories?

Have you ever felt the way any of the characters felt?

What lesson can you learn from these stories?

Guided Practice

Read and Practice

Remind children that often the things that characters say or do will remind them of other stories. Have heterogeneous partners take turns rereading page 200 as you circulate to provide support.

Teacher Talk: Find Evidence

Tell children that when reading they can look for ways that characters are alike and different. Say: *As I read, I'm thinking about how Jade acts toward Spider and how Snake acts toward Frog. I read that Spider tries to leave the hole, but can't. He calls for Jade's help. Jade agrees and calls for anyone to help them. I'll find the sentence that tells that Jade is going to help and underline it.*

Remind children that Snake is not willing to be Frog's friend. Say: *Snake is not like Jade. Snake follows nature. Snake knows he is going to have to eat Frog. What does Snake do that shows he is willing to eat Frog?*

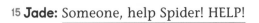

Comparing and Contrasting Characters

Words to Know

stomach
stuck
tasty

12 **Spider:** It is **tasty**, but I think I have had enough.

13 **Narrator:** Spider tries to leave the hole. His **stomach** is huge. He cannot get out!

14 **Spider:** Help me! I'm **stuck** in the hole! Please call for help.

15 **Jade:** Someone, help Spider! HELP!

16 **Narrator:** Remember, they were deep in the forest. No one could hear their calls.

Guided Practice

Teacher Talk: Find Evidence
Remind children that they can look for ways that characters' experiences are alike and different. Guide them to underline the sentence that tells what Jade says when Spider is stuck. Have pairs discuss how her words and actions are alike or different from Frog's.

200 Unit 9 ■ Reading Literature: Integration of Knowledge and Ideas

---

Words to Know

stomach (*noun*): body part that fills with food
stuck (*adjective*): unable to get out
tasty (*verb*): yummy; good to eat

Working with Word Meaning Help children understand the meaning of the words by answering the following questions:

How do you feel if your *stomach* is upset?

What does it mean to get a zipper *stuck*?

What is something that you think is *tasty*?

Integration of Knowledge and Ideas

17 **Jade:** Good luck, Spider. I'm going now. I have to pick oranges for my mother.

18 **Narrator:** Jade picks oranges, but Spider stays in the tree. He may even be there today!

Comprehension Check

MORE ONLINE sadlierconnect.com

1. Think about how these characters are alike or different from the characters in "Snake and Frog." Which word best tells how Spider and Snake act?

   a. friendly

   b. sneaky

   c. greedy

2. Think about the characters in this story and "Snake and Frog." Explain what is alike and different about the way Spider and Jade act and the way Snake and Frog act.

   Sample answer: Jade knows that Spider is greedy, so she

   plays a trick on him. Snake and Frog both want to be

   friends until they learn that snakes eat frogs.

Teacher Talk: Find Evidence
Have children circle the sentence that tells what each character does at the end of the story.

Independent Practice

Read and Apply

Have children read page 201 independently as you circulate. Provide support to struggling readers by reading the paragraphs chorally with them.

Teacher Talk: Find Evidence

Help children to recall the story endings. Say: *I know how Jade acts toward Spider at the end of the story and how Snake acts toward Frog. I can then think about how they are alike and how they are different.*

Comprehension Check

Answer Explanations:

1. Choice **A** describes the outward appearance of both animals, and **C** describes Spider. Answer choice **B** best describes the true nature of both animals' actions.

2. Remind children that to compare is to tell how things are the same. To contrast is to tell how they are different. Children should both compare and contrast.

Critical Comprehension

Use the following question to help children think critically about the selection. Children should be prepared to support their answers with evidence from the text.

Why do you think Jade tricked Spider? (She wanted him to stop following her.)

Assess and Respond
If children have difficulty answering the questions in the Comprehension Check . . .
Then have children highlight what each character says.

Peer Collaboration

Organize children into groups of four members. Assign each member a character: Snake, Frog, Jade, or Spider. Ask children to look back at the stories to review what their character says and does. Have children then share the most important things that the character says and does. After they have shared with their group, have each group create a chart listing ways the characters are alike and different.

OBJECTIVE
Read decodable text featuring long *o* words, long *u* words, long *e* words, and irregularly spelled words.

Prepare to Read

Tell children that you will be reading a story about a grandmother whose purse is missing. Tell children to look and listen for words that have the long *o*, long *u*, and long *e* vowel sounds as you read.

Introduce Phonics Skills

After you have read the selection once, read it again, this time focusing on the target phonics skills.

- Frame the word *close*. *The pattern of vowel-consonant-e stands for a long vowel sound. Find a long u word with the vowel-consonant-e pattern.* (use)

- Frame the word *moans*. *Vowel teams oa, ow, ue, ee, and ea also stand for long vowel sounds. Find a word with a long o, long u, or long e vowel team.* (own, clue, keeps)

- *I noticed words with unusual spellings,* behind *and* money. *I memorize these spellings so I can read the words automatically when I see them.*

Focus on Fluency

Remind children that reading with accuracy means paying attention to punctuation. Point out the punctuation marks in paragraph 3 and model reading the paragraph to show how to observe the punctuation marks. Then have children work in pairs to read the paragraph aloud.

Foundational Skills Read Together

As you read along, listen for words with the long *o*, long *u*, and long *e* vowel sounds.

The Missing Bag

1 Gram moans because her shiny red bag is missing. She keeps her money in the bag. She also keeps chocolate bars in it.

2 We look under the bed. We look behind the chair. We cannot find the bag in the house!

3 Then we look outside. Gram asks our cow, "Mina, did YOU take my bag?" The cow nods, but we know she did not.

4 Then we hear a fuss close by in the trees. The fuss is a clue. Two monkeys are fighting on a branch. "SCREECH! SCREECH!" They are tugging on something red and shiny.

5 "There's your bag!" I say. "The monkeys own it now."

6 Gram grins. "I should not use my bag to hold my chocolate!"

202 Unit 9 ■ Reading Literature: Integration of Knowledge and Ideas

---

Focus on Phonological Awareness

Phoneme Deletion and Addition

Use the following procedure for a quick phonological awareness activity focusing on phoneme addition and deletion.

- Say the word *coat*.
- Say: *Take off the /k/ sound. What word does it make?* (oat)
- *Add the /b/ sound at the beginning. What word does it make?* (boat)
- Continue in the same manner with the following words, having children replace each beginning sound with the indicated sound:

  cold /f/   feet /b/   mow /b/   face /r/   rose /n/

DIRECTIONS: Cut and fold the book.

Name

Robin's Trip to China

"I want to go to China," Robin says.
"I want to see my *first* home."

fold

fold

"I will go when I grow up. Until then,
I will stay in *this* home with you, Dad."

"A boat is too *slow*," Robin says.
"Can we fly in a jet?"

long o

203

Foundational Skills: Phonics Practice

Write the following words from the Read Together and Foundational Skills Reader 1 on the board or on a chart. Have children practice reading the words.

Read Together long vowels: moans, keeps, screech, know, close, own; **irregularly spelled words:** money, chocolate, behind, find

Foundational Skills Reader 1 long vowel o: home, grow, boat, slow, road, know, hope, show, globe; **irregularly spelled words:** China, says

OBJECTIVES

• **Read decodable text featuring long o words and irregularly spelled words.**

• **Read along orally, emphasizing words with special print.**

Prepare to Read

Tell children that they will be reading a story about a girl who talks about visiting China. They can take the book home to share. Have them follow the directions to cut and fold the book.

Review Phonics Skills

Explain that this book features words with long vowel sounds. Review the targeted phonics skills.

• *The pattern of o-consonant-e stands for the long o sound, as in hope. Find words with the o-consonant-e pattern in the story and say them.*

• *Remember that the vowel pairs oa and ow stand for the long o sound. Find long o words spelled oa or ow in the story and say them.*

• *Remember that some words, such as because, have unusual spellings. Find words in the story that have unusual spellings and say them.*

Introduce Reader 1

Divide the class into two groups. Assign each group to read even or odd pages. Have each group chorally read its corresponding page as you read each line aloud.

Read with a Partner

Select pairs of children to read together. Allow each pair to decide how it wants to read the text together several times: chorally, alternating by sentences, or alternating by pages. Once the pairs are comfortable with one of their oral readings, have them record it for playing back later.

Focus on Fluency

Remind children that fluent readers read with expression. Tell them to use a lively voice and pay attention to words that are treated differently, such as words in dark type, italic (slanted) type, and words that are all capital letters. Model fluency of the entire reader by using the Fluency Practice activity below.

Reading at Home

Once children are comfortable reading the book, send it home for children to read to family members.

Assess and Respond
If children have difficulty reading long *o* words . . .
Then place a square piece of colored transparent plastic on the end of a craft stick. Have children use the plastic square to highlight the vowel teams in long *o* words.

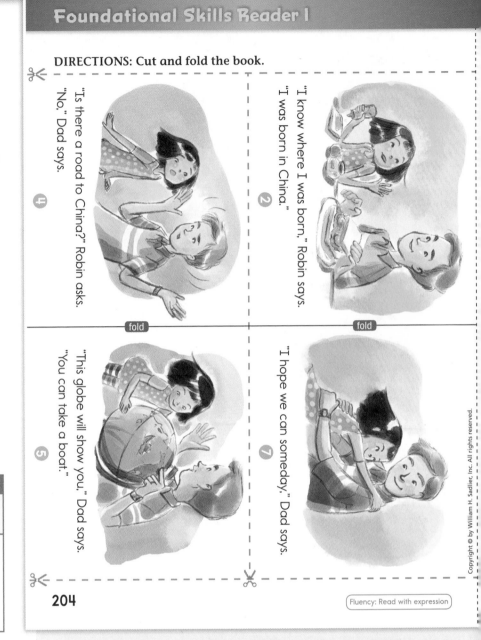

Foundational Skills Reader 1

DIRECTIONS: Cut and fold the book.

"Is there a road to China?" Robin asks. "No." Dad says.

4

"I know where I was born." Robin says. "I was born in China."

2

"This globe will show you." Dad says. "You can take a boat."

5

"I hope we can someday." Dad says.

1

204

Fluency: Read with expression

Foundational Skill: Fluency Practice

Explain to children that when reading aloud, they should read with expression. Point out that words in special type should often be stressed or read with excitement in order to read with expression. Have children turn to page 3 and identify the word in special type. (first) Demonstrate a fluent reading of the page, modeling an expressive reading of the dialogue, including the word *first*. Then chorally read the page. Follow this same procedure with pages 6 and 8. Additional fluency passages and activities can be found at **sadlierconnect.com**.

Foundational Skills Reader 2

DIRECTIONS: Cut and fold the book.

Name

Mule and the Deep Well

1

fold

Mule saw Fox in the well.
"Are you getting clean?" Mule asked.

3

fold

Fox ran away, and Mule learned a rule.
Always look before you leap.

8

"YIKES!" Mule said. "It is cold. We will turn blue in here."

9

long u; long e

Unit 9 ■ Reading Literature: Integration of Knowledge and Ideas **205**

Foundational Skill: Phonics Practice

Write the following words from Foundational Skills Reader 2 on the board or on a chart. Have children practice reading the words.

Long e words: deep, clean, leap, sweet, really

Long u words: mule, rule, June, true

OBJECTIVES
- **Read decodable text featuring long *u* words and long *e* words.**
- **Read along orally, emphasizing words with special print.**

Prepare to Read

Tell children that the next story they will be reading is a fable about a mule and fox. They can take the book home to share. Have them follow the directions to cut and fold the book.

Review Phonics Skills

Explain that there are several words in the book with long vowels. Review these elements.

- *The vowel-consonant-e pattern stands for a long vowel sound. Look for long* e *and long* u *words with this pattern. Read the words.* (mule, rule, June)

- *The vowel teams* ee and ea *stand for the long* e *sound. The vowel team* ue *stands for the long* u *sound. Look for words with* ee, ea, *and* ue *and read them.* (deep, clean, leap, sweet, really, true)

Introduce Reader 2

Have the class echo read the book with you: you read a sentence, and then they echo the sentence. When reading, be sure to model reading with expression. Point out the quotation marks that indicate what each animal says.

Read with a Partner

Have heterogeneous pairs of children take turns reading to each other. Have each pair read the text together several times, then take turns reading page by page.

Focus on Fluency

Remind children that fluent readers read with expression. Ask them to explain why this is important. (It makes the story more interesting and helps them to understand the characters' feelings and emotions.) Focus their attention on page 5 of the reader. Ask what they notice about the word *Wow*. Have them tell how they would read the word. Then have them identify the word in capital letters on page 6. Have them read the sentence. Then chorally read the two pages, using lively expression.

Reading at Home

Once children are comfortable reading the book, send it home for children to read to family members.

Assess and Respond

If children have difficulty reading long *u* or *e* words . . .

Then display the words *true*, *deep*, *clean*, *leap*, *sweet*, and *really*. Have children circle the vowel team in each word and then read the word.

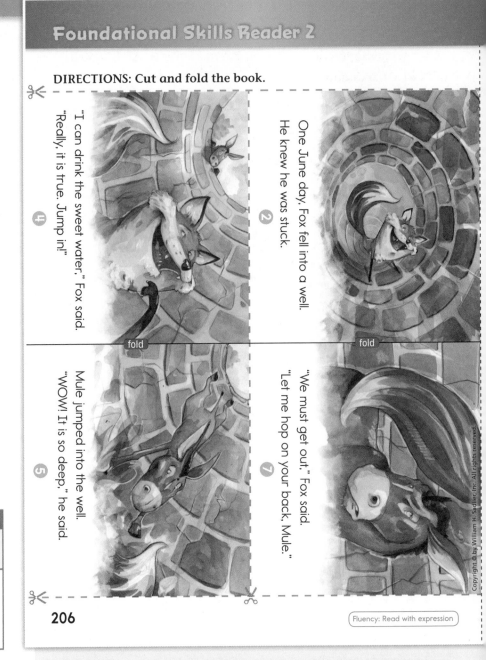

Foundational Skills Reader 2

DIRECTIONS: Cut and fold the book.

④ "I can drink the sweet water," Fox said. "Really, it is true. Jump in!"

② One June day, Fox fell into a well. He knew he was stuck.

⑤ Mule jumped into the well. "WOW! It is so deep," he said.

⑦ "We must get out," Fox said. "Let me hop on your back, Mule."

206

Fluency: Read with expression

Foundational Skill: Fluency Practice

Read the text on page 8 of the reader. Point out the different type (dark print), which indicates the moral, or lesson, of the story. Explain that the moral comes at the end of the story and tells the lesson learned. Model reading page 8, emphasizing how to read the moral. Then chorally read the entire reader. Have children practice; then record them reading aloud. Additional fluency passages can be found at **sadlierconnect.com**.

The Two Frogs

1 East Frog lived in a blue pond. The pond was east of the mountain. One June, he wanted to see the world. He said, "I'll go see the west side of the mountain."

2 West Frog lived in a green swamp. The swamp was west of the mountain. He said, "Is all the world like this? I want to know. I'll go see the east side of the mountain."

3 The frogs went up the mountain. West Frog hopped up a steep road. East Frog swam up a mountain stream. At the top, they met.

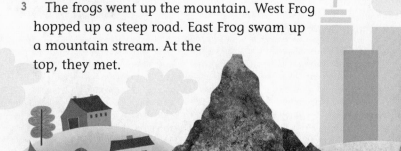

207

OBJECTIVES

- **Use story illustrations and text to describe characters, settings, or events.**
- **Make connections across texts by comparing characters.**
- **Answer questions about key details in a text read aloud.**

Genre: Fable

Tell children that this story is a fable and that fables are make-believe stories that often have animals as characters. Many fables end with a moral or a lesson learned. Ask children to think about the lesson the two frogs learn in this fable.

Path Options

You may wish to have children read the text independently and apply the skills learned in this unit. Or you may wish to do a close reading with children; if so, use the supports provided on these pages. As a third option, set up a buddy system with some heterogeneous and some homogenous pairs, to fit the needs of your class. Regardless, children should read the text more than once to facilitate understanding and to be able to answer the Comprehension Check questions correctly.

Support English Language Learners

If you do decide to have children read the text on their own, be aware that English language learners may struggle to read it independently. You may wish to allow children the option of partner reading the text with a more proficient reader. Ask readers to pause after each paragraph or page to summarize the plot to that point.

Support First Reading

Circulate to check children's understanding. As needed, use the following comprehension and strategy check-ins to support basic understanding of the selection as children read.

Check-in Questions

- **page 207** *Why did the frogs begin their journeys?* (They wanted to see what is on the other side of the mountain.)

- **page 208** *Why did the frogs stop before reaching the other side?* (They were tired. They held each other up to see, but they looked on the wrong side. They thought it looked just like their homes.)

- **page 209** *Why did the frogs return home?* (They thought they had seen the other side of the mountain.)

Review: Understanding Story Elements

Remind children that all stories have similar elements: characters, setting, and events. Have them talk with a partner and describe the characters, setting, and main events of this fable.

Review: Comparing and Contrasting Characters

Explain that strategic readers make connections when they read. One way to make connections is to compare and contrast characters. Ask: *How are the two frogs the same?* (They both want to see the other side. They are both tired. They both stop their journeys because they think the other side is the same as theirs.) *How are the two frogs different?* (One lives in the city, and one lives in the country. One lives in a swamp, and one lives in a pond.)

Close Reading

4   East Frog spoke first. He said, "I'm going to the west. I want to see the world."

5   West Frog said, "I do, too. I'm going to the east."

6   Both frogs had come a long way. They were very tired. East Frog had an idea. He said, "Why don't we look at each other's home? We can see what it's like!"

7   West Frog looked to the east. "I'm too short. I can't see anything!"

8   East Frog said, "Hop on my back. Take a look."

9   West Frog hopped on East Frog's back. As he looked down, he looked west. He was looking at his own home! "The east looks just like the west!" he cried.

208

Differentiate Instruction

For children who struggle with recalling story elements, provide a story map where they can list the characters, setting, and events. Remind them that they can use the illustrations and text to complete the story map. Once they are done, help them use two colors of highlighter pens. Have them highlight in one color ways that the experiences of the two frogs are the same. Have them highlight with a different color ways that the experiences of the two frogs are different.

Close Reading

10   East Frog jumped on West Frog's back. He looked east. He cried, "That's true! Now I know! The world is all the same!"

11   So the two silly frogs went back down the mountain. They thought they had seen the world. They were really just looking at their own homes.

Comprehension Check

1. In this story, both characters go to the top of a mountain. What is different about how they get there?

   (a.) One frog hops, and the other swims.

   b. One frog hops, and the other flies.

   c. One frog hops, and the other rides in a cart.

2. The characters have a reason for going up the mountain. What do they want to do?

   a. They want to live in a swamp.

   b. They want to have a large family.

   (c.) They want to see the world.

Unit 9 ■ Reading Literature: Integration of Knowledge and Ideas   **209**

Multiple Readings for Critical Comprehension

Have children reread this selection, and pose questions that focus on critical comprehension. Remind children that they can mark the text.

- *How was what the frogs experienced the same?* (They both had the same reason for traveling, and they both returned home without seeing the other side.)

- *What lesson can you learn from this story?* (Sample answer: Things are not always what they seem.)

Comprehension Check

Score children's understanding of unit skills and texts using the Comprehension Check on this page and the next. Use the children's total score to determine their readiness for the Unit 9 Review on page 213.

Multiple-Choice Questions: *1 point each*

1. Paragraph 3 describes that one frog hops, and the other swims, so answer choice **A** is correct.

2. The frogs could not see the other side of the world because of the tall mountain. Answer choice **C** is the correct answer, because it tells why they climbed the mountain.

Strategic Reading

Support all readers by reminding them of the importance of making connections to what they already know. As they read, children should be thinking about what they know about themselves, what they've read in other texts, and how things operate in the real world. Making connections helps them remember what they are reading and understand the characters and events better.

Short-Answer Questions: 2 points each

Item 3 Rubric

2	Children describe what each frog sees and explain what each frog thinks.
1	Children either describe what each frog sees or explain what each frog thinks but not both.
0	Children cannot describe what the frogs see or think.

Item 4 Rubric

2	Children make comparisons between homes and give details from the picture and the text to support their reason.
1	Children make comparisons between homes but do not offer details to support this reason.
0	Children are unable to compare homes.

Theme Wrap-Up

Lead children in a discussion on what they have learned from the theme: "In a Land Far Away." Ask them to share what they learned about the different settings in the stories.

Close Reading

3. What does each frog see from the top of the mountain? What does this tell them about the world?

Sample answer: East Frog sees a blue pond and the city.

West Frog sees a green swamp and some farmhouses.

Each thinks that the world is just like his home.

4. Is your home more like East Frog's home or West Frog's home? Use details in the pictures and the story to explain.

Sample answer: Children's responses should show that they

live in a more urban or rural area, and include details from

the story and illustrations.

210   Unit 9 ▪ Reading Literature: Integration of Knowledge and Ideas

Assess and Respond (pages 207–210)

If	Then
Children scored 0–2 points; they are **Developing** their understanding of unit skills …	Provide children with reading support and more intensive modeling of skills.
Children scored 3–4 points; they are **Improving** their understanding of unit skills …	Use children's scores to target areas that are weak and review those specific skills.
Children scored 5–6 points; they are **Proficient** in their understanding of unit skills …	Have these children move on. They are ready for the formal assessment.

Compare and Contrast Texts

Look at the pictures from the stories you have read. Think about the details in the stories. Be ready to talk about characters, settings, and events.

Snake and Frog

Spider's Greed

The Two Frogs

Return to the Essential Question

Why are characters, settings, and events important?

Talk about the characters and their adventures. How are they alike and different?

Unit 9 ■ Reading Literature: Integration of Knowledge and Ideas **211**

Compare and Contrast Texts

Read aloud the directions on page 211. Then provide some information about each of the featured texts, to help children as they recall the key details.

The selection "Snake and Frog" is the story about two animals that want to be friends but are not allowed to be. Why are they not friends in the end? (Their moms explained that snakes eat frogs.)

The selection "Spider's Greed" is the story about Spider, who only wants to be friends with Jade so he can get her fruit. How does Jade stop Spider? (She tricks him into going into a tree. He eats so much honey that he can't get out.)

The selection "The Two Frogs" is the story about two frogs that want to see what is on the other side of the mountain. What do they do when they get to the top? (They look at their own side of the mountain.)

Give children time to organize their thoughts about the texts. Remind them to ask questions about any confusion they have about the texts before you begin. Then lead the Essential Question discussion.

Support Essential Question Discussion

Read the Essential Question aloud. Then prompt children to share their ideas about their selections. Remind children to raise their hands and wait for you to call on them.

- *Why are the characters important to the stories?*
- *Why is the setting important in each story?*
- *What problems does each set of characters have?*

Discussion Skills

As children read the texts, encourage them to make connections. Review discussion skills with children reminding them that active participants listen to others and explain their reasoning. You can support them in responding to texts by providing prompts such as these to signal the relationships between the text and themselves, other texts, and the world.

I could relate to _____ because _____.

I read another story where _____.

This text taught me a lesson, because _____.

OBJECTIVE
Distinguish among words with similar meanings.

Guided Instruction

Read aloud the Guided Instruction section on page 212. Be sure children understand that all words have similar meanings, but each one has a little bit different meaning. Ask: *Why is* shove *the best choice in this sentence?* (*Ram* is too rough, and *push* could be too gentle.)

Guided Practice

Explain that children should read the sentences in order to choose the word that best describes the action.

Independent Practice

If children struggle to find the best answer, ask: *The sentence says the monkey was hungry. Which word best describes how someone who is really hungry eats?*

Apply to Reading

Have children return to page 199 of "Spider's Greed." Point to the word *skitter* in paragraph 10. Ask children to think of other words the author could have used, such as *glide, jump,* and *crawl.* Then have them turn to a partner and discuss whether *skitter* is the best word choice.

Language

Shades of Meaning

Guided Instruction Some words are very close in meaning. Read this sentence from "Spider's Greed."

Again, Spider **shoves** Jade aside.

> **shove** to push something with force
> **push** to press against something to move it
> **ram** to push into something very hard

Guided Practice Write the word from the box that best completes each sentence.

1. Do not _____ram_____ the wall with your bike!

2. I can _____push_____ the lawn mower over the grass.

3. If you _____shove_____ that player, he might get angry.

Independent Practice Choose the word that best completes the sentences. Write it on the line.

> **nibble   gobble**

4. A hungry monkey will _____gobble_____ the bananas!

5. The hens just _____nibble_____ on bits of corn.

Support English Language Learners

English language learners may need more support to understand shades of meaning. Bring in paint strips (or use crayons or markers) to illustrate different shades of a color such as blue. Explain that each square is blue, but they have a more precise name such as navy, turquoise, and aqua. Explain that words can have shades of meaning. Provide examples of words and discuss their meaning by giving examples to highlight their differences.

talk, whisper, mumble, shout

mad, cross, annoyed, furious

Read along with the following story.

Farmer Bill's Carrot

1   Farmer Bill planted a carrot in June. In ten weeks, it had grown a lot. He tried pulling it out. The carrot stayed where it was.

2   His wife helped him pull, but the carrot did not move. His son, Luke, helped too, but the carrot would not move.

3   Goat wanted to help. He came and tugged with everyone else. The carrot did not budge.

4   Mouse wanted to try. Farmer Bill said Mouse was too (weak) and small to pull. Mouse pulled anyway. Out came the carrot!

1. Who solves the problem in the story? Underline the sentences in the story that tell.

Unit 9 ■ Reading Literature: Integration of Knowledge and Ideas   213

Self-Assessment: Progress Check

Have children revisit the Progress Check on page 189 and respond to the questions again. Ask them to compare Before and After responses.

Review children's responses to get an idea of their confidence with the unit skills. Based on these responses and on children's success with the Comprehension Check in Close Reading, you may want to conduct additional review and practice of one or more of the unit skills.

Unit Summary

Children have had instruction and practice in reading different types of literature including fables, folktales, and realistic fiction that focus on adventures in lands far away. Children have learned that when reading they can use illustrations and details to describe characters, setting, or events. They can compare and contrast the experiences of characters in stories. Children have been able to compare texts on the same topics. They have progressed toward completing an independent close reading of text, practiced applying the concepts across texts, and identified shades of meanings in words. They have read words with long vowel teams and the vowel-consonant-e pattern. They should be well prepared for the review section.

Introduce the Review

Explain to children that they will read a new passage along with you that is related to the unit's theme and the selections they have already read. Then they will answer the questions on pages 213 and 214.

Answer Explanations

Scoring: Items 1, 6, and 7 on pages 213 and 214 are worth 1 point each. Explanations for the correct answers are given below and on the next page. Also see the rubrics on the next page for guidance in scoring the short-answer questions on page 214.

1. The illustration shows a garden, and characters who are not able to pull the carrot. The most confident and strongest character is the little mouse.

Answer Explanations

Item 2 Rubric

2	Child explains that both Luke and Goat pull, but the carrot does not come out.
1	Child explains that both Luke and Goat pull, but does not explain that the carrot will not come out.
0	Child is unable to compare the two events.

Item 3 Rubric

2	Child names the character that is most like him or her and gives a detail from the story to tell why.
1	Child names the character that most resembles him or her but does not tell why.
0	Child cannot make the connection between the character and himself or herself.

Item 4 Rubric

2	Child defines both words and explains why *weak* is a better word choice.
1	Child explains why *weak* is a good word choice.
0	Child is unable to explain why *weak* is the better word choice.

Item 5 Rubric

2	Child clearly explains what Farmer Bill does at the beginning of the story.
1	Child somewhat explains what Farmer Bill does at the beginning of the story.
0	Child is unable to explain what Farmer Bill does at the beginning of the story.

6. *Feet* and *weak* both have the long e sound.

7. Child identifies that Farmer Bill plants a carrot in a garden.

Unit 9 Review

2. In what way are Luke's and Goat's experiences alike?

They both pull, but the carrot doesn't come out.

3. Which character is most like you? In what way? Use details from the story and picture to explain.

Answers will vary, but should name a character and give

text evidence to support the comparison.

4. Why does the author use the word *weak* instead of *tired* to describe Mouse?

Sample answer: *Weak* tells that Mouse isn't very strong

because he is small. *Tired* just tells how he feels one day.

5. What does Farmer Bill do at the beginning of the story?

He plants a carrot.

Fill in the circle of the correct answer choice.

6. Which word has the vowel sound in *feet*?

○ ten
● weak
○ did

7. Where does this story take place?

● in a garden
○ in a yard
○ in a city

Analyze Scores

8–11 pts Strong	Child has a good grasp of the skills and concepts taught in this unit. Point out any mistakes the child has made and explain the correct answers if necessary.
4–7 pts Progressing	Child is struggling with some skills or concepts. Identify the specific skills that are problematic to target a review of instruction.
0–3 pts Emerging	Child has difficulty understanding the skills and concepts taught in this unit. Child may need further instruction with a higher level of support and detailed explanation of the unit's skills and concepts.

Introducing UNIT **10**

In this unit, you will learn facts about rainforests. You will make notes in a chart. Then you will write a research report. A research report gives facts about a topic. Good writers end reports by restating the topic. In your research report, you will share facts you learned from books or other places.

Progress Check — Can I?

Before Unit 10		After Unit 10
☐	Gather facts for a research report.	☐
☐	Write a topic sentence for a research report.	☐
☐	Write facts about the topic.	☐
☐	Write an ending for the research report.	☐
☐	Use different types of sentences.	☐
☐	Use the correct end marks for sentences.	☐

Unit 10 ■ Research to Build and Present Knowledge: Write Research Reports

Student Page 215

Progress Check

The Progress Check is a self-assessment feature that children can use to gauge their own progress. Research shows that when children take accountability for their own learning, their motivation increases.

Before children begin work on Unit 10, have them check the boxes next to any item that they feel they can do well. Explain that it is fine if they don't check any of the boxes. Tell them that they will have an opportunity to learn about and practice all of these items while studying the unit. Let them know that near the end of the unit they will have a chance to reconsider how well they can do each item on the list.

Before children begin their Unit 10 Review on page 228, have them revisit this page. You can use this information to work with children on any items they don't understand before they tackle the Review.

HOME ✦ CONNECT...

The Home Connect feature is a way to keep parents or other adult family members apprised of what their children are learning. The key learning objectives are listed, and some ideas for related activities and discussions are included.

Explain to children that they can share the Home Connect page with their parents or other adult family members in their home. Let children know how much time the class will be spending on this unit so they can plan their time accordingly at home.

Encourage children and their parents or other adult family members to share their experiences using the suggestions on the Home Connect page.

HOME ✦ CONNECT...

IN THIS UNIT, YOUR CHILD WILL...

- Participate in a shared research and writing project.
- Recall information from personal experiences or gather facts from print and online sources to answer a question.
- Write informative texts in which he or she names a topic, supplies facts about it, and writes a conclusion.
- Use end punctuation for sentences to tell, ask, show strong feeling, and give commands.
- Produce and expand simple sentences in response to prompts.

In this unit, children will learn about writing a **research report.** A research report tells about a topic that a person has researched. Talk to your child about who might write research reports and why. For example, a scientist might write a research report about an important discovery in science. Encourage your child to think of a topic that interests him or her, then ask how he or she could find out more about it.

When writing research reports, writers use many different kinds of resources for their research. Encourage your child to think of print and online sources that might have information about an interesting topic.

Invite your child to discuss the research topic that he or she will write about for this unit. Ask questions about the steps in writing the report, including gathering information, taking and organizing notes, and writing and revising a draft. Have your child tell about how he or she shared the final version with classmates.

WAYS TO HELP YOUR CHILD

Encourage your child's curiosity. When your child shows interest in topics such as bugs, kinds of transportation, or weather, help him or her find facts about these subjects. Look for books and magazines on the topics online or in print at the library or at home. Have your child share what he or she has learned with family members.

Activity: Brainstorm ideas for research that might involve your family. For example, you might want to research places to go camping or to find out the kinds of animals that make the best pets. Help your child look for print or online books and magazines on the topic and read them together. Have your child write several sentences explaining what he or she found out.

ONLINE
For more Home Connect activities, continue online at sadlierconnect.com

216 Unit 10 ■ Research to Build and Present Knowledge: Write Research Reports

Student Page 216

UNIT PLANNER

Theme: In a Place Far Away Curriculum Connection: Science	Focus
WRITING MODEL *pp. 218–219*	*Helpful Rainforest Plants*
LISTEN TO GATHER FACTS *p. 220*	*Animals of the Rainforest*
RESEARCH AND TAKE NOTES *p. 221*	**ORGANIZATIONAL STRUCTURE:** Chart
CREATE YOUR REPORT *pp. 222–223*	*Rainforest Animals*
LANGUAGE MINI-LESSON *pp. 224–225*	Sentences
SPEAKING AND LISTENING *pp. 226–227*	• Share Your Writing • Be a Good Listener • Return to the Essential Question
UNIT 10 REVIEW *p. 228*	Language Skills Summary

Objective(s)

Write a research report about rainforest animals (based on information learned from listening to a read aloud), clearly stating the topic at the beginning, supporting the topic throughout with facts, and restating it at the end.

Listen to a read-aloud about rainforest animals while looking at related photographs, in order to gather facts for use in writing a research report.

Recall facts about rainforest animals from a text they heard read aloud and, using a chart, organize the facts for inclusion in a research report.

Draw pictures, complete sentence starters, and use notes to compose a research report about rainforest animals.

Identify and correctly write and punctuate simple and compound declarative, interrogative, imperative, and exclamatory sentences.

- Orally present a research report, including personal feelings about the topic and answering questions after the presentation.

- Participate respectfully in presentations as an active listener who offers ideas he or she agrees or disagrees with and joins in the discussion.

Unit Assessment

- Unit 10 Review *p. 228*

Additional Assessment Options

- Performance Task 1 *pp. 141–144*
  ALSO ONLINE

- Performance Task 2 *pp. 259–262*
  ALSO ONLINE

Optional Purchase:

- iProgress Monitor ONLINE

- Progress Monitor Student Benchmark Assessment Booklet

ONLINE Digital Resources

- Home Connect Activities

- Additional Practice

- Teacher Resources

- iProgress Monitor (optional purchase)

Go to SadlierConnect.com to access your Digital Resources.

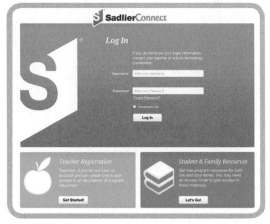

For more detailed instructions see page T3.

LEARNING PROGRESSIONS

In this unit, children will learn to write a research report based on details from a text that is read aloud. The report will include illustrations and sentences. In order to learn the skills necessary to craft a research report, children will further develop skills learned in kindergarten. They should be encouraged to retain these skills, as they will continue to build on them in second grade.

Naming the Topic

- By the end of kindergarten, children are able to name what they are writing about when composing informative texts by using a combination of drawing, dictating, and writing.

- In first grade, children understand what the topic of an informative text is and are readily able to name the topic as part of the introductions they write.

- Then, as second-graders, children work on creating effective openings for the informative texts they write, which includes introducing the topic.

Supplying Facts

- Proficient kindergartners include some information about their topics when writing informative texts.

- First-graders understand the need to provide facts about their topics and supply facts when writing informative texts.

- In second grade, children add definitions to the facts they supply and focus on using them to develop their points clearly in the body of an informative text.

Providing a Sense of Closure

- Kindergartners are not expected to provide closure when writing informative texts.

- Proficient first-graders are expected to provide some sense of closure at the end of an informative text.

- This expectation continues for second-graders, who should understand that the ending of an informative text should have a concluding statement or section.

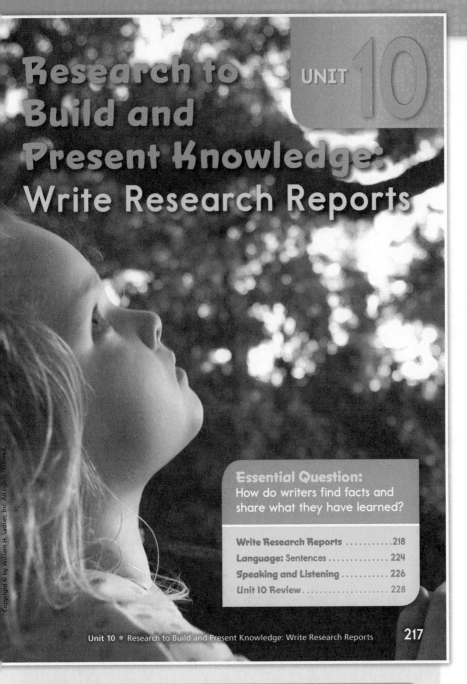

Research to Build and Present Knowledge: Write Research Reports

Essential Question:
How do writers find facts and share what they have learned?

Unit 10 ■ Research to Build and Present Knowledge: Write Research Reports **217**

Essential Question:
How do writers find facts and share what they have learned?

Children will learn the importance of clearly identifying the topic, supplying facts about it, and creating a sense of closure when writing a research paper.

Theme: In a Place Far Away

Children will carry forward from Unit 9 their thinking about rainforests as they read a research report model about a place featured as the setting for folktales in Unit 9—the rainforest.

Curriculum Connection: Science

As children learn facts about the plants and animals of the rainforest, they use these facts to develop a research report.

Connect Reading to Writing

Remind children that in Unit 9 they read several folktales set in lands far away. The stories "Snake and Frog" (Student Book, pages 194–197) and "Spider's Greed" (Student Book, pages 198–201) are both set in the rainforest. Now children will have an opportunity to learn facts about real plants and animals that live in the rainforest.

Writing Handbook

To assist children in writing a research report, use the *Writing Handbook* on pages 263–268 to guide them through the writing process. The *Writing Handbook* gives children detailed instruction on planning, drafting, revising, and editing their writing, as well as providing tips on producing and publishing.

Have children turn to page 263 and review all of the parts of the *Writing Handbook*. Then lead them through the suggestions on page 264 on selecting a topic and organizing their information. Once children get started on their research reports, return to the *Writing Handbook* for information on each part of the writing process.

OBJECTIVE
Write a research report about rainforest animals (based on information learned from listening to a read aloud), clearly stating the topic at the beginning, supporting the topic throughout with facts, and restating it at the end.

Introduce: Organizational Structure

Explain that a research report provides information about a topic. The topic is stated clearly at the beginning and at the end of the report. Facts that support the topic are given throughout. As you read the model together, identify the topic and the supporting facts.

Analyze a Student Model

Topic: Explain that the title of a research report often gives a clue about its topic. Read the title and the first sentence with children. Ask: *What words are the same in the title and in the first sentence? What does this tell you about the topic?* (Rainforest plants are helpful.)

Supporting Facts: Remind children that facts are statements that can be proven to be true. *What sentences in the paragraph are facts?* (Lipstick trees are used to make medicine and lipstick.)

Write Research Reports

Read a Student Model

Maya wrote a research report about plants in the rainforest. Think about how she states her topic. Look at the facts she uses in her report.

Helpful Rainforest Plants

Some rainforest plants are helpful to people. The lipstick tree is one useful plant. People use its leaves to make medicine. Its colorful seeds are used to make lipstick.

The lipstick tree is a helpful plant.

Teacher Talk: Find a Topic and Supporting Facts

Tell children that the topic is what the research report is about. Ask: *What sentence tells the topic?* Have children circle it. Explain that facts give more information about a topic. Ask: *What sentence tells a fact about the plant's leaves?* Have children underline it.

218 Unit 10 ■ Research to Build and Present Knowledge: Write Research Reports

Genre: Research Report

Emphasize to children that a research report is based on facts. It cannot be written unless facts have been gathered about the topic first.

Explain that facts can be gathered in different ways, but that only trusted sources should be used. Adults can help children access facts through appropriate sources. Tell children that it's important to use their own words to take notes about the information in the sources. Children should not use the exact words of another writer.

Point out that every fact used in a research report should relate to the topic. Sometimes while doing research, a writer might find interesting facts that are not on the topic. These facts should not be included.

The gumbo-limbo tree has many uses.

Another useful rainforest plant is the gumbo-limbo tree. People use its bark to keep bugs away. The bark is used in medicine, too.

(People need rainforest plants.) Aren't we lucky to have them?

Teacher Talk: Provide a Conclusion

Explain to children that a conclusion is a clear ending that restates the topic. Say: *Let's find a sentence at the end of Maya's report that restates the topic.* Have children circle the sentence.

Unit 10 ■ Research to Build and Present Knowledge: Write Research Reports **219**

Analyze a Student Model

Supporting Facts: Point out that the second paragraph of the research report gives facts about another helpful rainforest plant, the gumbo-limbo tree. So, this paragraph is definitely about the topic. Ask children how many facts are given to prove the tree's usefulness. (two)

Conclusion: Point out that the topic is restated in the final paragraph, but not in the final sentence. Explain that the topic should be introduced at the beginning of a research report, but it might not always be the very first sentence. Similarly, the topic should be restated at the end of the report, but not necessarily in the very last sentence. Sometimes, writers include an opinion for interest at the end of the research report.

Visual Literacy

Pictures and Captions: Ask children why the photographs included in this research report are helpful. (You can see what the plants described look like.) Point out the caption for the lipstick tree on page 218. Ask children to find the caption on page 219. Explain that the captions identify what is pictured and sometimes repeat information from the research report. So, the images and captions are an important part of the report.

Support English Language Learners

Teach plant part names to prepare children for this academic vocabulary included in the report.

Draw a simple tree. While drawing, say: *This tree grew from a small* **seed**. *The seed starts growing underground. Then plants grow from the seeds. The trunk of the tree is its biggest part. It is covered with* **bark**. *Bark feels rough when you touch it. The smaller parts are limbs. They have green* **leaves**.

Once the drawing is completed, ask: *What did the tree grow from?* (a seed) Then point to the trunk and ask: *What covers the trunk?* (bark) Finally, point to the leaves and ask: *What are these?* (leaves)

OBJECTIVE
Listen to a read-aloud about rainforest animals while looking at related photographs, in order to gather facts for use in writing a research report.

Using the Read Aloud: Listen to Gather Facts

Tell children that you will read a text aloud (see right) as they look at the pictures in their books. They should remember the facts they hear. Read the text, pausing at the numbers to discuss and pose the questions below.

Picture ①

In this text, the topic is stated in the last sentence of the first paragraph. Read the sentence again. What is this text about? (the animals of the rainforest)

Picture ②

What rainforest animal is this paragraph about? (howler monkeys) *What fact do you remember?* (Accept correct answers.)

Picture ③

What rainforest animal is this paragraph about? (leafcutter ants) *What fact do you remember?* (Accept correct answers.)

Picture ④

What rainforest animal is this paragraph about? (jaguars) *What fact do you remember?* (Accept correct answers.)

Turn and Talk

Have pairs discuss this question: *What makes each of the rainforest animals you learned about blend into the rainforest?* Then discuss the answers as a class. (Howler monkeys sound like wind. Leafcutter ants look like leaves. Jaguars have spotted coats that blend into the sun and shadows.)

Animals of the Rainforest

Rainforests are very moist places. They are found all around the world. More than 100 inches of rain can fall in a rainforest every year! Rainforests have a lot of trees and other plants. They also have many rivers and lakes. And rainforests are full of animals. ①

Many rainforest animals live in trees. Colorful birds are everywhere. Other animals, like howler monkeys, also live in the trees. Howler monkeys eat the fruits that grow on the trees. They also eat insects. Large groups of howler monkeys often live together. Their loud cries sound like a big windstorm. Who would guess the sound is coming from monkeys? ②

Some rainforest animals are very small. In fact, a rainforest has millions of insects! One of the most unusual insects is the leafcutter ant. This ant looks just like a green leaf. The way it looks helps the leafcutter ant hide while it works. Leafcutter ants chop up real leaves. They carry them to their home underground. There, the leaves help mushrooms to grow. Then the leafcutter ants eat the mushrooms. ③

Other rainforest animals are much bigger. These animals need a lot of room. They travel all around the rainforest. For example, jaguars are large cats. They hunt smaller animals. Jaguars are fast hunters and swift swimmers. They have beautiful spotted coats. Their coat helps them hide in the mixed sun and shadows of the rainforest. ④

If you ever go to a rainforest, you might not see very many animals. That's because they all blend in so well. Their colors match the rainforest colors. They also know how to be quiet when they need to hide. Fitting in helps rainforest animals survive

Write Research Reports

Listen to Gather Facts

Listen to the text. Try to remember important facts. Look at the pictures as you listen.

Animals of the Rainforest

1. rainforest
2. howler monkey
3. leafcutter ant
4. jaguar

Teacher Talk: Find a Topic and Supporting Facts

Read the text aloud from the Teacher's Guide. Then, remind children that they heard facts and details about animals in the rainforest. Say: *Name a fact that you learned about rainforest insects. Why is being hard to see helpful to animals in the rainforest?*

OBJECTIVE

Recall facts about rainforest animals from a text they heard read aloud and, using a chart, organize the facts for inclusion in a research report.

Research and Take Notes

Think About Organization

Remind children of how Maya organized her research report. She stated her topic in the first sentence. Each paragraph was about an example of a helpful plant. Then she restated her topic at the end.

Explain that children should follow this organization for their reports about rainforest animals. That means they need to have at least two facts about each animal they will include, to write a paragraph about it.

Plan

Explain that children will now use the graphic organizer on page 221 to take notes about the facts from the Read Aloud. They will use the notes when writing their reports.

Read the text a second time. Pause after paragraphs 2, 3, and 4 and ask: *What facts do we learn from this text about (name of rainforest animal)?* Record children's responses on the board or chart.

When the reading is complete, guide children to see how the information can fit into the graphic organizer on page 221. Discuss other facts about the leafcutter ant that might fit into the graphic organizer. Then have children complete the graphic organizer on their own.

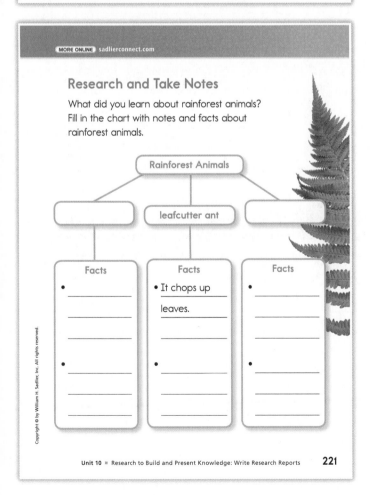

Research and Take Notes

What did you learn about rainforest animals? Fill in the chart with notes and facts about rainforest animals.

Rainforest Animals

leafcutter ant

Facts
•
•

Facts
• It chops up leaves.
•

Facts
•
•

OBJECTIVE
Draw pictures, complete sentence starters, and use notes to compose a research report about rainforest animals.

Introduce the Writing Process

Remind children that writing is a process that occurs in several steps over time. They have already completed the first step, planning. The next step is drafting.

Emphasize that the first draft of a research report is not the finished product. Children will have a chance to revise their drafts and edit them before they reach the final step, publishing.

Draft a Research Report

Point out the different areas for children to create their reports. Have children refer to their planning charts.

Ask: *What are all the facts about?* (rainforest animals) *How might you state the topic of your report?* (Example: Rainforests have many animals hidden in them.) Guide children to complete the first sentence starter as their statement of topic. Then ask: *Which animals will you include in your report?* (Example: howler monkeys, leafcutter ants, jaguars)

Remind children that they should have at least two facts about each animal. Guide children to complete the second sentence starter with the animal names. Explain that the remaining write-on lines are for a paragraph about each animal and a conclusion that restates the topic.

Write Research Reports

Create Your Report

In the boxes on pages 222–223, draw pictures of rainforest animals you have learned about.

Then use your research notes on page 221 to help you as you write. Start by completing the sentences below.

Rainforests have <u>a lot of animals</u>

_____.

Some examples are <u>the howler monkey, the leafcutter ant,</u>

<u>and the jaguar</u>_____.

Differentiate Instruction

As children continue drafting the body of the research report, circulate and provide the correct level of support for individuals who have not yet achieved independent literacy.

Emergent: Have these learners focus on creating illustrations that accurately show the facts they have learned about each rainforest animal. The write-on lines can be used to write captions (most likely phrases rather than sentences) about each animal illustrated.

Developing: Ask learners to express orally the facts they want to share about each animal. Provide corresponding sentence starters on the write-on lines for them to use in writing the facts.

Answers will vary. Children should introduce the topic, give

facts about rainforest animals, and then restate the topic

for a clear ending.

Unit 10 ■ Research to Build and Present Knowledge: Write Research Reports **223**

Revise and Edit: Peer Collaboration

Once children have finished their drafts, have them work in pairs to read their drafts to each other and suggest revisions. Explain that they should ask each other questions if anything is unclear. The answers can point to revisions that might need to be made. Partners might also suggest other facts to include or ways of stating and restating the topic more clearly.

Partners can then read each other's revisions and then make suggestions for ways to improve the draft.

Research Report Rubric

4	The research report includes a topic that is clearly stated at the beginning and end of the report, and facts that support the topic are presented in well-developed paragraphs.
3	The report has the elements listed under "4" above, though they are executed less successfully.
2	The report is missing one or more of the elements required.
1	The report is unfinished or shows a minimal understanding of required elements.

Assess and Respond

If children have trouble creating a research report from the planning chart . . .

Then guide them to compose a sentence(s) for each section of the chart. Help them see that the sentences for a section go together as a paragraph. Explain that these paragraphs form the body of the report. Help them to finish the report by guiding them to write a conclusion that restates the topic.

Digital Connection

As children create a final draft of their research reports, completing the publishing stage of the writing process, they might want to include realistic images of the animals they describe. Demonstrate for them how to do an image search using your preferred search engine on the Internet. Show them how to type in the key word and how to view, select, and print the images.

You might work with small groups of children at a time, helping each group member select just the right images to include in his or her final draft. Provide scissors, glue sticks, and other supplies for children to use in creating their finished products.

OBJECTIVE
Identify and correctly write and punctuate simple and compound declarative, interrogative, imperative, and exclamatory sentences.

Guided Instruction

Review the concept of a sentence as a group of words that gives a complete idea. Remind children that sentences include a naming part and an action part. Also review that sentences begin with a capital letter and end with a punctuation mark. Display and review the three end marks (**.** **!** **?**).

Then read aloud the introduction to sentences and the first four bulleted items. Clearly model the correct voice inflection for the example sentences, and have children echo-read the sentences with you.

Before reading the fifth bullet aloud, display and review the comma, explaining that this punctuation mark means you should pause while reading. Also review the word *and*, explaining that it shows that two things are connected.

Then read the fifth bullet aloud. Point out the comma and the connecting word *and* in the example compound sentence. Explain that both of these must appear in a compound sentence for it to be written correctly.

Sentences

Guided Instruction Sentences share thoughts or ideas in different ways. Their end marks are clues.

- Some sentences **tell information**. They have a period (.).

  A rainforest gets a lot of rain.

- Some sentences **ask a question**. They have a question mark (?).

  How much rain falls in the rainforest?

- Some sentences **give a command**. They have a period (.).

  Tell me more about rainforests.

- Some sentences **show strong feeling**. They have an exclamation point (*!*).

  Rainforests are so damp!

- Sometimes writers join two simple sentences to make one longer sentence.

  Simple *Rainforests are cool. I like them!*
  Compound Rainforests are cool, *and* I like them!

224 Unit 10 ■ Research to Build and Present Knowledge: Write Research Reports

Support English Language Learners

Be sure children see how each punctuation mark is formed and where it is placed. Spanish speakers, for example, are used to seeing exclamation and question marks at the beginning and the end of a sentence—written "upside down" at the beginning. Arabic speakers are used to seeing question marks and commas reversed.

Guided and Independent Practice Circle what each sentence does. Then add the correct end mark (. ? !).

1. Howler monkeys are loud . (tells)
   asks

2. How fast are jaguars ? gives a command
   (asks)

3. A jaguar is coming ! gives a command
   (shows strong feeling)

Write a sentence that gives a command.

4. Sample answer: Look in the box. _____

Write a sentence that tells information.

5. Sample answer: The box is heavy. _____

Look at the following short sentences. Write a longer sentence from the two short ones.

A jaguar is fast. A howler monkey is loud.

6. A jaguar is fast, and a howler monkey is loud. _____

_____

Unit 10 ■ Research to Build and Present Knowledge: Write Research Reports **225**

Guided and Independent Practice

Point out that items 1 through 3 require two responses. First, children should identify the purpose of each sentence. Then, they should write the end mark that matches the purpose. For children who need support, display these reminders:

. (period) = tells or commands

! (exclamation point) = shows strong feelings

? (question mark) = asks

For items 4 and 5, have children come up with their own sentences. To make the task for item 4 easier, tell children to think about the last time someone spoke a command to them, or for item 5 told them a piece of information. Circulate as children write these sentences, helping as needed. Ask how each sentence should end. (with a period)

For item 6, point out to children that to form the longer sentence, they need to add a comma and add the word *and*.

Assess and Respond

If children have difficulty writing different types of sentences . . .

Then give them more practice in identifying the types of sentences as you speak them, using a game-like format. Have children make four index cards, writing the purpose of one type of sentence on each card: *ask, tell, command, show feelings*. After you say a sentence, children hold up the card identifying it. (You can use the sentences from this lesson and simple variations on them.) Once children truly understand how each type of sentence functions, they will have an easier time coming up with their own sentences of each type.

Differentiate Instruction

Some children may be ready to learn how to form compound sentences using the connecting words *or* and *but*. Remind them that *and* is used to connect ideas, so the sentences that are combined with *and* give similar information, as in *We work hard in class, and we learn a lot.*

Then explain that *or* is used to suggest a choice, so this word connects sentences that present different ideas. Give an example: *We could go to a movie tonight, or we could go to the mall.* See if children can come up with an example of their own. Repeat for *but*, explaining that it suggests a difference between two ideas, as in *I like reading best, but my friend likes math.* Have children practice writing compound sentences using all three connecting words.

OBJECTIVE

Orally present a research report, including personal feelings about the topic and answering questions after the presentation.

Share Your Writing

Tell children that they will present their research reports by reading them aloud. Explain that they should tell how they felt about their topics at the beginning of their presentations. Provide a few sentence starters for children to use: This topic was interesting to me because _____.

Explain that children might be asked questions about their reports. Emphasize that since they wrote their reports, they should not be anxious about this part of the presentation. Tell children to answer questions using complete sentences.

Get Ready

Children can practice their presentations in pairs. Guide them to apply the speaking skills they have learned: speak clearly and loudly, show their drawings, use sentences with detail, answer questions, and tell how they feel.

Present

Have children give their presentations in small groups. Monitor to be sure children are applying the listening skills they have learned: wait their turn, listen carefully, ask questions, build on what others say, and tell if they agree or disagree.

Speaking and Listening

Share Your Writing

You will present your research report. Speak clearly and in complete sentences. Look at your listeners.

Tell your opinion. Explain your feelings about the topic.

This topic was really interesting and exciting!

Be ready to answer questions about your report.

226   Unit 10 ■ Research to Build and Present Knowledge: Write Research Reports

---

Discussion Skills

As you monitor the small group presentations, encourage children to participate in each presentation by encouraging them to engage in multiple exchanges after each speaker presents. Ask them the following questions to help with their discussion.

- Can you repeat what was just said in your own words?
- Can you say a little more about that?
- Would someone like to add anything?

Copyright © by William H. Sadlier, Inc. All rights reserved.

Be a Good Listener

Your role is to listen carefully when a classmate presents a report. As you listen, think of questions you have about what you hear.

I agree with what you said.

After a report, you will ask questions and discuss ideas.

Think about the ideas in the report. Tell what you agree or disagree with.

Return to the Essential Question

How do writers find facts and share what they have learned?

Think about these questions before the class discussion:

• Where did we find facts for our reports?

• Where else can we find facts?

Unit 10 ■ Research to Build and Present Knowledge: Write Research Reports **227**

OBJECTIVE
Participate respectfully in presentations as an active listener who offers ideas he or she agrees or disagrees with and joins in the discussion.

Be a Good Listener

Remind children that good listeners look at and listen to the speaker. When the speaker is finished, listeners can discuss the points, asking questions to clear up confusion. Tell them if they disagree, they should present their point of view respectfully. Encourage children to start with a positive comment and to express their opinions clearly by using the sentence stem "I like how you described the jaguar. I disagree that it is more beautiful because _____."

Return to the Essential Question

Give children time to think about the questions before the discussion. After discussing those questions, have children suggest other ways that writers might share what they learn from their research.

Support English Language Learners

English language learners who are at the beginning stages of language development will be most comfortable relying on visuals during their presentations. Support them by helping them find excellent visuals, each of which they can share with a single sentence. Allow them to practice until they are comfortable, and consider carefully the small groups you form. If listeners ask questions requiring complicated responses, rephrase the sentences so a single word or phrase can serve as the answer.

Remember that these same learners understand much more than they are able to express. Involve them as listeners by asking them yes/no questions such as "Do you agree with that? Did you enjoy hearing that fact, too?"

Introduce the Review

Explain to children that this review will give them a chance to use the language skills that they have studied and practiced in this unit. It will also give them a chance to share what they have learned about being a good speaker or listener.

Language Skills Summary

Let children know that they are going to use what they learned about the different types of sentences and how to write them. Briefly review the main concepts they learned. Say:

• *Some sentences tell information. What are three other things a sentence can do?* (ask, give a command, show strong feeling)

• *Which two types of sentences end with a period?* (sentences that tell and sentences that give a command)

Answer Explanations

1–2. Suggest that children try reading the sentences aloud softly to themselves, which will help them "hear" the sentence purpose.

3–4. Suggest that children think about a strong feeling and a question they have had recently, using these personal experiences to come up with the sentences.

Self-Assessment: Progress Check

Have children revisit the Progress Check on page 215 and compare their answers now with the answers they gave before completing Unit 10.

Unit 10 Review

Choose the correct answer. Fill in the circle.

1. Which end mark should you use?

I have one sister

● .   ○ ?   ○ !

2. What does the following sentence do?

How many legs does a spider have?

● asks   ○ tells   ○ gives a command

Write each kind of sentence.

3. Write a sentence that shows strong feeling.

Sample answer: I love that song!

4. Write a sentence that asks a question.

Sample answer: Did you learn a lot about rainforests?

Think about speaking and listening.

5. Write a sentence about what a good speaker or listener does.

Sample answer: A good speaker speaks clearly.

228   Unit 10 ■ Research to Build and Present Knowledge: Write Research Papers

---

Test-Taking Tip

Have children analyze the parts of questions 1 and 2—the question, the sentence, and the choices. Explain that when answering questions such as these, they should read the question, read the sentence, and read each answer choice before filling in a bubble.

Introducing UNIT 11

In this unit, you will learn about the sun, moon, and stars by reading informational texts. Authors who write informational texts use pictures and details to help readers understand their ideas. They use reasons to explain their opinions. Thinking about how informational texts are alike and different helps you understand them.

Progress Check Can I?

Before Unit 11 / After Unit 11

- ☐ Use pictures and details to describe key ideas. ☐
- ☐ Identify reasons that explain an opinion. ☐
- ☐ Tell what is alike and different in informational texts. ☐
- ☐ Use what I learn to read new words. ☐
- ☐ Sort words into groups. ☐
- ☐ Use word groups to give word meanings. ☐

Unit 11 ▪ Reading Informational Text: Integration of Knowledge and Ideas

Student Page 229

HOME✦CONNECT...

The Home Connect feature is a way to keep parents or other adult family members apprised of what their children are learning. The key learning objectives are listed, and some ideas for related activities and discussions are included.

Explain to children that they can share the Home Connect page with their parents or other adult family members in their home. Let children know how much time the class will be spending on this unit so they can plan their time accordingly at home.

Encourage children and their parents or other adult family members to share their experiences using the suggestions on the Home Connect page.

Progress Check

The Progress Check is a self-assessment feature that children can use to gauge their own progress. Research shows that when children take accountability for their own learning, their motivation increases.

Before children begin work on Unit 11, have them check the boxes next to any item that they feel they can do well. Explain that it is fine if they don't check any of the boxes. Tell them that they will have an opportunity to learn about and practice all of these items while studying the unit. Let them know that near the end of the unit they will have a chance to reconsider how well they can do each item on this list.

Before children begin their Unit 11 Review on page 257, have them revisit this page. You can use this information to work with children on any items they don't understand before they tackle the Review.

HOME✦CONNECT...

By using **pictures and details**, authors help readers to understand **key ideas**. Choose a print or online article on a topic your child might enjoy. As you read the text with your child, identify the key ideas on a page with him or her. Then look for details and pictures that support this key idea.

Authors use **reasons** to convince readers to share their opinions. Find a print or online opinion article. With your child, identify the opinion and look for reasons the author uses to support it. Ask your child if he or she thinks the author gives good reasons.

Comparing texts—identifying what is the same and different about them—helps children think about what they read. Choose two nonfiction books on the same topic. Look at the photos, illustrations, diagrams, maps, or other images in both books. Use the following questions to discuss similarities and differences: Do both books have the same types of images? Do the images show the same information?

Activity: Look at the night sky with your child and talk about what you see. Can you see stars, or do city lights make it hard to see them? Are some stars brighter or bigger than others? Is the moon out? If so, what shape is it? Try to go out at different times of the month and discuss how the night sky changes.

IN THIS UNIT, YOUR CHILD WILL...

- Use illustrations and details to describe the key ideas in a text.
- Identify the reasons an author gives to support ideas.
- Find what is similar or different about two texts on the same topic.
- Determine the number of syllables in words and break words into syllables to read them.
- Read words with -s, -ed, and -ing endings.
- Sort words into categories and use categories to define words.
- Compare and contrast three different texts on the same topic: an informational text, a how-to text, and an opinion piece.

WAYS TO HELP YOUR CHILD

Show respect for your child's opinions on topics while helping him or her develop the speaking and thinking skills to express and support opinions. Whether you are discussing food, sports, or clothing, ask for your child's opinions and reasons that support them. Share some of your opinions, too, and give reasons for them. Discuss how your opinions are similar to or different from your child's.

ONLINE
For more Home Connect activities, continue online at sadlierconnect.com

230   Unit 11 ▪ Reading Informational Text: Integration of Knowledge and Ideas

Student Page 230

UNIT PLANNER

Theme: Sky Lights	Focus
READ ALOUD pp. 232–233	*Lighting Up the Sky* **GENRE:** Informational Text with Procedure
USING PICTURES AND DETAILS pp. 234–237	*Sky Lights* **GENRE:** Informational Text **LEXILE®:** 450L **WORDS TO KNOW:** amount, center, grab, loose
IDENTIFYING AUTHOR'S REASONS pp. 238–241	*Lights Out!* **GENRE:** Opinion Piece **LEXILE®:** 470L **WORDS TO KNOW:** attract, avoid, confuse, harm, signal
COMPARING TEXTS pp. 242–245	*Movements of the Sun, Earth, and Moon; Make a Model* **GENRES:** Informational Text; Procedural Text **LEXILE®:** 360L; 510L **WORDS TO KNOW:** attach, insert, model, solid, surface
FOUNDATIONAL SKILLS READ TOGETHER p. 246	*Pictures in the Stars* **GENRE:** Informational Text
FOUNDATIONAL SKILLS READER 1 pp. 247–248	*Super Stars* **GENRE:** Informational Text
FOUNDATIONAL SKILLS READER 2 pp. 249–250	*Our Moon* **GENRE:** Informational Text
CLOSE READING pp. 251–254	*Sunlight Is Better* **GENRE:** Opinion Piece **LEXILE®:** 440L
CONNECT ACROSS TEXTS p. 255	Compare and Contrast Texts
LANGUAGE p. 256	Groups of Words
UNIT 11 REVIEW pp. 257–258	*Kids in Space* **GENRE:** Opinion Piece **LEXILE®:** 510L

Essential Question: How do authors use details to tell about key ideas?

UNIT 11

Objective(s)

- Match text to corresponding visuals, using both to describe in their own words the main ideas.
- Identify an author's opinions and the reasons given to support those opinions.
- Compare and contrast two texts on the same topic.

Match text to corresponding visuals, using both to describe in their own words the main ideas.

Identify an author's opinions and the reasons given to support those opinions.

Compare and contrast two texts on the same topic.

Read decodable text featuring two-syllable words and words with inflectional endings.

Read decodable text featuring two-syllable words.

Read decodable text featuring inflectional endings.

Same objectives as pages 234–237, pages 238–241, pages 242–245

Group words that are similar and then note the differences among them.

Unit Assessment

- Unit 11 Review *pp. 257–258*
- Unit 11 Performance Task ONLINE

Additional Assessment Options

- Performance Task 1 *pp. 141–144*
  (ALSO ONLINE)
- Performance Task 2 *pp. 259–262*
  (ALSO ONLINE)

Optional Purchase:
- iProgress Monitor (ONLINE)
- Progress Monitor Student Benchmark Assessment Booklet

ONLINE Digital Resources

- Home Connect Activities
- Unit Performance Task
- Additional Practice
- Full-Length Reading Selections
- Foundational Skills Practice
- Teacher Resources
- iProgress Monitor (optional purchase)

Go to SadlierConnect.com to access your Digital Resources.

For more detailed instructions see page T3.

231B

LEARNING PROGRESSIONS

In this unit, children will learn that being able to connect the information within and between texts helps them to comprehend the key ideas and understand why the author included the facts and visuals. In order to learn the skills in this unit, children will further develop skills learned in kindergarten. They should be encouraged to retain these skills, as they will continue to build on them in second grade.

Using Pictures and Details

- By the end of kindergarten, children can respond to prompts about how the images in a text go with the text.

- In first grade, children are able to independently link images and text when describing the key ideas presented.

- Then, second-grade children produce explanations of why images included in a text are helpful in fully comprehending the ideas presented.

Identifying Author's Reasons

- Proficient kindergartners are able to identify the specific reasons an author gives to support key ideas, but most children require support to do this.

- First-graders are then expected to accomplish this task independently.

- In second grade, children are further able to describe how the reasons included provide support for specific points.

Comparing Texts

- When prompted, children at the end of kindergarten can identify similarities and differences between two texts on the same subject.

- By the end of first grade, children are seeing the basic similarities and differences between two texts on their own.

- As second grade draws to a close, children should be thinking in a more sophisticated way as they compare and contrast the key ideas found in two texts on the same topic.

Reading Informational Text: Integration of Knowledge and Ideas

UNIT 11

Essential Question:
How do authors use details to tell about key ideas?

Unit 11 ■ Reading Informational Text: Integration of Knowledge and Ideas **231**

Vocabulary Overview

amount 236, attach 244, attract 239, avoid 239, center 234, confuse 239, grab 236, harm 240, insert 244, loose 235, model 243, signal 240, solid 242, surface 242

Essential Question:
How do authors use details to tell about key ideas?

In this unit, children will learn how to integrate knowledge and information when reading informational texts, with the emphasis on linking images to text, identifying the reasons an author uses to support key ideas, and seeing similarities and differences between two texts on the same topic.

Theme: Sky Lights

Children will read selections about objects in the sky, including the sun and other stars, the moon, and planets. They will learn about the movement of these objects and make a moon calendar and a model that shows how the movements are related; they will read opinion pieces about turning off lights at night and appreciating the superiority of sunlight over moonlight; and they will enjoy learning interesting facts about constellations, the life of a star, the phases of the moon, and the ways humans are able to study the skies.

Curriculum Connection: Science

As children enjoy the selections in this unit, they will learn key details and facts about the solar system and how the sun, moon, and stars are related to Earth.

OBJECTIVES

- **Match text to corresponding visuals, using both to describe in their own words the main ideas.**
- **Identify an author's opinions and the reasons given to support those opinions.**
- **Compare and contrast two texts on the same topic.**

Using the Read Aloud

Tell children that you will read aloud a text (see right) as they look at the pictures in their books. Read the text, pausing at the numbers to pose the questions below.

Picture

What is the sun? (a star) *What is the sun made of?* (gases) *What does the sun give off?* (bright light) Read caption 1 together.

Picture

Why can't we see the sun at night? (Earth is facing away from the sun.) *Is it night everywhere on Earth at the same time? Why or why not?* (No, because part of Earth faces the sun and has day.) Read caption 2 together.

Picture

Why do the stars in the night sky look so small? (They are very far away.) *In this picture, why does the moon look bright?* (Sunlight hits the moon and makes it look bright.) Read caption 3 together.

Picture

Let's look at picture 4 closely. What does this picture tell you about the moon? (It shows the different shapes we see.)

Turn and Talk

Have pairs discuss this question: What makes the moon's shape seem to change?

Lighting Up the Sky

What do you see when you look at the sky during the day? Do you see a bright light? That bright ball of light is the sun. The sun is a star. It's a huge ball of gases that gives off light. **1**

Earth turns all the way around each day. Because it turns, we have day and night. It is daytime where Earth faces the sun. In the daytime, you can see the sun's light. You can feel its warmth. It is night where Earth faces away from the sun. At night, you cannot see the sun. **2**

What do you see when you look at the sky at night? Do you see any little points of light? Those points of light are just like our sun because they are stars. They don't seem as bright as the sun, but they are. They don't seem big, either, but they are. They look tiny because they are very far away from Earth. Like the sun, they are made of gases that give off light.

You might see the moon in the night sky, too. The moon is a rocky sphere that travels around Earth. The moon can look bright, but it does not make its own light. The light you see is sunlight hitting the moon. **3**

Sometimes the moon looks like a big glowing ball. It looks large and round. Sometimes we cannot see the moon at all. You can make a moon calendar to show the changes in the moon's appearance. Here's how:

1. Copy or print out a blank calendar page for a month.
2. Draw a circle in the box for each day. Try to make all the circles the same size. The circle is the moon.
3. On the first night of a new moon, go outside and look at the sky. Try to find the moon.
4. In the first box of your calendar, shade the moon to show what you see. Write the date.
5. Keep looking at the moon every night. Shade the moon or the box to show what you see.
6. When your moon calendar is done, take a closer look at it. Think about how the moon's shape seems to change. Share your calendar with your family. **4**

Listen to the selection. Pay attention to important details.

Look at the pictures as you listen. How do they help you understand?

Lighting Up the Sky

1 We see the sun during the day.

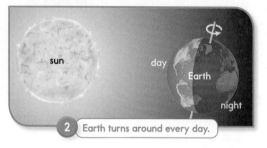

2 Earth turns around every day.

3 The moon goes around Earth.

Monday	Tuesday	Wednesday	Thursday	Friday	Saturday	Sunday
1	2	3	4	5	6	7
8	9	10	11	12	13	14

4 The moon seems to change shape.

Preview the Focus Skills

Do a second reading of the Read Aloud as children look at the pictures. As you read, pause briefly where indicated below. Use the suggested think alouds to preview the unit's targeted reading skills and model how children might use the skills independently during shared reading.

- Pause after reading the second paragraph. Say: *I am really glad the diagram shows what the text describes. I could not quite picture in my mind what the words say, but the diagram makes it easier to understand. Using both the picture and the text as I read helps me understand the text better.*

- Pause after reading the fifth paragraph. Say: *The author says the moon sometimes "looks like a big glowing ball. It looks large and round." I always thought that the moon looks like a person's face, but I can see why the author says it looks like a ball, because it is round. Finding the author's reasons behind his or her thinking helps me understand the information better.*

- After reading paragraph 5 and the procedural text, say: *The instructions for how to make a moon calendar are quite different from the rest of this text. Each sentence is a command. The directions are very clear, and the illustration helps me see what the finished project should look like. I did enjoy how the author wrote the rest of the text, though. I especially liked the descriptions of the sun, stars, and moon. Reading different texts on the same topic helps me understand the topic better.*

Digital Connection

If you do not typically have a good view of the moon in your area, you might want to find websites that provide daily moon images that children can use to make their calendars.

Guided Instruction

OBJECTIVES

- **Match text to corresponding visuals, using both to describe in their own words the main ideas.**
- **Answer questions about key details.**

Genre: Informational Text

Remind children that informational text presents facts. People read informational text to learn about a topic.

Set the Purpose

Help children understand the purpose for learning to use illustrations by asking: *Why do authors of informational text include pictures and diagrams? How do they help you understand the text?*

Model and Teach

Read the text aloud as children follow along in their books.

Teacher Talk: Find Evidence

Point out to children that details can describe information in a text and lead them to understand the text's key ideas. Reread paragraph 2 aloud. Then say: *There were a lot of details in that paragraph. I learned that a cloud is made of gas and dust. It spins and shrinks. I also learned that as the cloud shrinks everything gets closer to the center. The center heats up and starts to glow. How do all these details help me to understand the key idea? I'm going to look back now in the paragraph and find the sentence that tells me the key idea.*

Using Pictures and Details

Words to Know

center

loose

Sky Lights
(Genre: Informational Text)

1   The stars in the night sky look like they have always been there. However, they are changing all the time. Stars are like living things on Earth. They are born. They grow old. They die.

How a Star Is Born

2   A star starts out as a giant cloud in space. The cloud is made of cold gas and dust. Over time, the cloud shrinks and spins. As it spins, everything in the cloud gets closer together. The **center** of the cloud heats up and starts to glow. The center has become a brand new star!

A star is born.

3   Other parts of the cloud are left behind. A planet forms when those parts come together. Planets revolve, or circle, around the star.

Guided Instruction

Teacher Talk: Find Evidence

Tell children that they can use details in informational text to describe its key ideas. Ask: *What does paragraph 2 tell you about new stars?* Have children underline the words in paragraph 2 that tell the key idea of the paragraph.

234   Unit 11 ■ Reading Informational Text: Integration of Knowledge and Ideas

---

Words to Know

center (*noun*): the middle point of something
loose (*adjective*): not together in one place; scattered

Working with Word Meaning Use masking tape to create a large circle on the floor. Ask a child to stand in the *center* of the circle. Then say that you want to demonstrate *loose*. Take a small stack of paper and scatter the sheets in disarray in the circle. Have the child pick up the sheets and stack them all back together.

Guided Instruction

Our Star

4   The sun was born billions of years ago. Like all stars, it started from a cloud of dust and gas. The cloud became a spinning ball in space. The center of the ball began to glow, and our sun was born. Smaller clumps of dust and gas surrounded the sun. They became other space objects.

5   When the sun began to glow, it created winds. The winds blew away **loose** dust and gases. What was left? Eight planets, some moons, and large space rocks called asteroids. All revolve around the sun. They make up our solar system.

Eight planets go around the sun in our solar system.

Mars
Venus
Saturn
Neptune
Mercury
Jupiter
Earth
Uranus

Teacher Talk: Find Evidence

Tell children that they can also use pictures to understand a text's key ideas. Discuss the diagram. Ask: *Which part of the text does the diagram help explain?* Have children underline text that shows the key idea of the diagram. Ask: *What other details do you learn from the diagram?*

Guided Instruction

Unit 11 ▪ Reading Informational Text: Integration of Knowledge and Ideas   **235**

Teacher Talk: Find Evidence

Point out to children that photos and illustrations can add information in a text and help them understand the text's key ideas better. Say: *When I look at this illustration, I see 8 planets. The thin lines let me know that these planets revolve, or go around, the sun. I know I read some text about that. I'm going to look for words in paragraph 5 that tell the same idea.*

Explain that illustrations and diagrams sometimes include additional information. Say: *I know that the diagram shows 8 planets that revolve around the sun, and that's what the text tells me, too. But if I look closely at the diagram I see some words. I don't think these words are part of the text I read. Let's look more closely to see what this additional information is.*

After going through the Find Evidence instruction, help children sum up the key idea of the selection. Ask them to tell how they used the details from the text and the illustrations to determine the key idea. Ask them to tell how the illustrations and the text both helped them understand the text.

Use Visuals

To help children retell key ideas from information presented in visuals, have them look at the visuals on pages 234–235. Ask them to tell which part of "Sky Lights" each visual explains. Ask children to use a sentence to tell the key idea shown by the visual.

Support English Language Learners

Build an understanding of the solar system before reading. Assign a child to be the sun and others to be the planets. Help children arrange themselves in the proper order. Have them say the name of each planet in order and then revolve around the sun a few times if room is available in your classroom.

Guided Practice

Read and Practice

Read the first paragraph aloud. Have heterogeneous partners take turns rereading the paragraph as you circulate to provide support.

Teacher Talk: Find Evidence

Allow children a few moments to examine the picture. Ask them to describe what they see. Point out to children that pictures and illustrations can add to the information in a text and help them understand the text's key ideas better. Say: *When I look at this picture, the moon seems huge! I think of the moon as being very far away. But in this picture it looks really close. I'm going to look for words in the first paragraph that tell the same idea.*

Team Jigsaw

After children have finished page 237, use the following peer support activity as a wrap-up activity. Paragraphs 4, 5, 6, and 7 offer information about our sun and our moon. Place children in groups of four and assign each child in the group one of these paragraphs. Ask each child to decide the most interesting fact from the assigned paragraph and to write it in a sentence, using their own words. Then put the four sentences together and have the group share with the rest of the class. Discuss why different people find different facts interesting.

Using Pictures and Details

Words to Know

amount
grab

Hello, Neighbor!

6   We live on planet Earth. Our closest neighbor is the moon. It is more than 200,000 miles away from us. <u>Even so, sometimes it looks close enough to reach up and **grab**.</u>

7   Some objects, such as the moon, rotate in space. This means that they spin around. The moon also revolves around Earth. It does both in the same **amount** of time. That is why one half of the moon always faces Earth. Do you know what we call the side that faces away? It is called the dark side of the moon.

Sometimes the moon looks big and close to Earth.

Guided Practice

Teacher Talk: Find Evidence

Review how text details and pictures can be used to describe key ideas. Have children describe what the picture shows. Then have them underline the sentence in "Hello, Neighbor!" that goes with the picture.

236   Unit 11 ■ Reading Informational Text: Integration of Knowledge and Ideas

---

Words to Know

amount (*noun*): piece
grab (*verb*): to get

Working with Word Meaning Present children with a bowl of sand or soil and a small cup, such as a ¼-cup measure. Ask them to predict whether the *amount* of sand they can *grab* with one hand will fill the cup. Then have them do it! Were their predictions correct?

Integration of Knowledge and Ideas

8   Sometimes the <u>moon</u> looks round and bright. It lights up the night sky. The <u>stars</u> light up the night sky, too. Together with <u>the sun</u>, they are our (sky lights.)

Comprehension Check   (MORE ONLINE) sadlierconnect.com

1. Reread the "Hello, Neighbor!" section. Which detail does not belong in this part of the text?

   a. The moon is one of Earth's sky lights.

   (b.) Stars are born, grow old, and die.

   c. The moon is Earth's closest neighbor.

2. Look at the diagram on page 235. What planet is closest to the sun? How do you know?

   Mercury is closest to the sun. I know Mercury is closest to

   the sun because I can see it in the diagram.

   _____

   _____

Teacher Talk: Find Evidence
Have children circle the words *sky lights* in the last sentence. Ask them to underline the details in the last paragraph that name the sky lights.

Independent Practice

Unit 11 ■ Reading Informational Text: Integration of Knowledge and Ideas   **237**

Foundational Skills Review: Fluency Practice

Remind children that paying attention to punctuation helps them to read accurately. Have students find all of the sentence end marks in paragraph 7. Model a fluent reading of the paragraph, coming to a full pause at each end mark. Then go back to the beginning of the paragraph and have children chorally read the paragraph. Have them work in groups of three to continue practicing with paragraph 7 and paragraph 8. Additional fluency passages and activities can be found at **sadlierconnect.com**.

Independent Practice

Read and Apply

Have children read paragraph 8 on page 237 independently as you circulate. Provide extra support to struggling readers by choral reading with them.

Teacher Talk: Find Evidence

Say: *Stars make light, and they are in the sky. That's one kind of sky light. What other words in the paragraph make you think of light in the sky?*

Comprehension Check

Answer Explanations:

1. Choice **B** is a detail that does not support the key idea of the section.

2. Children should trace the planets' paths. Mercury is closest to the sun.

Critical Comprehension

Use the following question to help children think more deeply about the selection. Children should support their answers with evidence from the text.

• *How do the photos and illustrations help you understand the information in the text?* (Sample answer: The diagram helps me understand how the planets move around the sun. The picture helps me to see how it seems big and close.)

Assess and Respond
If children have difficulty answering the questions in the Comprehension Check . . .
Then work with them to create a graphic organizer showing the key details in "Hello, Neighbor!" Compare details with the choices. Review the diagram on page 235. Help children locate the planets in relation to the sun.

Guided Instruction

OBJECTIVES
- **Identify an author's opinions and the reasons given to support those opinions.**
- **Answer questions about key details.**

Genre: Opinion Piece

Tell children that opinion pieces are texts written to share an opinion with others. Authors of opinion pieces try to convince readers their opinions are right.

Set the Purpose

Help children understand the purpose for learning the reading skill by asking *What kinds of information do you find helpful when you read?*

Model and Teach

Read the text aloud as children follow along in their books.

Teacher Talk: Find Evidence

Tell children that an author often writes to give his or her opinion. Say: *An opinion is what an author believes or thinks. An opinion is neither right nor wrong. Certain words and phrases can help me figure out the author's opinion. Let's look at paragraph 1 together. The author states that people think lights are pretty but that all those lights are making the nights look like days. The author is telling me how he or she feels about those lights. Let's look to see what the author's opinion is about using the lights.*

Words to Know
attract
avoid
confuse

Lights Out!
(Genre: Opinion Piece)

1 Every night, lights come on in cities all over the world. Many people like the lights. They think the lights are pretty. But all those lights add up. Our nights are becoming like days. It is time for us to turn off some city lights.

2 Why do we need to turn off lights? One reason is that we cannot see the stars. Out away from a city, you can see thousands of stars on a clear night. You do not even need a telescope. They are very bright!

3 In a city, people sometimes see only a few stars on a clear night. That is a problem for scientists. City lights make it hard for them to study the stars.

Guided Instruction

Teacher Talk: Find Evidence
Tell children that an opinion is something a person thinks or believes. Explain that *think* and *believe* can signal opinions. Point out the opinion "the lights are pretty" and the clue *think* in paragraph 1. Ask: *What is the author's opinion at the end of paragraph 1?* Have children underline it.

238 Unit 11 ■ Reading Informational Text: Integration of Knowledge and Ideas

---

Words to Know

attract (*verb*): to pull or call to
avoid (*verb*): to stay away from
confuse (*verb*): to mix up

Working with Word Meaning Help children understand the words by naming something that would *confuse* you, something that would *attract* you, and something that you *avoid*. Then have children name things that *confuse* them, things that *attract* them, and things that they *avoid*.

Integration of Knowledge and Ideas

4   There is another reason for turning off some lights. Bright light at night makes problems for animals. For example, bright lights **confuse** some birds. They get day and night mixed up. Birds and bats end up hunting at the same time. Then both have a hard time finding food.

5   Bright streetlights **attract** many insects. The lights can hurt them. The insects do not survive. Animals that eat insects might go hungry.

6   Another animal hurt by bright light at night is the sea turtle. Female sea turtles lay their eggs on beaches. They lay their eggs only at night. The turtles **avoid** bright beaches. When they stay away, they do not lay eggs. That means we have fewer sea turtles.

sea turtle

Teacher Talk: Find Evidence

Explain that authors give reasons to support an opinion so they can convince readers to share the opinion. Tell children that *why* and *reason* signal reasons. Point out the reason the author gives in paragraph 2. Have children circle the reason in paragraph 4.

Guided Instruction

Unit 11 ■ Reading Informational Text: Integration of Knowledge and Ideas   **239**

Guided Instruction

Teacher Talk: Find Evidence

Pause before continuing to read the text on page 239. Say: *I want to be sure I understand the first reason the author gives to support the opinion that we should turn off some lights. The author introduces it with the words "One reason is . . . ."*

Direct children to find and underline this sentence in paragraph 2. Explain: *The fact that we can't see the stars seems like a good reason to turn off some lights. I know I think the stars are beautiful. However, that is an opinion, not a fact. In paragraph 3, the author makes the reason stronger by saying that not being able to see the stars is bad for scientists.*

Then read aloud the text on page 239: *Now let's go back and see if the author gives another reason in paragraph 4 for turning the lights out. Remember words such as* reason *help us find the author's reason.* Have children give the reason.

Review: Using Pictures and Details

Focus attention on the photographs on pages 238–239. Ask: *How does each of these photographs help you better understand the text?* (Sample answers: Seeing all the bright lights burning in the city helps me realize that some of them really could be turned off. When I see the turtle on the beach I understand that it needs to be protected.)

Differentiate Instruction

To help children understand the opinion/supporting reasons structure of "Lights Out!" present children with an opinion from their world of experience, such as "Students should get exercise." Then invite children to think of reasons that support this opinion. Return to "Lights Out!" and explain that the title is a clue to the opinion of the piece. Point out that when they are deciding if an author's idea is a reason, the word *because* makes sense in front of it. Give children this example: Why do we need to turn off lights? Because bright light at night makes problems for animals.

Guided Practice

Read and Practice

Remind children that the author should continue providing reasons for the opinion expressed in this piece. Have heterogeneous partners take turns rereading page 240 as you circulate to provide support.

Teacher Talk: Find Evidence

Tell children they can use clue words in the text to find an author's reasons. Say: *I know that the author wants people to turn off lights at night. I have read some reasons why the author feels this way. As I read, I look for words such as* reason *to help me find the reasons. When I look at paragraph 7, I will look for that word to find another reason.*

Identifying Author's Reasons

Words to Know

harm
signal

7   Maybe the best reason for turning off some bright lights is that it can **harm** our health. Our brains get a **signal** from light. The signal tells our brains that it is day. But what if it is really night?

8   Our bodies get confused. They do not know if it is day or night. It is hard for us to get to sleep. Then we have trouble waking up! We need enough sleep to stay healthy.

Guided Practice

Teacher Talk: Find Evidence
Explain that on this page the author gives another reason why people should turn off some lights at night. Have children underline the reason the author gives.

240   Unit 11 ■ Reading Informational Text: Integration of Knowledge and Ideas

---

Words to Know

harm (*verb*): to hurt
signal (*noun*): sign; notice

Working with Word Meaning Have children name *signals* that they see every day, such as a stoplight, stop sign, or a crossing guard's flag. Then have them tell how such signals help keep them from *harm*.

Integration of Knowledge and Ideas

9 Now is the time to turn off some of our lights at night. Then we can all look up at the stars in the night sky. That is a truly beautiful sight!

Comprehension Check
MORE ONLINE
sadlierconnect.com

1. What is the author's opinion about city lights?

   a. We need them to sleep.

   (b.) We should turn some of them off.

   c. We need them to see.

2. Which of the author's reasons do you think is the best?

   Sample answer: The author's best reason is that too many

   lights can hurt us. We need sleep to be healthy.

Teacher Talk: Find Evidence
Tell children that the last paragraph is the author's ending and that the author repeats her opinion in the paragraph. Have them underline the sentence that repeats the author's opinion.

Independent Practice

Unit 11 ■ Reading Informational Text: Integration of Knowledge and Ideas   **241**

Peer Collaboration

Have children work in teams of three. Remind them that the author has given three reasons to support the opinion that some lights should be turned off. Assign each team one of the reasons and have them explain why it is a good reason.

Once children have completed this work, they will share their ideas with other teams' members and then answer any questions.

Independent Practice

Read and Apply

Have children read the paragraph on page 241 independently as you circulate. Provide extra support to struggling readers by choral reading with them.

Teacher Talk: Find Evidence

Remind children that the ending repeats the opinion the author stated earlier. Then have them explain which sentence they underlined.

Comprehension Check

Answer Explanations:

1. Choice **B** is the only answer that repeats the opinion in paragraph 9.

2. Accept answers that correctly identify a reason given by the author.

Critical Comprehension

Use the following questions to help children think critically about the selection. Children should support their answers with evidence from the text.

- *Which facts make the author's reasons more believable?* (facts based on science)

- *If readers do what the author suggests at the end, what does that show?* (They support the opinion.)

Assess and Respond

If children have difficulty answering the questions in the Comprehension Check . . .

Then work with them to make a concept map, with the author's opinion in the center, the reasons on the spokes extending out from the center, and supporting facts along branching lines from the spokes.

Guided Instruction

OBJECTIVES
- Compare and contrast two texts on the same topic.
- Answer questions about key details.

Genre: Procedural Text

Tell children that the procedural text (starting on page 243) tells how to do something. The author includes a list of materials and numbers the instructions.

Set the Purpose

Help children understand the purpose for learning to make comparisons by asking: *How can comparing two texts on the same topic be useful?*

Model and Teach

Read the text aloud as children follow along in their books.

Teacher Talk: Find Evidence

Tell children that the topic is what the text is all about. Say: *I can usually find the topic by looking at a title or reading the first paragraph. The title tells me that this selection is about the way the sun, Earth, and the moon move. Now I'm going to read the first paragraph. Then I'll ask myself what this paragraph is mostly about. Now I'll look for other sentences that also tell about the topic.*

Comparing Texts

Words to Know

model
solid
surface

Movements of the Sun, Earth, and Moon

(Genre: Informational Text)

1 Have you ever watched the sun rise in the sky? Have you ever seen the moon change shape? The sun and the moon both light our sky. The light changes because Earth and the moon move.

2 The sun is a star. It is not **solid** like our planet. Earth has a hard, rocky **surface**. The sun is a ball of hot gases. That is why it is so bright.

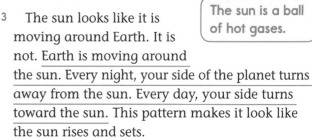

The sun is a ball of hot gases.

3 The sun looks like it is moving around Earth. It is not. Earth is moving around the sun. Every night, your side of the planet turns away from the sun. Every day, your side turns toward the sun. This pattern makes it look like the sun rises and sets.

Guided Instruction

Teacher Talk: Find Evidence
Explain that a text's topic usually appears in the title or first paragraph. Ask: *What is the topic of this text?* Have children underline text that tells the topic in paragraph 1.

242 Unit 11 ■ Reading Informational Text: Integration of Knowledge and Ideas

Words to Know

model (*noun*): a small copy of something that shows what the larger thing looks like
solid (*adjective*): hard
surface (*noun*): top layer

Working with Word Meaning Ask quick yes/no questions to confirm children's understanding of meanings: Is my desk *solid*? (yes) Is the *surface* of my desk bumpy? (no) Is a toy train a kind a *model*? (yes)

Integration of Knowledge and Ideas

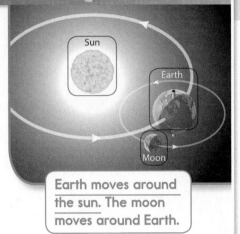

Sun

Earth

Moon

Earth moves around the sun. The moon moves around Earth.

4   The moon is rocky like Earth. It is a lot smaller, though. It does not give off its own light. It mirrors back the light of the sun. It moves around Earth in space.

Make a Model

(Genre: Procedural Text)

You can make a **model** to show how the sun, Earth, and the moon move. Read on to find out how.

What You Need

- Construction paper
- Small, medium, and large circles for tracing
- Hole punch
- Scissors
- Three paper fasteners, or brads

Teacher Talk: Find Evidence

Reread the introduction of "Make a Model." Ask: *What is the topic?* Discuss the "What You Need" section. Have children explain how this text is different from "Movements of the Sun, Earth, and Moon." Have them circle text features that are clues to these differences.

Guided Instruction

Unit 11 ■ Reading Informational Text: Integration of Knowledge and Ideas   **243**

Guided Instruction

Teacher Talk: Find Evidence

Remind children that the topic is what the selection is all about. Say: *I know that if I read the first section, it will probably tell me what this topic is.*

Point out that "Make a Model" is a different type of text from the type of text in "Movements of the Sun, Earth, and Moon." Say: *"Make a Model" is going to show me how to make a model of how the sun, Earth, and the moon move. The text looks different from the text in "Movements of the Sun, Earth, and Moon." I'm going to look for clues that show me how the text is different.*

Review: Using Pictures and Details

Remind children that they identified the way that pictures and text details work together in "Sky Lights." Focus attention on the diagram on page 243. Ask: *How does this diagram help you better understand the text?*

Support English Language Learners

English language learners may have difficulty understanding the use of *mirror* as a verb in the sentence "It mirrors back the light of the sun." You can demonstrate the concept for them. Use a mirror and a flashlight. Explain that the mirror is the moon. The flashlight is the sun. Hold up the mirror and say: *No light is coming from the mirror. That's the same way that no light comes from the moon.* Then have a child shine the flashlight directly at the mirror. Say: *Now light is coming from the mirror. That's the same way that the sunlight bounces off the moon and makes it seem to shine.*

Guided Practice

Read and Practice

Remind children that a procedural text tells how to do something. Have heterogeneous partners take turns rereading the rest of the steps while you circulate and provide support.

Teacher Talk: Find Evidence

Have children look at the illustrations from the two selections on pages 243 and 244. Point out that the illustrations share some of the same information. Say: *When I look at the illustrations, I see the sun, Earth, and the moon. The illustrations are similar. Now I'm going to look at the caption to see what words might be the same.*

Peer Collaboration

As children within the groups work on comparing the illustrations, have them think about this question: *How is being able to compare the two illustrations helpful in understanding both texts?* Then have children share their ideas within the group, coming up with a statement in response to the question that they would like to share with the whole class.

Digital Connection

Many animated models of the interaction of the sun, Earth, and moon are available online, as part of educational Web sites devoted to the study of space. Share with children as appropriate.

Comparing Texts

Words to Know

attach

insert

What to Do

1. Cut a small circle (moon) from the paper. Next, cut a medium-size circle (Earth). Then, cut a large circle (sun).

2. Cut two rectangles from the paper. They should be about an inch wide. One should be twice as long as the other.

3. Punch holes in the middle of each circle. Then punch holes at the ends of the rectangles.

4. **Insert** a fastener into the Earth circle. Then insert the same fastener into one end of each rectangle.

5. **Attach** the other end of the long rectangle to the sun circle with the second fastener. Attach the other end of the short rectangle to the moon circle with the third fastener.

A model shows how Earth and the moon move around the sun.

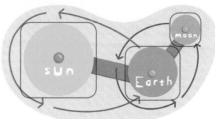

Guided Practice

Teacher Talk: Find Evidence
Have children look at the two illustrations on pages 243 and 244 and circle parts of the pictures that are similar. Then tell them to underline words in the captions that are the same.

244   Unit 11 ■ Reading Informational Text: Integration of Knowledge and Ideas

---

Words to Know

attach *(verb)* to fasten together
insert *(verb)*: to put something inside something else

Working with Word Meaning Give children cloze sentences in which the words *attach* and *insert* belong, in order to broaden their knowledge of the contexts in which these words are commonly used.

Use tape to _____ the card to the gift.

How can we _____ the kite to the frame?

After you fold the letter, _____ it in the envelope.

_____ the key into the lock and then turn it.

Integration of Knowledge and Ideas

6. Move the moon around Earth. Then move Earth around the sun. Use the model to show how Earth and the moon move in space.

Comprehension Check   **MORE ONLINE** sadlierconnect.com

1. How does the model help you understand "Movements of the Sun, Earth, and Moon"? It shows that

   a. stars are made of very hot gases.

   (b.) Earth and the moon move in space.

   c. the sun and the moon give off light.

2. What is the same about "Movements of the Sun, Earth, and Moon" and "Make a Model"? What is different? Use examples from the two texts to explain your answers.

   Sample answer: Both texts are about the sun, Earth,

   and moon. The first text tells about how the light changes.

   The second text tells how to make a model.

Teacher Talk: Find Evidence
Move your model as you read step 6 on page 245. Tell children to underline information in paragraphs 3 and 4 in "Movements of the Sun, Earth, and Moon" that describe how the sun, Earth, and the moon move.

Independent Practice

Unit 11 ▪ Reading Informational Text: Integration of Knowledge and Ideas **245**

Extend Thinking: Design a Model

Provide children with some 3-D objects they could use to design their own models for showing the movement of the sun, Earth, and moon. For example, foam balls, wooden blocks, or math manipulatives might spark ideas. You might also simply give children access to your art supplies, and let them go from there.

Give children time to create their models. Then have each child share his or her model with the class. Encourage children to use complete sentences and to use details describing the movements of the sun, Earth, and moon.

Independent Practice

Read and Apply

Have children read Step 6 on page 245 independently as you circulate. Provide extra support to struggling readers by choral reading with them.

Teacher Talk: Find Evidence

Help children understand how the model works to show the movements of the sun, Earth, and moon. Say: *Now I'll go back to the other selection and find the paragraphs that tell how the sun, Earth, and moon move.*

Comprehension Check

Answer Explanations:

1. Choice **B** shows what the model does.

2. Both selections are on the same topic. The informational text explains why light changes. The procedural text tells how to make a model.

Critical Comprehension

Use the following questions to help children think critically about the selections. Children should support their answers with evidence from the text.

- *How did making the model help you to understand "Movements of the Sun, Earth, and Moon"?* (Sample answer: The model helped me to understand how the light from the sun shows on Earth and the moon.)

Assess and Respond
If children have difficulty answering the questions in the Comprehension Check . . .
Then use a two-column chart to compare the two texts' topics.

OBJECTIVE
Read decodable text featuring two-syllable words, inflectional endings, and irregularly spelled words.

Prepare to Read

Tell children that you will be reading an informational text about how the stars appear in the sky. As you read, children should listen for two-syllable words and look for words with inflectional endings.

Introduce Phonics Skills

After you have read the selection once, read it again, this time focusing on the target phonics skills.

- *Look at the word* ago *in paragraph 2. It has two syllables because it has two vowel sounds. When I say it aloud, a-go, I can hear that the syllables divide between the a and the g. What other two-syllable words do you find in paragraph 2?* (people, pictures)

- *Endings such as* -ed, -s, *and* -ing *are added to base words. The word* watched *in paragraph 2 has the ending* -ed *added to the word* watch. *The* -ed *ending means that the action takes place in the past. The word* hunting *in paragraph 3 has the* -ing *ending added to the word* hunt *to tell more about* dogs. *The word* wears *in paragraph 4 has the* -s *ending added to the word* wear *to agree with the subject* Orion. *Endings change words.*

- *I see words with unusual spellings,* group *and* people. *I memorize these spellings so I can read the words automatically when I see them.*

Focus on Fluency

Have children read paragraph 4 aloud, using their voice to show the question at the end.

Foundational Skills Read Together

As you read along with the selection, listen for syllables. Look for word endings.

Pictures in the Stars

1 Look up at the stars on dark nights. Try to find the same stars. How can you tell which star is which? You can look for groups of stars that form images, or pictures. People use the star pictures to make a map of the sky.

2 Long ago, people watched the stars and saw pictures. They gave the pictures names.

3 Some pictures are named for animals. There is a crab named Cancer and a bull named Taurus. Other pictures are named for hunting dogs, a goldfish, and a rabbit. There is even a winged horse named Pegasus.

4 Some pictures are named for people. There are a queen, a princess, and a hunter named Orion. Orion wears a belt and holds a bow. Orion's belt has three stars. What pictures do you see when you look at the stars?

Orion

246 Unit 11 ■ Reading Informational Text: Integration of Knowledge and Ideas

---

Focus on Phonological Awareness

Phoneme Segmentation

Use CVC words for a quick phoneme awareness warm-up. Follow the steps below for the words *tap, ran, log,* and *hat.*

- Tell children to listen as you pronounce the word.

- Ask how many sounds they hear.

- Have them pronounce the sounds in sequence (/t/ /a/ /p/) and then blend them to say the whole word.

Foundational Skills Reader 1

DIRECTIONS: Cut and fold the book.

Name

Super Stars

The sky is full of many stars.
No two stars are the same.

There are more stars than people on Earth.
That is an amazing number of stars!

Sailors used stars to guide them.
They knew to follow the North Star.

syllables

Unit 11 ■ Reading Informational Text 247

OBJECTIVES
- **Read decodable text featuring two-syllable words.**
- **Read along orally, paying special attention to reading in phrases.**

Prepare to Read

Tell children that they will be reading an informational text that will help them learn many more facts about stars, and that they can take the book home to share. Have them follow the directions to cut and fold the book.

Review Phonics Skills

Explain that this book features many words with two syllables and irregular spellings that they learned about in the Read Together. Review the targeted phonics skill.

- *Remember that a word with two vowel sounds has two syllables. Find two-syllable words in the book.*
- *Remember also the two words with unusual, or irregular, spellings,* people *and* group. *What words in the book have unusual spellings?*

Introduce Reader 1

Divide the class into two groups. Assign each group to line 1 or 2. Have each group chorally read its corresponding line on each page of the book as you read each line aloud.

Foundational Skills: Phonics Practice

Write the following words from the Read Together and Foundational Skills Reader 1 on the board or on a chart. Have children practice reading the words.

Read Together 2-syllable words: pictures, ago, Cancer, Taurus, goldfish, rabbit, princess, hunter; **irregularly spelled words:** you, people, wears

Foundational Skills Reader 1 2-syllable words: super, objects, really, planet, around, rabbit, follow, study, number; **irregularly spelled words:** many, two, Earth, people, guide, through

Read with a Partner

Select pairs of children to read together. Ask each to read the text together several times, first chorally and then individually. Once the pairs are comfortable with one of their oral readings, have them record it for playing back later.

Focus on Fluency

Tell children that fluent readers read the way that people speak. To demonstrate what you mean, read aloud fluently page 6 of Foundational Skills Reader 1. Model fluency of the entire reader by using the Fluency Practice activity below.

Reading at Home

Once children are comfortable reading the book, send it home for children to read to family members.

Assess and Respond

If children have difficulty decoding two-syllable words . . .

Then show children where the syllables break in each of the target words on page 247. Have children focus on decoding one syllable at a time and then blending the two syllables. Emphasize that each syllable has a vowel sound.

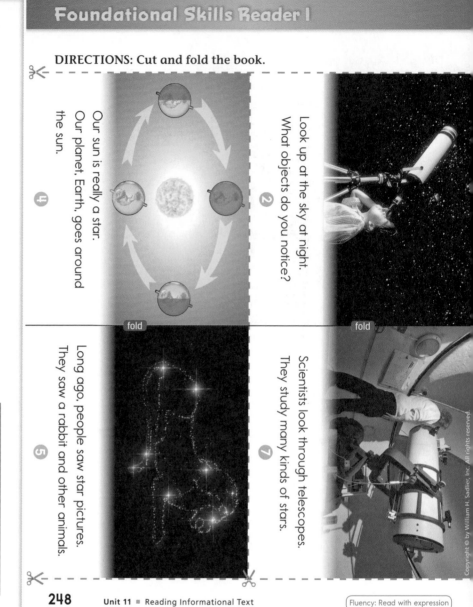

Foundational Skills Reader 1

DIRECTIONS: Cut and fold the book.

Our sun is really a star.
Our planet, Earth, goes around the sun.

4

Look up at the sky at night.
What objects do you notice?

2

Long ago, people saw star pictures.
They saw a rabbit and other animals.

5

Scientists look through telescopes.
They study many kinds of stars.

7

Fluency: Read with expression

Foundational Skills: Fluency Practice

Explain to children that when we read with expression, we group words together just as we do when we talk. Tell children to listen for words that you group together as you read the book. Then model a fluent reading of the book to demonstrate reading in phrases, or groups of words. Ask children where you grouped words together as you read. Have students echo read after you so that they can imitate fluent phrasing. Additional fluency passages and activities can be found at **sadlierconnect.com.**

Foundational Skills Reader 2

DIRECTIONS: Cut and fold the book.

Name

Our Moon

fold

The moon does not always look round.
We can see only part of the moon.

fold

Then the lit part seems to get smaller.
We say the moon is waning.

The lit part gets bigger.
Soon it looks like half a circle.

inflectional endings -s, -ed, -ing

Unit 11 ■ Reading Informational Text **249**

Foundational Skills: Phonics Practice

Write the following words from Foundational Skills Reader 2 on the board or on a chart. Have children practice reading the words.

words ending in -s: seems, circles, looks, gets

words ending in -ed: called

words ending in -ing: growing, waning, waxing

OBJECTIVES
- **Read decodable text featuring inflectional endings.**
- **Read along orally, paying special attention to reading in phrases.**

Prepare to Read

Tell children that the next informational text they will be reading gives facts about the moon, including why it seems to change shape. They can take the book home to share. Have them follow the directions to cut and fold the book.

Review Phonics Skills

Explain that there are several words in the book with inflectional endings. Review these endings (-s, -ed, -ing).

- First look for words ending in -s (circles). *What is the base word for that word?* (circle) *What does the -s ending show about the word?*
- Next look for a word ending in -ed (called). *What is the base word? What does the -ed ending show about the word?*
- Now look for words ending in -ing. *Read each word, with and without the -ing ending.*

Introduce Reader 2

Have the class echo read the book with you. You read a sentence, and children echo the sentence. When reading, model grouping words together to sound natural.

Read with a Partner

Have heterogeneous pairs of children take turns reading to each another. Have each pair read the text together several times, and then take turns reading page by page. Once the pairs are comfortable with one of their oral readings, have them record it for playing back later.

Focus on Fluency

Explain to children that reading in chunks—groups of words that work together—is part of reading with expression. Read the first sentence on page 5 of Foundational Skills Reader 2 to demonstrate reading in phrases in order to read with expression. Have children repeat after you.

Reading at Home

Once children are comfortable reading the book, send it home for them to read to family members.

Assess and Respond
If children have difficulty decoding the words with inflectional endings . . .
Then have them cover up the endings on the target words in the text and decode the base word. Remind them that then all they need to do is add /s/, /d/, or /ing/.

Foundational Skills Reader 2

DIRECTIONS: Cut and fold the book.

4 — Sometimes we cannot see the moon. It is called the start of a new moon.

2 — The moon is a big, round ball of rock. It circles Earth. Earth circles the sun.

fold

fold

5 — Other times, it seems to be growing. We say the moon is waxing.

7 — Next, the lit part looks like a circle. That is called a full moon.

250   Unit 11 ■ Reading Informational Text

(Fluency: Read with expression)

Foundational Skills: Fluency Practice

Identify some word groups on page 7 of the reader, such as "the lit part" and "looks like a circle." Model reading page 7 to show how the groups sound when read aloud, emphasizing your phrasing and expression. Chorally read the entire reader. Have children practice; then record them reading aloud. Additional fluency passages can be found at **sadlierconnect.com**.

Sunlight Is Better
(Genre: Opinion Piece)

The sun shines during the day.

The moon shines at night.

1   Both the moon and the sun light up the sky. Moonlight is pretty. Light from a full moon helps us see at night. But sunlight is better than moonlight.

2   One reason why sunlight is better is that it keeps us warm. A sunny day keeps me warm outside. I can play baseball when it is sunny!

Baseball is a good sport for a sunny day!

Unit 11 ■ Reading Informational Text: Integration of Knowledge and Ideas   **251**

OBJECTIVES
- **Match text to corresponding visuals, using both to describe in their own words the main ideas.**
- **Identify an author's opinions and the reasons given to support those opinions.**
- **Compare and contrast two texts on the same topic.**

Genre: Opinion Piece
Remind children that the author of an opinion piece is sharing his or her beliefs about a topic. In order for readers to agree with the opinion, the author must include strong reasons to support the opinion. Instruct children to identify the opinion and reasons for it while reading this text. Then they can decide whether or not the reasons are strong enough for them to accept the author's opinion.

Path Options
You may wish to have children read the text independently and apply the skills learned in this unit. Or, you may wish to do a close reading with children; if so, use the supports provided on these pages. As a third option, set up a buddy system, with some heterogeneous and some homogeneous pairs, to fit the needs of your class. Regardless, children should read the text more than once to facilitate understanding and to be able to answer the Comprehension Check questions correctly.

Support English Language Learners

If you decide to have children read the text on their own, be aware that English language learners may struggle to read it independently. You may wish to assign them reading buddies who have strong reading skills. Instruct reading buddies to point out the opinion stated in the first paragraph. Then, they should similarly point out each reason given for the opinion and help their buddies see the other key ideas and details of the text.

Support First Reading

Circulate to check children's understanding. As needed, use the following comprehension and strategy check-ins to support basic understanding of the selection as children read.

Check-in Questions

- **page 251** *What is the author's opinion in this text?* (Sunlight is better than moonlight.)
- **page 252** *Why does the author say sunlight is so important for people and animals?* (Sunlight helps plants grow, and people and animals eat plants.)
- **page 253** *How does the author feel about moonlight?* (The author likes moonlight but doesn't think it is as important as sunlight.)

Review: Using Pictures and Details

Ask children which text details the photographs on page 252 support. (Top photo: Sunlight makes plants grow. Bottom photo: Sunshine helps us see.)

Review: Identifying Author's Reasons

Reread paragraph 4 with children. Ask them to restate the reason given in this paragraph. (Sunlight helps us see.) Then prompt them to recall the first reason given by the author in paragraph 2. (Sunlight keeps us warm.)

Close Reading

3   Sunlight is also better because it makes plants grow. Then animals and people eat the plants. We eat plants like carrots and peas. These fresh foods keep us healthy!

Animals and people eat plants.

4   Sunlight also helps us see. Then it is easy to know where we are going. My family can see well when we ride our bikes. Mom can see well when she drives. I can see well when I walk to the park.

Sunshine lets us see outside very well.

252

Differentiate Instruction

To help children understand the key ideas of this opinion piece, provide them with a frame to fill in as they read. Write these frames on the board or chart paper:

Paragraph 1: The author's opinion is that sunlight is _____ than moonlight.

Paragraph 2: One reason that sunlight is better is _____.

Paragraph 3: Another reason that sunlight is better is _____.

Paragraph 4: The most important fact is _____.

Paragraph 5: The most important fact is _____.

5   Moonlight can be really nice, too. I enjoy walking with my family when the moon is full. But we need sunlight to live. I am glad we have both!

The moon is brightest when it is full.

Comprehension Check

1. Which is the key idea of the text?

   a. Sunlight helps us get exercise.

   b. The moon is not as bright as the sun.

   c. We need lights in the night.

2. Which photograph best describes the key idea of paragraph 5?

   a. photograph of the baseball player

   b. photograph of the family riding bicycles

   c. photograph of the moon at night

Unit 11 ■ Reading Informational Text: Integration of Knowledge and Ideas   **253**

Strategic Reading

Support all readers by reminding them of the importance of setting a purpose for reading and remembering that purpose while reading. Explain that when they are reading an opinion piece, their purpose should be to understand the author's opinion and see if they agree with it. Therefore, while reading, they should remain on the lookout for the reasons given by the author. This means they must remain more focused than when they are reading for enjoyment. They should ask themselves: *Does this reason make sense to me? Is it strong enough to make me think the author's opinion is correct?*

Review: Comparing Texts

Ask children to recall the information that they read in "Our Moon." Ask: *How does the information from "Our Moon" compare with the author's information in this text? Which author gives more information about the moon and how it appears in the sky? Which author gives more facts? Which author gives more opinions?*

Multiple Readings for Critical Comprehension

Have children reread this selection, and pose questions that focus on critical comprehension. Remind children that they can mark the text.

- *Do you think the author wishes the sun would shine all of the time?* (No, the author enjoys the moonlight and is glad we don't have to choose between sunlight and moonlight.)

- *Some parts of Earth don't get much sunlight. What might it be like there?* (It wouldn't be very warm. There might not be very many plants, animals, or people. There would have to be a lot of human-made lights.)

Comprehension Check

Score children's understanding of unit skills and texts using the Comprehension Check on this page and the next. Use children's total score to determine their readiness for the Unit 11 Review on page 257.

Multiple-Choice Questions: *1 point each*

1. Answer choice **B** is correct because it relates to the paragraph about sunlight helping us to see.

2. Answer choice **C** is correct. Since the key idea of paragraph 5 is that the author enjoys the moonlight, this idea is best supported by a picture of the moon.

Short-Answer Questions:
3 points each

Item 3 Rubric

3	Children make valid comparisons between the two texts and cite corresponding evidence from each text.
2	Children make valid comparisons between the two texts but cite evidence from only one text.
1	Children make valid comparisons between the two texts but fail to cite any evidence.
0	Children cannot make a valid comparison between the two texts.

Item 4 Rubric

3	Children correctly identify both the author's opinion and a reason given to support it.
2	Children correctly identify the author's opinion but are not completely accurate in the reason they give to support it.
1	Children correctly identify either the author's opinion or a reason given in the text.
0	Children cannot identify either the author's opinion or any of the author's reasons.

Theme Wrap-Up

Lead children in a discussion on the facts they have learned about the lights in our sky. Ask them to recall the most fascinating thing they learned while studying this topic.

Close Reading

3. "Movements of the Sun, Earth, and Moon" explains that the moon mirrors back the sun's light. You also learned about moonlight in "Sunlight Is Better." Tell how the information is the same or different.

Sample answer: The information is different because

"Movements of the Sun, Earth, and Moon" tells what

happens to make the moonlight that we see. "Sunlight Is

Better" tells how we use the moonlight.

4. What is the author's opinion about sunlight in "Sunlight Is Better"? What is a reason the author uses to support this opinion?

Sample answer: The author says sunlight is better because

it keeps us warm.

Assess and Respond (pages 253–254)

If	Then
Children scored 0–3 points, they are **Developing** their understanding of unit skills …	Provide children with reading support and more intensive modeling of skills.
Children scored 4–6 points, they are **Improving** their understanding of unit skills …	Use children's scores to target areas that are weak and review those specific skills.
Children scored 7–8 points, they are **Proficient** in their understanding of unit skills …	Have these children move on. They are ready for the formal assessment.

Compare and Contrast Texts

Look at the pictures from the texts you have read. Be ready to talk about the pictures and the key ideas.

Sky Lights

Make a Model

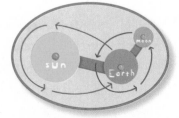

Sunlight Is Better

Return to the Essential Question

How do authors use details to tell about key ideas?

Talk about the pictures and the ideas in the texts. How are they the same? How are they different?

Compare and Contrast Texts

Read aloud the directions on page 255. Then provide some information about each of the featured texts to help children as they recall the key ideas.

The selection "Sky Lights" is an informational text. The sections are titled "How a Star Is Born," "Our Star," and "Hello, Neighbor!" What is our star? (the sun) *Who is our neighbor?* (the moon)

The selection "Make a Model" is a procedural text. It gives instructions for making something. Why was this procedural text included? (so readers could better understand how the sun, moon, and Earth move)

The selection "Sunlight Is Better" is an opinion piece. What is the author's opinion? (Sunlight is better than moonlight.)

Give children time to organize their thoughts about the texts. Have them ask any questions they have about the texts before you begin. Then lead the Essential Question discussion.

Support Essential Question Discussion

Read the Essential Question aloud. Then prompt children to share their ideas about the selections. Remind children to raise their hands and wait for you to call on them.

- *Which image from these selections do you remember the most? Why?*
- *Which image was most helpful to you in understanding the text? Why?*
- *Which text presented the most ideas?*
- *Which text was mostly about one idea?*

Discussion Skills

Some of the Essential Question prompts call for opinions. Be sure to establish an environment that encourages the voicing of opinions. You might begin by expressing your own opinion in response to a question. (Example: *I really liked the photo of the moon over the ocean in "Sunlight Is Better" because I enjoy walking on the beach at night.*)

After someone expresses an opinion, it is appropriate to ask children if they agree or not and why. Lead children to express their opinions clearly by using the sentence stem "I agree/disagree because . . ." As more children express their opinions and the class sees that this is not a threatening thing to do, you can then encourage non-participating children by asking, "Would you like to add on? We'd like to hear what you think, too."

OBJECTIVE
Group words that are similar and then note the differences among them.

Guided Instruction

Read aloud the Guided Instruction section on page 256. Be sure children understand that carrots and peas are similar because they are both plants that we eat. Ask: *What is different about carrots and peas?* (Sample answer: Carrots are orange. Peas are green.)

Guided Practice

Explain that two of the four words in the box belong in the group *plant parts*. Have children identify the two words and choose the one that belongs in the sentence.

Independent Practice

If children struggle to fill in the two blanks, have them first find the word that describes the group a fly is in and write it in the first blank. Then have them choose the word that fits in the last blank.

Apply to Reading

Have children return to "Pictures in the Stars." Point out that the star pictures are named after two different groups. Have partners identify the two groups (animals, people), write words from the text in each group, and discuss the differences.

Language

Groups of Words

Guided Instruction Words that are the same in some way can be put into a group. Read this sentence from "Sunlight Is Better."

> We eat plants like carrots and peas.

The group is **plants**. The plants in the group are *carrots* and *peas*. Each word in the group is different in some way. We can understand a word by saying what is different about it.

> The words *dog* and *cat* belong to the group **pets**.
> A dog is a pet that barks. A cat is a pet that purrs.

Guided Practice Choose a word from the box to complete the sentence. Write the word on the line.

> animal   leaves   petals   wings

1. A **tree** is a plant that has _____leaves_____ .

Independent Practice Choose words from the box above to complete the sentence. Write the words on the lines.

2. A **fly** is a(n) _____animal_____ that has _____wings_____ .

256   Unit 11 ■ Reading Informational Text: Integration of Knowledge and Ideas

---

Support English Language Learners

Create cards with words and pictures for children to sort into two piles. Use yes/no questions to help learners decide if words and pictures belong in a group and to check their comprehension of the concept. For Guided Practice, for example, ask: *Is a (tree) a plant?* Assign a native speaker of English to help check their piles and discuss any incorrect answers.

Read along with the following selection.

Kids in Space

1   Do you think a kid will be able to go into space someday? I do. Many people have traveled safely into space. Animals have traveled into space, too. Astronauts have even walked on the moon.

2   Scientists are planning how people can live in space. Astronauts are working, cooking, and playing in space. They have (stayed) at a space station for a few months. I think that someday a family may be able to live in space. That would be really cool for a kid!

Astronauts can do many things in space.

Fill in the circle of the correct answer choice for questions 1 and 2.

1. Which key idea of the text does the picture show?

○ Astronauts have walked on the moon.

○ Animals have traveled in space.

● Astronauts have lived in space.

Unit 11 ■ Reading Informational Text: Integration of Knowledge and Ideas   **257**

Self-Assessment: Progress Check

Have children revisit the Progress Check on page 229 and respond to the questions again. Ask them to compare their Before and After responses.

Review children's responses to get an idea of their confidence with the unit skills. Based on these responses and on children's success with the Comprehension Check in Close Reading, you may want to conduct additional review and practice of one or more of the unit skills.

Unit Summary

Children have had instruction and practice in reading different types of informational texts that provide facts and opinions about Earth and the sun, moon, and stars of our solar system.

Children have learned that authors may use visuals (illustrations and diagrams) and details to support key ideas in their texts. Children have also learned that authors provide reasons to support points in their texts. Children have compared texts on the same topics. They have progressed toward completing an independent close reading of text, practiced applying the concepts across texts, and used word categories to refine their understanding of word meanings.

They have read words with -s, -ed, and -ing endings, and have read words with two syllables. They should be well prepared for the review section.

Introduce the Review

Explain to children that they will read a new passage along with you that is related to the unit's theme and the selections they have already read. Then they will answer the questions on pages 257 and 258.

Answer Explanations

Scoring: Items 1, 2, 4, 5, and 6 on pages 257–258 are worth 1 point each. Explanations for the correct answers are given below and on the next page. Also see the rubrics on the next page for guidance in scoring the short-answer questions on page 258.

1. The photo shows an astronaut doing much more than walking, which is why the third choice is the best one.

Answer Explanations

2. Only the middle response is supported by the text.

Item 3 Rubric

2	Answer correctly identifies the author's opinion.
1	Answer comes close to identifying the author's opinion; for example, a family might live in space.
0	The author's opinion is not correctly identified.

4. The following sentence should be underlined: *Many people have traveled safely into space.*

5. The following word should be circled: *stayed.*

6. The following words may be identified with a line drawn between the two syllables (in paragraph 1): *people, traveled, safely, into.*

Item 7 Rubric

2	Child has chosen a category that all three words fit into.
1	Child has chosen a category that two of the words fit into.
0	An incorrect category or no category has been chosen by the child.

Item 8 Rubric

2	Answer correctly identifies a new piece of information found in "Kids in Space."
1	Answer correctly identifies a piece of information from "Kids in Space" but it is not a new piece of information.
0	Answer does not identify a piece of information that is found in "Kids in Space."

---

2. What details describe what astronauts do in space?

- ○ Astronauts fly around the spacecraft.
- ● Astronauts work, cook, and play.
- ○ Astronauts live on the sun.

3. What is the author's opinion?

Sample answer: A family might be able to live in space.

4. Underline a sentence in paragraph 1 that tells a reason for the author's opinion.

5. Circle one word in paragraph 2 with the *-ed* ending.

6. Find a word in the text that has two syllables. Draw a line between the syllables.

Answers will vary.

7. What group do the words *working, cooking,* and *playing* belong to?

Sample answers: activities; words that end with -ing

8. Listen as your teacher rereads "Hello, Neighbor!" in "Sky Lights." What new information did you learn about the moon in "Kids in Space"?

Sample answer: Astronauts have walked on the moon.

258   Unit 11 ■ Reading Informational Text: Integration of Knowledge and Ideas

Analyze Scores

9–11 pts Strong	Child has a good grasp of the skills and concepts taught in this unit. Point out any mistakes the child has made and explain the correct answers if necessary.
5–8 pts Progressing	Child is struggling with some skills or concepts. Identify the specific skills that are problematic to target a review of instruction.
0–4 pts Emerging	Child is having serious problems understanding the skills and concepts taught in this unit. Child may need to redo the work with a higher level of support.

There are three parts to this performance task. Your teacher will give you a copy of the text "A Trip to the Eye Doctor."

Part 1: Text Questions

☐ Listen to and read along with "A Trip to the Eye Doctor."

☐ Then answer the questions on pages 260–261.

Part 2: Text Analysis

☐ Listen to and read along with "A Trip to the Eye Doctor" again.

☐ Then listen to and read along with the directions for Text Analysis on page 262. Use the page your teacher gives you to write your answer.

Part 3: Informative Writing

☐ Listen to and read along with "A Trip to the Eye Doctor" again.

☐ Then listen to and read along with the directions for Informative Writing on page 262. Use the page your teacher gives you to write your answer.

Performance Task 2   **259**

Part 1   Text Questions

Listen to and read the questions and answer choices. Fill in the circle next to the correct answer.

1. What does the author think about visits to the eye doctor?

   ○ The author thinks the visits are scary.

   ● The author thinks the visits are helpful.

   ○ The author thinks the visits are not important.

2. Which sentence from the text helps you know the answer to question 1?

   ○ "Keep your eyes open wide."

   ○ "The eye test feels like a game!"

   ● "The eye doctor can help you."

3. Which part of the text tells something about you and your eyes?

   ● "Getting to Know You"

   ○ "The First Eye Test"

   ○ "More Eye Tests"

Performance Task Overview

Overview

The Performance Tasks are designed to determine a student's ability to understand a read-along text, locate evidence to support text analysis, and create extended responses that show comprehension of the text. Each has one part devoted to text questions and two parts devoted to writing.

Performance Task 2

Go to **sadlierconnect.com** to download the following resources for Performance Task 2:

ONLINE   Digital Resources

- **Text:** "A Trip to the Eye Doctor" (informational text)
- **Prompts:** response sheet; model responses
- **Answer Keys and Rubrics**

Administration Procedure

Part 1 Introduce the Task Explain that children will read along as you read an informational text. Then they will answer questions and write about what they read.

- **Selected response items** ask about the text; some items ask children to find evidence from the text that points to the correct answer.

- **Constructed response items** are writing prompts based on the text; they require children to use text details for support.

Reading Children follow along as you read the text aloud.

Selected Response Children complete the multiple choice items.

Part 2 Reading Children follow along as you read the text aloud.

Constructed Response (Text Analysis) Distribute the prompt. Read the prompt, and make sure children understand the directions. Then have children respond.

Part 3 Constructed Response (Informative Writing) Repeat the steps followed for the Text Analysis Constructed Response.

Text Questions

ONLINE Download "A Trip to the Eye Doctor" and the Answer Key.

Core Task: Children read along with an informational text and respond to six selected response items. In answering the items, children must analyze the informational text and identify the evidence that supports their answers.

Depth of Knowledge Levels:

Item 1:	Item 2:	Item 3:	Item 4:	Item 5:	Item 6:
Level 2	Level 2	Level 2	Level 3	Level 3	Level 2

Text Analysis

ONLINE Download "A Trip to the Eye Doctor" and the Answer Key and Rubric.

Core Task: Children read along with the text and respond to a prompt that requires text analysis. In writing a response, children must: 1) recall and write details from the text that support the key idea; 2) use linking words and provide a conclusion; 3) construct sentences properly; 4) demonstrate command of spelling, punctuation, and capitalization.

Depth of Knowledge Level: Level 3

Informative Writing

ONLINE Download "A Trip to the Eye Doctor" and the Answer Key and Rubric.

Core Task: Children read along with an informational text and respond to a prompt that requires them to write a description of a helpful place in their community. In writing a response, children must: 1) name and describe the place; 2) use relevant details and provide a sense of closure; 3) construct sentences properly; 4) demonstrate a general command of conventions.

Depth of Knowledge Level: Level 3

Scoring
Selected response items: 1 point per item (up to 6 points)
Constructed response items: up to 3 points per item (possible total of 12 points)
Note: When analyzing constructed responses, have student volunteers share their responses. Discuss key elements of the scoring rubric and ask children to make one significant change to improve their responses.

4. How do you learn what a first eye test might look like?

○ by reading "More Eye Tests"
● by looking at the picture of the eye charts
○ by reading the last paragraph

5. Look at the picture of the eye mask. What does it show that you also read in the text?

○ "The doctor may put drops in your eyes."
○ "The doctor writes down what he learns."
● "The doctor turns the round pieces of the mask."

6. What does the word **revisit** mean in this sentence from "A Trip to the Eye Doctor"?

You can **revisit** the eye doctor every year or so!

● come back to
○ go around
○ never see again

Part 2 Text Analysis

Listen to and read the directions. Use the paper your teacher gives you to respond.

The author of "A Trip to the Eye Doctor" says that a visit to an eye doctor can help you. What details does the author give to describe this key idea? Write a paragraph. Use your own words to write about the details that the author uses.

Part 3 Informative Writing

Listen to and read the directions. Use the paper your teacher gives you to respond.

What place in your community can help you? Write a paragraph to tell how this place is helpful. Begin by naming the place. Use details to describe how this place is helpful. Write a conclusion for your paragraph.

See online rubric for scoring.

STEP 1: Planning.... 264
STEP 2: Drafting 265
STEP 3: Revising.... 266
STEP 4: Editing 267
STEP 5: Producing
and Publishing 268

Writing Handbook **263**

Writing Handbook

Writers follow steps when they write. These steps will help you write well.

STEP 1 Planning

Let's say you choose polar bears for a topic. You will need information about polar bears. You can find facts in books and on the Internet. A chart can help you organize the facts.

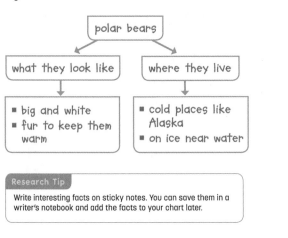

Research Tip

Write interesting facts on sticky notes. You can save them in a writer's notebook and add the facts to your chart later.

The Writing Handbook: What is the writing process?

The *Writing Handbook* explains the steps in the writing process. Once familiar with the steps, children can use them to create a finished piece for any type of writing.

Writing Process Overview
Step in the Writing Process
Planning: Assignment/genre; topic and details; researching
Drafting: Student model draft
Revising: Working with a partner; using a revising checklist
Editing: Using an editing checklist; using editing marks; focused editing
Producing and Publishing: Sharing writing; neatness; visuals; text features; technology use

How to Use the Handbook

Use the handbook at the beginning of the school year to introduce children to the writing process. You may then help children use the handbook with any writing assignment.

Step 1: Planning

Assignment/Genre Tell children that writing that gives facts about a topic is called a research report. Writers find the facts by doing research—reading books and other sources of information in a library or online.

Brainstorming Offer children a short list of topics they could write a research report about, and have children select a topic. Group children according to topic and have groups brainstorm a list of questions to find answers to as part of doing research for their report. Remind children that they will answer questions with facts.

Digital Integration: Research Tip Model how to use a search engine to locate facts about topics. You may provide QR codes or links to safe sites with child-friendly information. Circulate to assist children as they look for facts about their topics. Help children record the facts on self-stick notes to be added to their organizer. Help children with the same topic to perform shared research together.

Writing Handbook: Drafting and Revising

Step 2: Drafting

Explain to children that drafting is the step where they turn their ideas into sentences. Each sentence should tell a fact about the topic. Explain that their writing does not need to be completely correct. They will have time to make changes and fixes later.

Digital Integration Some children may be ready to use a word-processing program to draft their reports. Other children may wish to write a first draft on paper and type the final draft or have an adult type the final draft.

Step 3: Revising

Discuss the notes and marks in the draft. Explain to children that they can use the Revising Checklist to check their own work and to read a partner's draft.

Peer Review Allow partners time to read each other's drafts. Encourage children to be polite and respectful when they make comments. Children may add symbols such as a happy face to indicate they like a sentence, a question mark to indicate they have a question, and a plus sign to show places where more information is needed. Display drafts with revision feedback and use a shared revising activity to discuss ways to revise.

Peer Collaboration If children are new to peer review when revising, you may wish to provide sentence frames such as the following to guide their discussions: I like _____. I would add _____.

Differentiated Instruction For children who need extra support in adding details to their writing, present pictures related to their topic. Have children turn to partners and describe the pictures. Use questions such as the following to help children add elements of their description to their writing: *I heard you say the polar bear is white. That is a great detail. Where can we add that to your writing?* Then model using a caret mark to add the detail.

Assignment: Planning, Drafting, and Revising

Provide time for children to use a chart, web, or other organizer to organize their facts. Then have them use their organizer to write a draft. Remind children that when drafting, the goal is to get their ideas on paper. After they finish drafting, engage the children in revising to make sure their writing gives facts that describe or explain their topics.

STEP 2 Drafting

Use your planning chart to write a draft. In a draft, you write your ideas in sentences. You can use a computer or write on paper. You can make changes later. Right now, just get your ideas on paper. Here is a draft of a report about polar bears.

Polar Bears

Polar bears are big white animals. They have thick fur. Their fur keeps them warm.

Polar bears liv in cold places like alaska. They walk on the ice. They swim in the cold water Seals live in Alaska, too.

Writing Handbook **265**

STEP 3 Revising

When you revise, you make your writing better. Use the checklist below to revise your writing. Use the marks on page 267 to make changes.

REVISING CHECKLIST
- ☐ Does my writing have a topic?
- ☐ Do my sentences tell facts about my topic?
- ☐ Do any of my sentences not belong?
- ☐ Does my writing have an ending?

Here is a revised draft. The notes and marks show how the writer made the draft better.

Polar Bears

Polar bears are big white animals. They have thick fur. Their fur keeps them warm.

Polar bears liv in cold places like alaska. They walk on the ice. They swim in the cold water ∧ ~~Seals live in Alaska, too.~~

Polar bears keep warm in a cold place!

Add an ending.

The topic is polar bears, not seals. Take out the last sentence.

266   Writing Handbook

---

265 and 266   Writing Handbook

Writing Handbook

STEP 4 Editing

You have made some changes to your writing. Now make your writing correct. Use the editing checklist on page 268. Read carefully to find mistakes. Show corrections with the editing marks below.

EDITING MARKS

∧ Add   — Take out   ⊙ Period   ◯ Check spelling

Polar Bears

Polar bears are big white animals. They have thick fur. Their fur keeps them warm.

Polar bears ◯liv◯ in cold places like ∧alaska. They walk on the ice. They swim in the cold water⊙ Polar bears keep warm in a cold place!

Writing Handbook **267**

Writing Handbook

EDITING CHECKLIST

- Every sentence begins with a capital letter.
- Every sentence ends with an end mark.
- Names of people, specific places, and dates have capital letters.
- All words are spelled correctly.

STEP 5 Producing and Publishing

Share your writing with others. What can you do?

- Make a final copy. You can type your work on a computer or write a neat copy.
- You can add pictures.
- You can add other features like bold words, headings, and diagrams. Here is an example of a diagram.

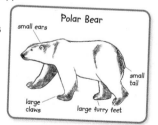

Polar Bear
small ears
small tail
large claws
large furry feet

Digital Connection

You can use a computer to make interesting text features like bold words and colorful headings.

268   Writing Handbook

Step 4: Editing

Tell children that editing helps to make their writing correct. Have children use the Editing Checklist on page 268 to check their writing. Until children gain competency with editing, have them perform a focused edit, where they look for only one checklist item at a time, such as capital letters.

Using Editing Marks Explain that editing marks are used to make changes to writing. Display an unedited draft and model with remarks such as the following to show how to use editing marks to correct the writing: *I think a word has been left out here. When I need to add a word, I use a caret mark. See how it points up? It shows where a word should go. Watch as I add the word.* Continue thinking aloud to demonstrate how and where to use the remaining editing marks.

Step 5: Producing and Publishing

Digital Integration Assist children by using a word-processing program to type their final drafts. Then model how to create a text box, showing children how to place a text box and adjust its size. Children can cut and paste photos or diagrams into the text boxes or leave the boxes blank and add pictures that they create.

Managing Class Presentations Allow children the opportunity to share their work by dividing the class into small sharing circles. While in the circles, children should take turns being the reader and a member of the audience. Review the attributes of an effective speaker, such as using a voice that can be heard but is not too loud and showing the audience the pictures. Then discuss with children the appropriate behaviors of the audience, such as looking at the speaker, sitting quietly, thinking about the writing that is being presented, and asking questions after the writing is shared.

Assignment: Editing and Publishing

Have children mark off each item on the Editing Checklist when it is true of their reports. For children who need support, use small-group focused edits. For example, for spelling, have children touch each word to look carefully at the letters. If a word is misspelled, have children stretch out the sounds and try to spell the word correctly on a white board. Guide the children in recognizing and learning spelling patterns.

Encourage children to use technology and to work with a partner to produce and publish their final drafts. To provide an authentic audience, you may wish to post the reports on a classroom or school Web site.

A

air the gas that helps things live

alarm very loud noise to get attention

amount piece

appear to show up

attach to fasten together

attract to pull or call to

avoid to stay away from

B

blaze burning

bloom to open into flowers

bottle glass container

bud unopened flower

build to make something out of wood or other materials

C

carrier person who takes things from place to place

caught stuck; trapped

center middle

certain sure

check to look at to see if everything is all right

clear see-through

confuse to mix up

cover wrapping that goes over or around something

D

dash to run

delicious yummy; very good to eat

drill going through steps to prepare for a real situation

E

exercise regular activity to keep healthy

F

fancy special

G

gather to collect; pick up

gently carefully, trying not to hurt anything

gill body part that lets underwater animals breathe in the water

grab to get

H

harm to hurt

heavy hard to lift up

I

ignore to pay no attention to

insert to put something inside something else

L

librarian person who works in a library

list names or items written in order; note

loose not connected to or part of something else

lungs body parts used to breathe air

M

mayor leader of a town or city

message something someone wants to tell someone else

mine belonging to me

model small copy of something that shows what the larger thing looks like

N

nature the way animals and plants live and behave

P

practice to do something to get better, often over and over

prance to dance and skip around

pupa stage of a butterfly's life when it turns from a caterpillar into a butterfly

R

rake to scrape or sweep up

rescue to save; help

rot to fall apart

rule what is allowed or not allowed; law

S

scary something that makes someone afraid

serious not teasing

shape shadow; figure of something

shone glowed with light; gave off light

shower type of bath where water falls down from above

signal sign; notice

silver shiny gray or white

skitter to run in little steps

soil dirt; ground

solid hard

spin to turn around and around

spray to squirt, like water from a hose

sting sharp hurt

stomach body part that fills with food

strange hard to understand

stuck unable to get out

sudden fast and surprising

surface top layer

T

tadpole a stage in a frog's life when it is like a fish

talent something someone is good at doing

tasty yummy; good to eat

toward in the direction of

trash things people no longer need or want; garbage

treat something special and good to eat

V

vegetable plant grown as food

W

warn to tell someone about danger

weigh to be the size of

worry to feel upset about something or about what might happen